CONTENTS

FISH & SEAFOOD RECIPES 50

VEGETABLES & SIDES RECIPES 75

BEEF RECIPES 98

SAUCES, RUBS & MORE RECIPES 126

OTHER FAVORITE RECIPES 138

PORK RECIPES... 148

RECIPE INDEX 176

INTRODUCTION

So, you have an electric smoker and after reading the walkthroughs, you're very excited about using it. There are some other tools you should think about having, however, before you really dive in. Must-haves like quality grilling gloves, a meat thermometer, and a smoker cover keep smoking safe, convenient, and enjoyable:

BBQ gloves

Smokers are hot. To protect yourself, invest in a good pair of heat-resistant gloves. Expect to pay between $15 and $30. Try on a pair before buying, so you can see how well they grip tongs and fit on your hands.

A Meat Thermometer

You need to know the internal temp of your meat, so a meat thermometer is a must. There's a variety to choose from, but a lot of people like the wireless ones. This lets you check the temp of the meat without opening the smoker and losing heat. The range on most wireless units is about 100-300 feet. If you're buying a digital electric smoker, we would also suggest getting a separate thermostat to confirm that the one on the smoker is accurate.

Long Meat Tongs

Your old pair of pasta tongs aren't going to cut it when it comes to smoking. You want a sturdy, long pair that lets you grip and turn meat around in the smoker. Pay attention to the actual "claw" part, too, because you don't want the tongs to accidentally tear about the meat when you're turning a piece. For shredding meat, bear claw tongs are very useful.

A Smoker Cover

To protect your smoker against the elements, you need a cover to keep it clean and dry. Waterproof covers made from polyester material are very popular.

III. Cleaning Your Electric Smoker

Once you've used your smoker and eaten your fill of delicious food, it's time for cleanup. This part is never fun, but it's essential for your smoker. Keeping it clean ensures it has a long life and keeps producing great food. You should always clean your smoker after each use and then every once and a while, give it a really big clean. Keep an eye out for mold, rust, and scale.

The After-Each-BBQ Clean:

1. Unplug the smoker and wait until it's completely cool.

2. Take out everything that you can remove - the racks, smoker box, water pan, and drip tray.

3. With a grill brush, scrape off the black, carbonized bits of food off the racks. Don't scrub too hard or you'll rub off the protective seasoning. You should also never use an abrasive cleaner, like an oven cleaner. A natural cleaner from Traeger should work.

4. Open the smoker box and toss out the ash. Wipe down the box with hot soapy water, rinse, and dry.

5. Clean the drip tray with degreasing soap and water. Rinse and dry. Repeat with the water pan.

6. For the wood chip drawer, wipe it down with a clean cloth and degreaser. Fill a spray bottle with water to rinse if the drawer isn't removable. If it is, you can just rinse it out under a sink. Dry well before returning to the smoker.

7. For the rest of the smoker, you can use a mixture of apple cider vinegar and hot water. You don't need to rinse off this solution. A spray bottle is a convenient tool. Wipe down the areas you've sprayed with a clean cloth to remove all the smoke residue. Note: Avoid any actual electrical parts.

8. If you see ash hanging around anywhere in your smoker, vacuum it up. Ash attracts moisture, which in turn attracts mold and causes rusting.

9. Put the removable parts back into your smoker. It's ready to be used again!

POULTRY RECIPES

Smoked Brick Chicken

Servings: 4
Cooking Time: 3 Hours

Ingredients:

- 2 chickens, whole
- ¼ cup ground ancho chile pepper
- 2 tablespoons paprika
- 2 tablespoons ground coriander
- 4 thyme sprigs, leaves stripped and finely chopped
- 4 rosemary sprigs, leaves stripped and finely chopped
- 8 garlic cloves, finely chopped
- Extra-virgin olive oil, for drizzling
- Flaked sea salt
- Freshly ground black pepper

Directions:

1. To prepare the chickens, place them breast-side down on a cutting board. Working one at a time, locate the spine. Using poultry shears or heavy-duty kitchen shears, cut on either side of the spine, one side at a time, cutting as close to the spine as possible. Remove the spine and separate the chicken halves. Repeat.
2. Preheat the electric smoker to 275°F. Ensure the drip tray is clean and in place. Seal the door.
3. Place the wood chips in the smoking tray or firebox, get a good smoke rolling, and seal the door.
4. Wrap 4 clean bricks in several layers of aluminum foil. Place them on the smoking racks to preheat.
5. In a large bowl, whisk together the chile pepper, paprika, coriander, thyme, rosemary, and garlic. Set aside.
6. Rinse the chicken in cold water and pat it dry with a paper towel. Drizzle the chicken all over with olive oil and season with salt and pepper.
7. Completely coat the chicken with the spice mixture, rubbing the mixture into the skin and flesh. Place the chicken, skin-side down, on a smoking rack. Place 1 brick on top of each chicken half. Insert a probe thermometer (if available) into the thickest part of the meat, not touching the bone. Set the target temperature for 165°F. Smoke for 3 hours, or until the internal temperature reaches 165°F.
8. Gently remove the chicken from the racks, being careful to keep the skin intact.

Whole Smoked Jerk Chicken

Servings: 4 To 6
Cooking Time: 2 To 3 Hours

Ingredients:

- FOR THE JERK SPICE RUB
- 2 tablespoons dark brown sugar
- 2 tablespoons ground allspice
- 1 tablespoon garlic powder
- 1 tablespoon onion powder
- 1 tablespoon ground cinnamon
- 1 tablespoon fine sea salt
- 1 teaspoon ground cayenne pepper
- 1 teaspoon ground cloves
- 1 teaspoon ground nutmeg
- 1 teaspoon freshly ground black pepper
- FOR THE CHICKEN
- 2 chickens, whole, rinsed, drained, and patted dry
- Flaked sea salt
- Freshly ground black pepper
- 1 garlic bulb, halved
- 8 thyme sprigs
- 8 rosemary sprigs
- 2 navel oranges, quartered and seeded
- Olive oil, for coating
- ½ cup wildflower honey, divided

Directions:

1. TO MAKE THE JERK SPICE RUB
2. In a medium bowl, whisk the sugar, allspice, garlic powder, onion powder, cinnamon, salt, cayenne, cloves, nutmeg, and black pepper to blend. Transfer to an airtight container for storage.
3. TO MAKE THE CHICKEN
4. Preheat the electric smoker to 275°F. Ensure the drip tray is clean and in place. Seal the door.

5.   Place the wood chips in the smoking tray or firebox, get a good smoke rolling, and seal the door.

6.   Season the chicken cavities with salt and pepper. Stuff each chicken with ½ head of garlic, 4 thyme sprigs, 4 rosemary sprigs, and 4 orange pieces.

7.   Lightly coat the chickens with olive oil and generously rub them all over with the jerk spice. Season the outside of the chickens with salt and pepper. Snugly truss the chickens for uniform smoking and to keep the ingredients in the cavity.

8.   Arrange the chickens on smoking trays, leaving space between them. Drizzle the chickens with ¼ cup of honey. Insert a probe thermometer (if available) into the thickest part of the meat, not touching the bone. Set the target temperature for 165°F. Smoke for 2 to 3 hours, or until the internal temperature reaches 165°F when tested in the thigh, not touching the bone.

9.   Remove the chickens from the smoker. Remove the trussing and loosely tent the chickens with aluminum foil. Let them rest for 10 minutes.

10.   To finish, drizzle with the remaining ¼ cup of honey.

Standing Whole Chicken

Servings: 4 To 6
Cooking Time: 15 Minutes

Ingredients:
- 12 cloves garlic, divided
- ½ onion, quartered
- ½ lemon, quartered
- 1 tablespoon salt
- 1 teaspoon black pepper
- 1½ tablespoons ground sage
- 1½ tablespoons dried thyme
- 1½ tablespoons dried rosemary
- 1 teaspoon paprika
- 1 whole chicken (4 to 6 pounds)
- 3 tablespoons canola or vegetable oil

Directions:
1.   Prepare the smoker's water pan according to the manufacturer's instructions and remove one or two top racks from smoker to make room for the standing chicken. Smash 8 of the garlic cloves and add to the water in the pan along with the onion and lemon pieces. Preheat the smoker to 250°F. While it heats, fill a medium bowl with water and add 3 or 4 handfuls of hickory wood chips to soak.

2.   Finely mince the remaining 4 garlic cloves and combine in a small bowl with the salt, pepper, sage, thyme, rosemary, and paprika; set aside. Remove the package of giblets from the cavity of the chicken, then rinse the bird and dry well. Rub with oil and then coat heavily with the seasoning mixture on both the inside and outside of the chicken.

3.   Set the chicken on the vertical roaster and place it in the smoker. Add a small handful of the soaked hickory chips to the chip loading area, and keep adding chips at least every 30 minutes. The chicken is done when it reaches an internal temperature of 165°F, about 1½ to 2 hours.

4.   Let stand 10 to 15 minutes to cool before removing from the vertical roaster and carving.

Beef Ribs

Servings: 2
Cooking Time: 3 Hours

Ingredients:
- 2 tablespoons brown sugar
- 2 tablespoons garlic, chopped
- 1 tablespoon paprika
- 2 tablespoons onion powder
- 2 pounds beef ribs
- 3 tablespoons lemon juice

Directions:
1.   Preheat smoker for 30 minutes at 200 degrees F.
2.   First mix first 4 ingredients together in a large bowl.
3.   Sprinkle the spice mixture over the pork ribs.
4.   Rub well for fine coating.
5.   Next, smoke it in an electric smoker for 3 hours at 250°F.
6.   After 2 hours, take out the ribs and pour lemon juice on top.
7.   Serve warm and enjoy.

Smoked Chicken Quarters

Servings: 3
Cooking Time: 2 Hours

Ingredients:

- 2 cups water
- 2 teaspoons brown sugar
- ⅓ cup maple syrup
- ⅓ cup Sriracha sauce
- ½ teaspoon salt
- ⅓ teaspoon pepper
- ⅓ teaspoon paprika
- 3 pounds chicken meat

Directions:

1. In a large pan, add water along with brown sugar, Sriracha, salt, pepper, paprika, maple syrup, and heat it over the low flame.
2. Cook it for 5 minutes.
3. Then, once the sugar dissolves, removes it from the heat to let it get cool off.
4. Reserve this sauce for later use.
5. Set the electric smoker to 250 degrees F.
6. Cook the chicken in it for 2 hours.
7. Remember to baste the chicken with the prepared sauce every 20 minutes with a brush.
8. Once the digital thermometer meets 165 degrees F, serve with the reserve dripping and remaining sauce.

Citrus Chicken Fajitas

Servings: 6
Cooking Time: 20 Minutes

Ingredients:

- ½ cup canola or vegetable oil, divided
- zest and juice of 1 lemon
- zest and juice of 1 orange
- zest and juice of 3 limes, divided
- 3 cloves garlic, smashed
- 2 tablespoons coarse kosher salt
- 1 tablespoon Worcestershire sauce
- ½ tablespoon chili powder
- 2 teaspoons ground cumin
- 2 teaspoons black pepper
- 2 teaspoons onion powder
- 4 boneless, skinless chicken breast halves (1½ to 2 pounds)
- 4 bell peppers (any color), seeded
- 2 onions
- 4 tablespoons oil, divided
- 4 green onions (whites and greens), finely minced
- ¼ cup finely minced fresh cilantro
- 12 tortillas (corn or flour)
- fajita toppings: grated cheese, sour cream, salsa, guacamole

Directions:

1. In a 1-gallon zip-top plastic bag, combine ¼ cup oil with the zest and juice from the lemon, orange, and 2 limes. Add the garlic, salt, Worcestershire, chili powder, cumin, pepper, and onion powder. Mix well to combine and then add the chicken breasts, turning them in the bag to coat them. Seal the bag and place in the refrigerator to let the chicken marinate for at least 6 hours, or overnight.
2. Prepare the smoker's water pan according to the manufacturer's instructions and preheat the smoker to 275°F. While it heats, fill a medium bowl with water and add 3 or 4 handfuls of hickory wood chips to soak.
3. While the smoker is heating, slice the bell peppers and onions in thin strips and place in a grill basket that has been sprayed with cooking spray. Remove the chicken breasts from their marinade and place directly on a low smoker rack. Place the grill basket with the peppers and onions on the top rack. Add a small handful of the soaked hickory chips to the chip loading area, and add more 30 minutes in. The chicken is done when it reaches an internal temperature of 165°F, about 1 hour. Remove the chicken, onions, and peppers from the smoker and let the chicken rest under a foil tent for 15 to 20 minutes before thinly slicing it.
4. While the chicken is resting, preheat the grill to high heat. Pour 2 tablespoons oil into a large cast-iron skillet and set directly over the heat. Add the smoked onions and peppers and cook until soft and caramelized over high heat, about 15 minutes; stir occasionally to make sure they are caramelizing and not burning. If the onions are burning, lower the temperature to medium or medium-high. Transfer the grilled vegetables to a large bowl. Add 2 more tablespoons oil to the pan on the grill.

Add the sliced chicken and allow it to slightly caramelize, stirring occasionally, for about 5 minutes. Return the onions and peppers to the pan for a quick toss with the chicken.

5. Wrap tortillas in foil and place on the grill with indirect heat to gently warm while the chicken cooks on the grill. Flip them once or twice to warm.

6. Remove the pan from the grill. Top the chicken mixture with fresh-squeezed juice from the remaining lime, the green onions, and the cilantro. Serve hot with the tortillas, cheese, sour cream, salsa, and guacamole.

Spicy Sriracha Chicken Wings Recipe

Servings: 2
Cooking Time: 2 Hours

Ingredients:
* 2 pounds chicken wings
* 2 teaspoons garlic powder
* Sea salt, to taste
* Freshly ground black pepper, to taste
* 2 teaspoons fresh cilantro leaves, minced
* ⅓ cup raw honey
* ⅓ cup Sriracha sauce
* 2 tablespoons coconut amino
* 3 limes, juice

Directions:
1. Combine all the sauce ingredients in a separate bowl and set aside for further use.
2. Season the chicken with garlic, salt, and pepper.
3. Preheat the smoker for a few minutes at 250 degrees F.
4. Add cherry or apple wood chip to the smoker.
5. Place the chicken into the smoker once the smoke starts to come out.
6. Close the door and cook for about 2 hours.
7. Cook until the internal temperature reaches 165 degrees F.
8. Use the digital meat thermometer to measure the temperature.
9. Serve and enjoy with the prepared sauce.
10. Enjoy.

Herbed And Smoked Chicken

Servings: 2-3
Cooking Time: 90 Minutes

Ingredients:
* 15 cups filtered water
* 4 cups nonalcoholic beer
* Salt, to taste
* 1 cup brown sugar
* 1 tablespoon rosemary
* 1 teaspoon sage
* 2 pounds whole chicken, trimmed and giblets removed
* 4 tablespoons butter
* 3 tablespoons olive oil, for basting
* 1 cup Italian seasoning
* 2 tablespoons garlic powder
* Zest of 3 small lemons

Directions:
1. Add water to a large cooking pot, then add salt and sugar.
2. Let it boil until dissolved.
3. Add the herbs and let it cook for a few minutes until aromatic.
4. Pour in the beer and then immerse chicken in it.
5. Let it refrigerate for a few hours.
6. Now, remove the chicken from the brine, and then pat dry with a paper towel.
7. Uncover and let it sit for one more hour in room temperate.
8. Next, butter the chicken.
9. Massage the chicken for fine coating.
10. Next, rub the chicken with Italian seasoning, garlic powder, and lemon zest.
11. Load electric smoker with the wood chips, and preheat to 250 degrees F until smoke starts to build.
12. Then, slow roast it for 1.5 hours to 2 hours, and keep basting with olive oil every 30 minutes.
13. Once, the internal temperature reaches 165 degrees F and juices run clear, serve and enjoy.

Beer-brined Applewood-smoked Chicken Wings

Servings: 6
Cooking Time: 2 Hours

Ingredients:

- 3 limes, thinly sliced, plus 3 limes, quartered lengthwise, for serving
- ¼ cup coarse sea salt
- ¼ cup wildflower honey
- 1 jalapeño pepper, thinly sliced, plus more for additional heat (optional)
- 2 tablespoons fresh thyme leaves, stripped and finely chopped
- 3 fresh bay leaves
- 3 (12-ounce) bottles pilsner beer
- 6 pounds bone-in skin-on chicken wings, rinsed and drained
- Flaked sea salt
- Freshly ground black pepper

Directions:

1. In a large bowl, stir together the lime slices, coarse sea salt, honey, jalapeño, thyme, lime, bay leaves, and beer. Transfer to a large food-grade plastic bag and add the wings. Remove as much air as possible from the bag and seal it. Refrigerate for 24 hours, turning the bag occasionally.
2. Drain the wings and pat them dry.
3. Preheat the electric smoker to 275°F. Ensure the drip tray is clean and in place. Seal the door.
4. Place the wood chips in the smoking tray or firebox, get a good smoke rolling, and seal the door.
5. Arrange the wings on smoking trays, leaving space between each one. Top with additional jalapeño, if desired. Season with salt and pepper. Smoke for about 2 hours, or until the wings reach an internal temperature of 165°F.
6. Serve with lime wedges on the side.

Smoked Javanese-style Chicken Satay With Spicy Peanut Sauce

Servings: 4

Cooking Time: 1 Hour 30 Minutes

Ingredients:

- ⅓ cup well-shaken canned light coconut milk
- ¼ cup sesame oil
- 2 tablespoons fresh lime juice, divided
- 1 tablespoon grated peeled fresh ginger
- 3 garlic cloves, minced
- 1 ½ teaspoons smoked paprika
- 1 teaspoon ground turmeric
- 1 teaspoon salt
- 1 teaspoon freshly ground black pepper
- 2 pounds boneless, skinless chicken breasts, cut into 1 ½-inch cubes
- 2 cups Spicy Peanut Sauce, divided
- 2 tablespoons chopped fresh cilantro

Directions:

1. In a medium bowl, whisk together the coconut milk, sesame oil, 1 tablespoon lime juice, the ginger, garlic, smoked paprika, turmeric, salt, and pepper. Add the chicken to the marinade and coat it completely. Cover and chill for 1 hour.
2. Take the chicken out and let it reach room temperature before smoking, about 30 minutes.
3. Preheat the smoker to 275°F. If you are using wooden skewers, soak them in water for at least 30 minutes.
4. Thread the skewers through the chicken cubes, leaving about 1 inch of space on each end.
5. Smoke the skewers for 30 minutes, then rotate. Smoke for another 30 minutes.
6. Remove the chicken and coat with 1 cup peanut sauce. Smoke for another 30 minutes, or until the internal temperature reaches 165°F.
7. Sprinkle the chopped cilantro over the chicken and serve with the remaining 1 cup peanut sauce.

Crispy-skin Orange Chicken

Servings: 4

Cooking Time: 30 Minutes

Ingredients:

- FOR THE POULTRY SPICE RUB
- 4 teaspoons paprika
- 1 tablespoon chili powder

- 2 teaspoons ground cumin
- 2 teaspoons dried thyme
- 2 teaspoons salt
- 2 teaspoons garlic powder
- 1 teaspoon freshly ground black pepper
- FOR THE MARINADE
- 4 chicken quarters
- 2 cups frozen orange-juice concentrate
- ½ cup soy sauce
- 1 tablespoon garlic powder

Directions:

1. TO MAKE THE SPICE RUB
2. In a small bowl, mix together the paprika, chili powder, cumin, thyme, salt, garlic powder, and pepper. Set aside.
3. TO MAKE THE MARINADE
4. Place the chicken quarters in a dish that will accommodate the marinade and chicken.
5. In a medium bowl, whisk the orange-juice concentrate (do not add water), soy sauce, garlic powder, and half the spice-rub mixture. Pour the marinade over the chicken, cover, and refrigerate for a minimum of 8 hours.
6. Preheat the smoker with the applewood to a stabilized 275°F.
7. Discard the marinade and rub all surfaces of the chicken generously with the remaining spice rub. Place the chicken quarters in the smoker for 1½ to 2 hours.
8. Remove the chicken from the smoker once a digital thermometer inserted in the breast has reached 160°F. Let it rest for 10 minutes, after which the temperature should have risen to 165°F.

Spicy Smoked Chicken Wings

Servings: 4
Cooking Time: 1 Hour

Ingredients:

- 32 chicken wingettes (flats) or 16 whole wings cut in half at the joint
- 1 ½ cups all-purpose flour
- ½ cup Poultry Rub
- ½ cup hot sauce
- ½ cup store-bought barbecue sauce or Bacon-Flavored BBQ Sauce

Directions:

1. Pat the wings dry with paper towels.
2. Put the flour in a shallow bowl and mix in the rub. Coat the wings in the mixture, a few at a time, then place them on a sheet pan.
3. Refrigerate the wings, uncovered, for about 45 minutes. The air in the fridge dries them a little, which will make them extra-crispy.
4. Preheat the smoker to 250°F.
5. Smoke the wings for 30 minutes.
6. Take them out and increase the temperature of a pellet smoker to 425°F (if you don't have a pellet smoker, finish the wings in the oven). Place the wings in a bowl and douse them with the hot sauce and barbecue sauce.
7. Return the wings to the smoker and smoke for 1 hour, or until their internal temperature reaches 165°F. Serve the wings warm.

Smoked Boneless Leg Of Lamb

Servings: 8
Cooking Time: 8 Hours

Ingredients:

- 6 pounds legs of lamb, boneless
- ½ cup olive oil
- 4 teaspoons fresh rosemary, chopped
- 5 teaspoons fresh thyme, chopped
- 10 teaspoons BBQ sauce
- 1 teaspoon garlic powder

Directions:

1. Rub ½ cup of olive oil on the leg of lamb.
2. Mix chopped rosemary, garlic powder and fresh thyme in a bowl.
3. Rub this mixture onto the leg of lamb.
4. Put it in the refrigerator for 1 hour.
5. After 1 hour, put the leg of lamb in the electric smoker at 225°F for 8 hours.
6. After 2 hours, take out the lamb and drizzle BBQ sauce on top.
7. Enjoy!

Sweet Sriracha Barbecue Chicken

Servings: 3 Or 4

Cooking Time: 30 Minutes

Ingredients:

- 1 cup sriracha
- ½ cup (1 stick) butter
- ½ cup molasses
- ½ cup ketchup
- ¼ cup firmly packed brown sugar
- ¼ cup prepared yellow mustard
- 1 teaspoon salt
- 1 teaspoon freshly ground black pepper
- 1 whole chicken, cut up
- ½ teaspoon chopped fresh parsley leaves

Directions:

1. Preheat the smoker to 250°F with the cherrywood.
2. In a medium saucepan over low heat, stir together the sriracha, butter, molasses, ketchup, brown sugar, mustard, salt, and pepper until the sugar and salt dissolve. Set aside.
3. Divide the sauce into two portions. Brush the chicken with half the sauce and reserve the remaining sauce to serve with the meat. Make sure you divide the sauce before basting the chicken, and discard any remaining sauce used to baste the chicken, to eliminate cross-contamination.
4. Place the chicken on the smoker rack and smoke for 1½ to 2 hours, or until an instant-read thermometer reads 165°F.
5. Sprinkle the chicken with the parsley and serve with the reserved barbecue sauce.

Herbed Chicken Recipe

Servings: 6

Cooking Time: 5 Hours

Ingredients:

- 6 pounds whole chicken
- 2 tablespoons dried oregano
- 2 tablespoons dried thyme
- 1 tablespoon dried rosemary
- 1 teaspoon smoked paprika
- Salt and pepper, to taste
- 2 teaspoons garlic powder
- 3 teaspoons lemon pepper
- 40 ounces chicken stock
- 2 carrots, diced
- 2 celery stalks, diced
- 2 onions, diced
- 4 tablespoons dill weed
- ½ cup extra-virgin olive oil

Directions:

1. Preheat the electric smoker to 250 degrees F.
2. Combine thyme, oregano, paprika, rosemary, salt, pepper, lemon pepper, and garlic powder in a small bowl.
3. Remove all the giblets and neck of the chicken.
4. Brush the chicken with the oil, and then massage spices from the bowl all over the chicken
5. Pour the stock into a large rack, and lower the spice-rubbed chicken on to the beer.
6. Adjust the chicken upright.
7. Now, place this rack inside the smoker and toss in the diced veggies onto the rack.
8. Let it cook for 5 hours.
9. Once, the internal temperate reaches 165 degrees F, the dish is ready.
10. Just before 20 minutes remaining, add the dill weeds.
11. Then allow cooking for next 20 minutes.
12. Carefully remove the rack and then shred the chicken into pieces.
13. Mix it with the juices.
14. Serve it with orzo pasta.
15. Enjoy.

Herb-smoked Quail

Servings: 4 To 6

Cooking Time: 10 Minutes

Ingredients:

- 4 to 6 quail
- 2 tablespoons olive oil
- Salt
- Freshly ground black pepper
- 1 package dry Hidden Valley Ranch Dressing Mix
- ½ cup (1 stick) butter, melted

Directions:

1. Preheat the smoker to 225°F with the hickory wood.
2. Brush the quail with the olive oil and season with salt and pepper. Place the quail in the smoker and smoke for about 1 hour.
3. In a small bowl, stir together the ranch-dressing mix and melted butter.
4. Thirty minutes into the smoking process, brush the quail with the ranch-butter sauce and repeat at the end of the cook time. The quail are done when the internal temperature reaches 145°F.

Smoked Korean Turkey Tacos With Pickled Slaw

Servings: 4
Cooking Time: 2 Hours

Ingredients:
- FOR THE TURKEY
- 1 cup fresh cilantro leaves, finely chopped, plus more for garnish
- 3 garlic cloves, minced
- 1 jalapeño pepper, trimmed, seeded, and diced
- ¼ cup packed dark brown sugar
- 3 tablespoons canola oil
- 3 tablespoons soy sauce
- 1 tablespoon toasted sesame oil
- 1 teaspoon ground coriander
- 1 teaspoon freshly ground black pepper
- 1 (4- to 6-pound) bone-in skin-on turkey breast
- Flaked sea salt
- Freshly ground black pepper
- FOR THE PICKLED SLAW
- 1 red onion, very thinly sliced
- 1 cup apple cider vinegar
- 4 cups finely sliced Savoy cabbage
- 4 scallions, trimmed and thinly sliced on a sharp angle
- 1 carrot, trimmed and very thinly sliced with a vegetable peeler
- 1 cup fresh cilantro leaves
- Flaked sea salt
- Freshly ground black pepper
- FOR THE TACOS
- 12 large flour tortillas
- 2 avocados, peeled, halved, pitted, and cut into slices

Directions:
1. TO MAKE THE TURKEY
2. In a large bowl, whisk together the cilantro, garlic, jalapeño, sugar, canola oil, soy sauce, sesame oil, coriander, and pepper.
3. Add the turkey to the marinade and massage the marinade into the turkey.
4. Cover the bowl with plastic wrap and refrigerate for at least 4 hours, or overnight for best results, turning the turkey occasionally.
5. Preheat the electric smoker to 275°F. Ensure the drip tray is clean and in place. Seal the door.
6. Place the wood chips in the smoking tray or firebox, get a good smoke rolling, and seal the door.
7. Remove the turkey from the marinade, reserving the marinade in the refrigerator. Season the turkey all over with salt and pepper. Place the turkey breast on a smoking tray. Insert a probe thermometer (if available) into the thickest part of the meat, not touching the bone. Set the target temperature for 165°F. Smoke the turkey for about 2 hours, or until it reaches an internal temperature of 165°F.
8. Remove the turkey from the smoker, loosely tent it with aluminum foil, and let it rest for 10 minutes.
9. Thinly slice the turkey across the grain (across the width rather than the length).
10. TO MAKE THE PICKLED SLAW
11. While the turkey smokes, in a small saucepan combine the red onion and vinegar. Place the pan in the smoker and cook for 30 minutes, until tender. Remove.
12. In a large bowl, combine the cabbage, scallions, carrot, and cilantro. Season with salt and pepper.
13. Add the warm pickled red onion and liquid to the slaw. Toss until evenly mixed.
14. TO MAKE THE TACOS
15. In a small saucepan over medium heat, cook the reserved marinade for about 15 minutes, until reduced to a rich sauce.
16. Arrange the tortillas on the smoking racks, spaced evenly apart. Smoke for 5 minutes to warm.
17. Build tacos on the warmed tortillas with layers of slaw, avocado, and turkey, topped with the marinade sauce.

Applewood-smoked Chicken

Servings: 4
Cooking Time: 20 Minutes

Ingredients:

- 1 (5- to 6-pound) whole chicken
- ½ lemon
- 1 tablespoon olive oil
- 7 cups Poultry Rub
- 4 or 5 rosemary sprigs

Directions:

1. Pat the chicken dry with paper towels. Rub the chicken with the lemon half, then drizzle the olive oil over it. Generously sprinkle the rub all over the inside and outside of the chicken. Rub it into the skin.

2. Put the rosemary sprigs inside the chicken. Truss the chicken by crossing the drumsticks and tying them together with kitchen twine. Then, tie the wings close to the body with another length of twine.

3. Preheat the smoker to 275°F.

4. Place the chicken breast-side down in the smoker and cover it with aluminum foil. Smoke for 30 minutes.

5. Turn the chicken breast-side up, then smoke, covered, for 1 hour, or until the internal temperature in the thickest part of the thigh reaches 165°F.

6. Wrap the cooked chicken in butcher paper or aluminum foil and let rest for 10 minutes. Cut the twine and serve.

Jamaican Jerk Chicken

Servings: 4
Cooking Time: 15 Minutes

Ingredients:

- 4 chicken leg quarters, scored
- ¼ cup canola oil
- ¼ cup cane syrup
- 8 whole cloves
- 6 habanero peppers, sliced
- 1 scallion, white and green parts, chopped
- 2 tablespoons whole allspice (pimento) berries, plus more for smoking (see tip)
- 2 tablespoons salt
- 2 teaspoons freshly ground black pepper
- 2 teaspoons ground cinnamon
- 1 teaspoon cayenne pepper
- 1 teaspoon dried thyme
- 1 teaspoon ground cumin

Directions:

1. Preheat the smoker to 275°F with the mesquite wood. Throw in a handful of whole allspice (pimento) berries with the mesquite.

2. Brush the chicken with the canola oil.

3. In a blender or food processor, combine the cane syrup, cloves, habaneros, scallion, allspice, salt, pepper, cinnamon, cayenne, thyme, and cumin. Pulse until smooth and sticky. Reserve 2 tablespoons of the mixture. Brush the chicken with the remaining mixture, on and under the skin. Place the chicken on the smoker rack and smoke for about 1½ hours.

4. Remove the chicken from the smoker when the internal temperature reaches 160°F, and let the meat stand for about 10 minutes so it reaches the targeted temperature of 165°F by the time you are ready to eat.

5. Baste the chicken with the reserved jerk seasoning before serving.

Sesame Chicken Wings

Servings: 2
Cooking Time: 2 Hours

Ingredients:

- ⅓ cup rice vinegar
- 3 tablespoons honey
- ½ cup soy sauce
- ⅓ cup sesame oil
- 2 tablespoons garlic sauce
- 1 tablespoon garlic salt, to taste
- 12 chicken thighs, skinless, boneless

Directions:

1. Combine rice vinegar, honey, soy sauce, sesame oil, chili garlic sauce and salt in a small bowl, then coat the chicken thighs with the mixture.

2. Refrigerate it for a few hours.

3. Preheat the smoker for 30 minutes at 255 degrees F.

4. Add cherry wood chips to the smoker.

5. Place the marinated chicken into the smoker.

6. Cook for about 2 hours, or until the internal temperature reaches 165 degrees F.

7. Use the digital meat thermometer to measure the temperature.

8. Serve and enjoy.

Honey Balsamic Glazed Lamb Chops

Servings: 4

Cooking Time: 3 Hours

Ingredients:

- ½ teaspoon salt
- ½ teaspoon paprika
- ¼ teaspoon garlic powder
- 1 teaspoon dried mustard
- ½ teaspoon thyme
- Other Ingredients:
- 12 lamb chops
- 4 teaspoons honey
- 2 teaspoons balsamic vinegar

Directions:

1. Cut the lamb into pieces with a sharp knife.
2. Mix all dry spices together in a large bowl.
3. Rub the spices on the lamb and massage for fine coating.
4. Place the lamb in a zip-lock plastic bag and then marinate in the refrigerator for an hour.
5. Grease skillet with oil spray and then add the marinated lamb in it.
6. Cook in the smoker at 220 degrees F for 3 hours.
7. Drizzle some honey and vinegar at the very end after taking out the lamb for a little sweetness.
8. Enjoy.

Herb-brined Smoked Chicken

Servings: 4

Cooking Time: 5 Hours

Ingredients:

- 3 cups water
- ⅓ cup coarse salt
- ⅓ cup packed light brown sugar
- 1 small onion, halved
- 1 celery stalk with leaves
- 2 tablespoons minced garlic
- 2 teaspoons grated lemon zest
- 1 tablespoon chopped fresh parsley
- 1 tablespoon chopped fresh oregano
- 2 thyme sprigs
- 1 rosemary sprig
- 1 bay leaf
- 3 cups ice
- 1 (4-pound) whole chicken
- 2 tablespoons olive oil
- 3 tablespoons Poultry Rub
- 5 fresh sage leaves

Directions:

1. In a large pot, heat the water to almost boiling. Add the salt, stirring until it's dissolved. Add the brown sugar and stir to dissolve. Add the onion, celery, garlic, lemon zest, parsley, oregano, thyme, rosemary, and bay leaf. Remove the pot from the heat.
2. Add the ice to the brine. Cover the pot and put it in the refrigerator for about 45 minutes.
3. When the brine is cold, put the chicken in a 1-gallon zip-top bag. Discard the onion and celery from the brine and pour the brine over the chicken. Seal the bag and refrigerate for 4 hours, turning it once each hour.
4. Preheat the smoker to 275°F.
5. Take the chicken out of the brine. Use paper towels to dry the chicken inside and out. Rub the olive oil all over the skin, then rub with the poultry rub. Place the sage leaves inside the bird.
6. Smoke the chicken for 3 hours, or until the internal temperature reaches 165°F.
7. Let it rest for 10 minutes, then serve.

Mesquite Maple-bacon Chicken

Servings: 4

Cooking Time: 20 Minutes

Ingredients:

- 4 boneless, skinless chicken breasts
- Salt
- Freshly ground black pepper
- 12 bacon slices, uncooked
- 1 cup maple syrup
- ½ cup (1 stick) butter, melted
- 1 teaspoon liquid smoke

Directions:

1. Preheat the smoker to 250°F with the mesquite wood.
2. Season the chicken with salt and pepper.

3. Wrap each breast with 3 bacon slices to cover the entire surface, and secure with toothpicks.

4. In a medium bowl, stir together the maple syrup, butter, and liquid smoke to make maple butter. Reserve about one-third of the maple butter.

5. Submerge each breast in the maple butter to coat and place it on a grill pan. Place the pan in the smoker and smoke for 1 to 1½ hours.

6. Brush the chicken with the reserved maple butter. Continue to smoke for about 30 minutes more until the internal temperature reaches 165°F.

Drunken Drumsticks

Servings: 8 To 12
Cooking Time: 45 Minutes

Ingredients:

- FOR THE RUB
- ¼ cup light-brown sugar
- 2 tablespoons paprika
- 1¼ teaspoons kosher salt
- 1 teaspoon cayenne pepper
- ½ teaspoon garlic powder
- ½ teaspoon onion powder
- ¼ teaspoon freshly ground black pepper
- FOR THE BEER BARBECUE SAUCE
- 2 cups ketchup
- 1 cup beer
- ⅓ cup chopped onion
- 2 tablespoons minced garlic
- 2 tablespoons Worcestershire sauce
- 2 tablespoons honey Dijon mustard
- 1 tablespoon molasses
- 1 tablespoon firmly packed brown sugar
- ½ teaspoon salt
- ½ teaspoon freshly ground black pepper
- ⅓ teaspoon hot sauce
- FOR THE BRINE
- 1 quart water
- 2 (12-ounce) bottles of beer
- ½ cup salt
- ½ cup firmly packed brown sugar
- 8 to 12 chicken legs
- Olive oil, for basting

- 2 tablespoons chopped fresh parsley leaves
- 2 tablespoons chopped fresh chives

Directions:

1. TO MAKE THE SPICE RUB

2. In a small bowl, mix together the brown sugar, paprika, salt, cayenne, garlic powder, onion powder, and pepper. Set aside.

3. TO MAKE THE BEER BARBECUE SAUCE

4. In a medium saucepan over medium-high heat, stir together the ketchup, beer, onion, garlic, Worcestershire sauce, mustard, molasses, brown sugar, salt, pepper, and hot sauce. Bring to a boil, remove from the heat, and let cool.

5. TO MAKE THE BRINE

6. In a container large enough to hold the brine and the chicken legs, combine the water and beer.

7. Add the salt and stir until dissolved.

8. Add the brown sugar and stir until dissolved.

9. Add the chicken legs to the container, making sure they are covered with the brine. Cover and refrigerate for 3 hours.

10. Preheat the smoker to 250°F with the pecan wood for indirect heat. Keep the smoke going the entire time for great flavor.

11. Discard the brine and rinse the chicken. Pat the chicken dry with paper towels.

12. Baste the chicken with olive oil, making sure all sides are well coated.

13. Season the chicken generously with the spice rub and sprinkle with the parsley and chives. Place the chicken legs directly on the smoker rack and smoke for 1½ to 2 hours. After about 45 minutes, use an instant-read thermometer to check the temperature, or you can use a thermometer with a leave-in probe to keep you aware of the temperature throughout the smoking process.

14. When the drumsticks reach 160°F, spoon some beer-barbecue sauce onto them. The chicken is done at 165°F.

Smoked Turkey And Andouille Poblano Poppers

Servings: 8
Cooking Time: 4 Hours

Ingredients:

- FOR THE SAVORY RICE
- 1 tablespoon unsalted butter
- 1 tablespoon extra-virgin olive oil
- 1 cup diced yellow onion
- Flaked sea salt
- Freshly ground black pepper
- 2 cups long-grain white or brown rice
- 1 tablespoon fresh thyme leaves, stripped and finely chopped
- 1 fresh bay leaf
- 4 cups chicken (or vegetable) stock
- FOR THE POPPERS
- 2 andouille sausages, casings removed and thinly sliced
- 2 Roma tomatoes, quartered lengthwise, seeded, and diced
- 2 scallions, trimmed and thinly sliced on an angle
- 2 cups shredded Monterey Jack cheese
- 8 poblano peppers, halved lengthwise, ribbed, and seeded
- 2 (4-pound) fresh bone-in skin-on turkey breasts
- Flaked sea salt
- Freshly ground black pepper
- 4 limes, halved
- Finely chopped fresh cilantro leaves, for garnish
- Sour cream, for garnish

Directions:

1. TO MAKE THE SAVORY RICE
2. Preheat a large saucepan over medium-high heat.
3. In the pan, combine the butter, olive oil, and onion. Season with salt and pepper. Sauté the onion for about 10 minutes, until golden brown.
4. Add the rice, thyme, and bay leaf, stirring to coat the rice in the butter and oil.
5. Add the chicken stock. Stir gently, cover the pan, and reduce the heat to low. Cook for 45 to 60 minutes, until the liquid is absorbed. Remove and discard the bay leaf.
6. TO MAKE THE POPPERS
7. Preheat the electric smoker to 275°F. Ensure the drip tray is clean and in place. Seal the door.
8. Place the wood chips in the smoking tray or firebox, get a good smoke rolling, and seal the door.
9. In a large bowl, fold together the sausage, tomatoes, scallions, 4 cups of the savory rice, and Monterey Jack cheese. Spoon the mixture into the pepper halves, mounding and gently pressing to fill the cavity. Arrange the stuffed peppers in a single layer, spaced evenly without touching, on the smoking racks.
10. Season the turkey all over with salt and pepper. Place the turkey breasts on the smoking racks, spaced evenly without touching. Insert the probe thermometer (if available) into the thickest part of the meat, not touching the bone. Set the target temperature for 165°F. Smoke for 4 hours, or until golden brown and the internal temperature reaches 165°F.
11. Let the turkey cool slightly. Gently remove the bones and thinly slice across the breast on an angle.
12. Top the stuffed peppers with turkey slices. Serve with lime halves, fresh cilantro, and sour cream.

Delicious Rib-eye Steak

Servings: 4
Cooking Time: 4 Hours

Ingredients:

- 4 rib-eye steak, 2-inches thick
- 2 cups sharp cheddar cheese, grated
- Spice Ingredients:
- 1 teaspoon black pepper
- Sea salt, to taste
- 3 tablespoons chipotle powder
- ½ tablespoon paprika
- ½ cup olive oil

Directions:

1. Combine the entire spice ingredient in a bowl and rub it all over the meat.
2. Let it sit for few hours before cooking.
3. Afterward, put the steaks in the electric smoker for 4 hours at 225°F.
4. After 4 hours take out the lamb and sprinkle cheese on top.
5. Let the cheese get melted, and then serve.

Chicken & Rice–stuffed Peppers

Servings: 4

Cooking Time: 20 Minutes

Ingredients:

- 4 bell peppers (any color)
- ½ small onion, finely minced
- 2 cups cooked rice
- 1 (10-ounce) can Rotel tomatoes and green chiles
- 2 cups shredded cooked chicken
- 2 tablespoons chopped fresh cilantro
- salt and black pepper

Directions:

1. Prepare the smoker's water pan according to the manufacturer's instructions and preheat the smoker to 275°F. While it heats, fill a medium bowl with water and add 1 or 2 handfuls of hickory wood chips to soak.

2. Slice ½ inch off the top of each bell pepper, discarding the stems but saving the rest. Scoop out the membranes and seeds and set the peppers aside.

3. To make the filling, in a large bowl combine the onion, rice, Rotel, chicken, and cilantro. Finely mince the reserved pepper tops and add to the mixture. Season with salt and pepper to taste. Gently spoon the filling into the peppers—no need to press it in firmly.

4. Set the peppers directly on the smoker rack. Add a small handful of the hickory chips to the chip loading area, and add more chips again in 30 minutes. Smoke until the peppers are soft and the filling is heated through, about 50 minutes. Remove and let cool slightly before serving.

Smoked Lamb Rib

Servings: 4

Cooking Time: 3 Hours

Ingredients:

- 2 pounds lamb rib chop
- 1 teaspoon black pepper
- 2 teaspoons BBQ Sauce
- ½ teaspoon salt
- 2 teaspoons apple vinegar
- 1 teaspoon thyme
- 2 teaspoons garlic powder
- ½ teaspoon onion powder
- 1 teaspoon ketchup

Directions:

1. Combine all the listed ingredients in a bowl to make a glaze excluding meat.

2. Pour the glaze on top of lamb rib and transfer it to the plastic zip lock bag.

3. Place in freezer for 2 hours before start cooking.

4. Afterward, put the lamb rib in a smoker and cook for 3 hours at 225 degrees F.

5. Brush the dripping on top and serve.

Jack Daniel's Meatloaf

Servings: 4

Cooking Time: 6 Hours

Ingredients:

- 4 pounds lamb meatloaf
- Glaze Ingredients:
- 4 cloves garlic
- 2 teaspoons light soy sauce
- 2 tablespoons lemon juice
- 4 tablespoons brown sugar
- ½ tsp cayenne pepper
- ½ cup pineapple juice
- ½ cup water
- ½ cup teriyaki sauce
- ½ cup Jack Daniels Whiskey
- 1 tablespoon olive oil

Directions:

1. Poke the lamb loaf with a fork.

2. Combine all of the glaze ingredient in a bowl and brush it all over the meatloaf.

3. Let it sit for few hours before cooking.

4. Afterward, put the meatloaf in the electric smoker for 6 hours at 225°F.

5. After every 30 minutes, baste the meat with the glaze.

6. After 3 hours, take out the lamb and let it sit for 20 minutes at room temperature.

7. Serve with the remaining glaze on top if desired.

8. Enjoy!

Bbq Chicken Wings Recipe

Servings: 4
Cooking Time: 2 Hours

Ingredients:

- 4 pounds turkey wings
- 1 cup of BBQ sauce

Directions:

1. Cut the chicken wings and discard the tips.
2. Marinate the wings in the BBQ sauce for about 2 hours.
3. Now preheat the smoker for a few minutes at 250 degrees F.
4. Add the cherry wood chip to the smoker and let the smoker release smoke.
5. Place the chicken into the smoker.
6. Cook for two hours or until the internal temperature reaches 165 degrees F.
7. Use the digital meat thermometer to measure the temperature.
8. Serve and enjoy.

Smoky Turkey Tenders

Servings: 4
Cooking Time: 1 Hour

Ingredients:

- 1 boneless skinless turkey breast
- 2 tablespoons dried mustard
- 2 tablespoons paprika
- 1 tablespoon ground chipotle chile pepper
- 1 tablespoon flaked sea salt, plus more for seasoning
- 1 tablespoon freshly ground black pepper, plus more for seasoning
- 2 cups all-purpose flour
- 3 large eggs, lightly beaten
- 4 cups panko bread crumbs
- 1 cup wildflower honey, for dipping

Directions:

1. On a large cutting board, slice the turkey across the grain into ½-inch strips. Set aside.
2. In a large bowl, whisk the mustard, paprika, chile pepper, 1 tablespoon of salt, and 1 tablespoon of pepper to combine. Add the turkey and toss to coat.
3. Place the flour in a large shallow bowl, the eggs in another large shallow bowl, and the bread crumbs in a third large shallow bowl.
4. Working in batches, dip each seasoned turkey strip into the flour, then dip it into the eggs, and finally into the bread crumbs. Set aside the strips on baking sheets, leaving space between each piece. Season with salt and pepper.
5. Preheat the electric smoker to 275°F. Ensure the drip tray is clean and in place. Seal the door.
6. Place the wood chips in the smoking tray or firebox, get a good smoke rolling, and seal the door.
7. Arrange the turkey strips on smoking trays, leaving space between each piece. Insert a probe thermometer (if available) into the thickest part of the meat. Set the target temperature for 165°F. Smoke for about 1 hour, or until the internal temperature reaches 165°F.
8. Remove the turkey strips from the smoker, loosely tent them with aluminum foil, and let them rest for 5 minutes. Divide the turkey into 4 equal portions and serve with ¼ cup of wildflower honey on the side of each portion for dipping.

Salted Brisket

Servings: 3
Cooking Time: 3 Hours

Ingredients:

- 2 teaspoons salt
- 1 teaspoon black pepper
- 1 teaspoon garlic paste
- 1 teaspoon ginger paste
- ½ teaspoon lemon juice
- 2 pinch five-spice powder
- 2 pounds of brisket

Directions:

1. Cut the brisket into pieces.
2. Mix all the remaining listed together in a bowl.
3. Coat the brisket with the mixture.
4. Put the brisket in the fridge for 1 hour.
5. After 1 hour, transfer to the electric smoker and cook for 3 hours at 225 degrees F.
6. Enjoy!

Buffalo Chicken Balls

Servings: 20
Cooking Time: 30 Minutes

Ingredients:

- FOR THE BALLS
- 1 pound ground chicken
- 2 cups dry Bisquick mix
- 2 cups grated Cheddar cheese
- ¼ cup water
- 1 teaspoon chicken bouillon powder
- 1 (8-ounce) block blue cheese, cut into 20 cubes
- FOR THE BUFFALO SAUCE
- ½ cup (1 stick) butter, melted
- 1 cup Frank's RedHot sauce
- 2 teaspoons cayenne pepper
- 1 teaspoon chopped fresh parsley leaves

Directions:

1. Ranch dressing, for dipping
2. Preheat the smoker to 275°F with the applewood, which offers a light, sweet flavor contrasted with the spicy ingredients.
3. TO MAKE THE BALLS
4. In a medium bowl, mix together the chicken, Bisquick mix, Cheddar cheese, water, and bouillon powder. Take a cube of blue cheese, and form about 2 tablespoons (just enough to cover the cube) of the chicken mixture around the cube. Roll it into a ball. Repeat with the remaining cheese cubes and chicken mixture.
5. Place the balls on the smoker rack and smoke for 1 to 1½ hours until firm and the internal temperature reaches 160°F.
6. TO MAKE THE BUFFALO SAUCE
7. While the balls smoke, stir together the butter, hot sauce, and cayenne in a small bowl.
8. Dredge the cooked chicken balls in the hot sauce and sprinkle with the parsley before serving with ranch dressing.

Turkey With Chimichurri

Servings: 5
Cooking Time: 4 Hours

Ingredients:

- 5 pounds bone-in, skin on turkey pieces
- Salt and pepper
- 1teaspoon paprika
- ½ teaspoon cayenne
- 2 tablespoons olive oil
- 1 pepper
- 1 onion
- 2 carrots, chopped
- 2 scallions
- 2 tomatoes, chopped
- Homemade Chimichurri Sauce
- ½ cup olive oil
- 1 teaspoon parsley
- 1 teaspoon red pepper flakes
- 2 garlic cloves
- 2 red onions

Directions:

1. Season the washed and clean turkey with the salt, pepper, paprika and cayenne pepper.
2. Rub it gently all over.
3. Arrange the wood chip inside the smoker and then preheat the smoker to 230 degrees F.
4. Transfer the turkey to the sheet pan and arrange peppers, onions, carrots, scallion, and tomatoes beside it.
5. Drizzle the olive oil on top.
6. Place the pan sheet inside the smoker.
7. Close the electric smoker door and then cook for 4 hours at 250 degrees F.
8. Check the turkey to an internal temperature of 165°F.
9. Now, it is time to make the chimichurri.
10. Blend all the homemade chimichurri ingredients in a blender and puree until combined.
11. Serve the cooked turkey and veggie with the ready to serve the sauce.

Chipotle-lime–marinated Chicken Skewers

Servings: 4

Cooking Time: 2 Hours

Ingredients:

- ½ cup extra-virgin olive oil
- 2 tablespoons fresh mint leaves, finely chopped
- 2 limes, thinly sliced
- 2 tablespoons finely chopped canned chipotle peppers in adobo sauce
- 2 tablespoons tomato paste
- 1 tablespoon dark brown sugar
- 2 boneless skinless chicken breasts, cut into bite-size pieces
- 2 boneless skinless chicken thighs, cut into bite-size pieces
- Flaked sea salt
- Freshly ground black pepper

Directions:

1. In a large bowl, stir together the olive oil, mint, lime slices, chipotle, tomato paste, and brown sugar to blend. Add the chicken and turn to coat completely. Season with salt and pepper and then cover the bowl with plastic wrap and refrigerate for 12 to 24 hours, turning the chicken 2 or 3 times.

2. Divide the chicken breast and thigh pieces into 8 portions, reserving the marinade in the refrigerator. Press the chicken onto 8 (10- to 12-inch) bamboo or metal skewers, alternating breast and thigh meat.

3. Preheat the electric smoker to 250°F. Ensure the drip tray is clean and in place. Seal the door.

4. Place the wood chips in the smoking tray or firebox, get a good smoke rolling, and seal the door.

5. Arrange the skewers on smoking trays, leaving space between each skewer.

6. Insert a probe thermometer (if available) into the thickest part of the meat. Set the target temperature for 165°F. Smoke for about 30 minutes, then baste the chicken with the reserved marinade. Smoke for another 30 minutes and baste again. Test for doneness: The internal temperature of the chicken should reach 165°F.

Applewood-smoked Turkey Breast

Servings: 4 Or 5

Cooking Time: 20 Minutes

Ingredients:

- 4 tablespoons unsalted butter, at room temperature
- 8 teaspoons Dijon mustard
- 2 tablespoons chopped fresh thyme leaves
- 1 teaspoon freshly ground black pepper, divided
- ½ teaspoon kosher salt
- 1 (6- to 7-pound) bone-in turkey breast

Directions:

1. In a small bowl, stir together the butter, mustard, thyme, ¼ teaspoon of pepper, and salt. Rub the turkey breast all over with the butter mixture. Cover and refrigerate overnight.

2. Preheat the smoker to 250°F with the applewood.

3. Sprinkle the turkey breast with the remaining ¾ teaspoon of pepper and place it on the smoker rack. Cover and cook for 3½ to 4 hours (about 30 minutes per pound).

4. When a thermometer registers 165°F, remove the turkey from the smoker and let it stand for at least 10 to 15 minutes before serving.

Sichuan-inspired Tea-smoked Duck

Servings: 4

Cooking Time: 7 Hours

Ingredients:

- 4 cups water
- ⅓ cup coarse salt
- ⅓ cup packed light brown sugar
- 1 teaspoon coarsely ground black pepper
- 4 tablespoons black tea leaves, divided
- 2 cups ice
- 2 pounds boneless, skin-on duck breasts
- 3 tablespoons sesame oil

Directions:

1. In a large pot, bring the water to a boil. Add the salt and brown sugar and let dissolve. Add the pepper and 2

tablespoons tea, then remove it from the heat. Add the ice and place the brine in the refrigerator until it's cold, about 45 minutes.

2. Place the duck breasts in a 1-gallon zip-top bag. Pour in the cooled brine. Seal the bag, pressing out all the air. Put the bag back in the pot and refrigerate for 5 hours.

3. Remove the duck from the bag and pat it dry with paper towels. Put it on a plate and refrigerate, uncovered, for 1 hour.

4. Preheat the smoker to 275°F.

5. Rub the duck with the sesame oil and place it in the smoker. Place the remaining 2 tablespoons tea in a small metal dish in a rack below the duck (when the tea stops smoking, remove the container).

6. Smoke the duck for 2 hours 30 minutes, or until the internal temperature reaches 165°F.

7. Serve warm.

Hickory-smoked Spatchcocked Chicken

Servings: 4
Cooking Time: 2 Hours

Ingredients:
- 1 quart apple cider
- 4 garlic cloves, crushed
- 4 thyme sprigs
- 3 fresh or dried bay leaves
- 1 lemon, thinly sliced
- 2 chickens, whole, spatchcocked (see tip)
- Flaked sea salt
- Freshly ground black pepper

Directions:
1. In a very large food-grade plastic bag, combine the cider, garlic, thyme, bay leaves, and lemon slices. Add the chickens, turn to coat, and remove as much air as possible from the bag before sealing it. Refrigerate for 12 to 24 hours, turning the chickens occasionally.

2. Preheat the electric smoker to 275°F. Ensure the drip tray is clean and in place. Seal the door.

3. Place the wood chips in the smoking tray or firebox, get a good smoke rolling, and seal the door.

4. Strain the chickens, reserving the brine, and pat the chickens dry. Strain the brine. Using an injection needle, inject the chickens with all the brining liquid. Space your injections evenly around the chicken.

5. Season the chickens on both sides with salt and pepper. Place the chickens, skin-side up, on a smoking rack. Insert a probe thermometer (if available) into the thickest part of the meat, not touching the bone. Set the target temperature for 165°F. Smoke for about 2 hours, or until the internal temperature reaches 165°F.

6. Transfer the chickens to a cutting board, loosely tent them with aluminum foil, and let them rest for 10 minutes before carving and serving.

Rum-brined And Smoked Turkey Legs

Servings: 6
Cooking Time: 11 Hours

Ingredients:
- 10 cups water, divided
- ¼ cup coarse salt
- ½ cup maple syrup or ¼ cup light brown sugar
- 1 cup dark rum
- 4 bay leaves
- 1 tablespoon mixed peppercorns
- 6 turkey drumsticks
- ¾ cup plus 2 tablespoons Poultry Rub

Directions:
1. In a large pot, bring 2 cups water to almost boiling. Add the salt and maple syrup and stir until the salt has dissolved. Remove from the heat and stir in the rum, bay leaves, peppercorns, and remaining 8 cups water. Set aside to cool.

2. When the brine has cooled, add the turkey. Store in the refrigerator for 10 hours or overnight.

3. Preheat the smoker to 275°F.

4. Take the turkey legs out of the brine and quickly rinse them under cold water. Then pat them well with paper towels. Season the turkey with the poultry rub.

5. Smoke the turkey for about 2 hours 30 minutes, or until the internal temperature in the thickest part of the leg reaches 165°F.

6. Let the turkey rest for at least 10 minutes before serving.

Smoked Spatchcocked Turkey

Servings: 8
Cooking Time: 1 Day

Ingredients:

- 1 (12-pound) whole turkey
- ¼ cup coarse salt
- 2 tablespoons dried rosemary
- ¼ cup Poultry Rub

Directions:

1. To spatchcock the turkey, place the bird breast-side down on a large cutting board. Use poultry shears to cut along both sides of the backbone from front to back. Remove the backbone. Turn the bird over and press firmly on the breast with the heels of your hands until it cracks to flatten out the turkey.
2. One day before smoking, dry-brine the turkey. Place it skin-side up and rub with the salt. Where possible, rub the salt under the skin and in the cavity. Place the turkey in a plastic bag or wrap it in plastic wrap. Refrigerate it overnight.
3. When you're ready to cook the turkey, preheat the smoker to 225°F.
4. Rinse the salt off the turkey. In a small bowl, mix together the rosemary and poultry rub. Generously spread the mixture all over the turkey.
5. Smoke the turkey for 6 hours, or until the internal temperature in the thickest part of the thigh reaches 165°F.
6. Let the turkey rest for 15 minutes before carving.

Smoked Turkey Soup With Bulgur Wheat

Servings: 4 To 6
Cooking Time: 3 Hours

Ingredients:

- 1 tablespoon canola oil
- 1 tablespoon unsalted butter
- 2 turkey thighs
- 1 cup diced carrots
- 1 cup diced celery hearts
- 1 cup diced yellow onions
- 4 garlic cloves, minced
- Flaked sea salt
- Freshly ground black pepper
- 2 quarts hot water
- 1 quart chicken (or vegetable) stock
- 4 Yukon gold potatoes, peeled and diced
- 1 cup cored and diced Roma tomatoes
- 2 tablespoons fresh flat-leaf parsley leaves, minced
- 3 fresh or dried bay leaves
- 1 cup bulgur wheat
- Grated Parmesan cheese, for garnish

Directions:

1. Preheat the electric smoker to 250°F. Ensure the drip tray is clean and in place. Seal the door.
2. Place the wood chips in the smoking tray or firebox, get a good smoke rolling, and seal the door.
3. Place a large cast iron Dutch oven on a smoking rack to preheat, then pour in the canola oil and add the butter to melt.
4. Arrange the turkey thighs on smoking trays, leaving space between them. Insert a probe thermometer (if available) into the thickest part of the meat, not touching the bone. Set the target temperature for 165°F.
5. Add the carrots, celery, onions, and garlic to the Dutch oven. Season with salt and pepper. Smoke for 1 hour.
6. Stir in the hot water and chicken stock to deglaze the pan, scraping up any browned bits from the bottom.
7. Add the potatoes, tomatoes, parsley, and bay leaves to the Dutch oven. Smoke for 1 hour more.
8. Add the bulgur wheat and turkey thighs to the Dutch oven. Smoke for 1 hour more and remove from the smoker.
9. Remove the thighs from the pot and remove all the meat from the bones. Cut the meat into bite-size pieces and return it to the soup. Taste and season with more salt and pepper, as needed. Remove and discard the bay leaves.
10. Finish with a sprinkle of Parmesan cheese.

Pecan Wood–smoked Turkey With Sourdough And Sausage Stuffing

Servings: 6 To 8
Cooking Time: 4 To 5 Hours

Ingredients:
- FOR THE BRINE AND TURKEY
- 2 gallons cold water
- 2 cups coarse sea salt
- 1 cup wildflower honey
- ¼ cup peppercorns
- 12 garlic cloves, unpeeled and smashed
- 2 lemons, thinly sliced
- 6 fresh bay leaves
- 6 rosemary sprigs
- 6 thyme sprigs
- 6 flat-leaf parsley sprigs
- 1 (about 12-pound) fresh or frozen turkey, thawed thoroughly in cold, running water or in the refrigerator 2 to 3 days in advance of cooking
- Flaked sea salt
- Freshly ground black pepper
- FOR THE SOURDOUGH AND SAUSAGE STUFFING
- ½ loaf sourdough bread, cut into bite-size cubes
- ½ loaf pumpernickel bread, cut into bite-size cubes
- 1 pound fresh pork sausage, casings removed
- 1 quart chicken (or vegetable) stock
- 8 ounces (2 sticks) unsalted butter, plus more, melted, for brushing
- 2 cups diced celery hearts
- 2 cups diced yellow onions
- 2 cups leeks, white parts only, quartered lengthwise and thinly sliced
- 1 tablespoon fresh thyme leaves
- 1 tablespoon fresh rosemary leaves
- 1 tablespoon thinly sliced fresh sage leaves
- 3 fresh or dried bay leaves
- Flaked sea salt
- Freshly ground black pepper

Directions:
1. TO MAKE THE BRINE AND TURKEY
2. In a large stockpot over high heat, combine the cold water, salt, honey, peppercorns, garlic, lemons, bay leaves, rosemary, thyme, and parsley. Bring the brine to a boil, then reduce the heat to maintain a simmer and cook for 5 minutes. Whisk to fully incorporate all the ingredients, remove from the heat, and let cool completely (to below 39°F) before using. Never place the turkey into hot or warm brine because bacteria will develop before the brine cools completely.
3. Completely submerge the turkey in the cooled brine and cover the pot. Refrigerate for 24 hours.
4. Remove the turkey from the brine. Rinse it and pat it dry with a paper towel. Season the turkey cavity with salt and pepper.
5. TO MAKE THE SOURDOUGH AND SAUSAGE STUFFING
6. If possible, the day before making the stuffing, leave the sourdough and pumpernickel bread cubes uncovered on the counter to dry. Place the bread cubes in a large bowl and set aside.
7. In a large skillet over high heat, sauté the sausage for about 10 minutes until browned. Remove the sausage and set aside.
8. Return the skillet to the heat and combine the chicken stock, butter, celery, onions, leeks, thyme, rosemary, sage, and bay leaves. Sauté for about 20 minutes, until golden brown. Remove and discard the bay leaves.
9. Transfer the vegetables and herbs to the bowl with the bread cubes. Add the sausage and fold the mixture together. Refrigerate the stuffing until fully cooled.
10. Stuff both cavities of the turkey with the stuffing, tucking the skin beneath it to seal. Using a bamboo skewer, sew the front cavity closed; tie the legs together with butcher's twine.
11. Preheat the electric smoker to 275°F. Ensure the drip tray is clean and in place. Seal the door.
12. Place the wood chips in the smoking tray or firebox, get a good smoke rolling, and seal the door.
13. Brush the turkey skin with melted butter and season with salt and pepper. Place the turkey on a smoking rack, in the center of the smoker. Insert a probe thermometer (if available) into the thickest part of the meat, not touching the bone. Set the target temperature for 165°F.

Smoke for about 4 hours (20 minutes per pound), or until the internal temperature reaches 165°F, when checked near the thigh, not touching the bone or the stuffing.

14. Remove the turkey from the smoker and loosely tent it with aluminum foil. Let the turkey rest for at least 20 minutes, or up to 1 hour, before slicing and serving.

Bacon-wrapped Smoked And Stuffed Chicken

Servings: 6
Cooking Time: 1 Hour 20 Minutes

Ingredients:
* 6 boneless, skinless chicken breasts
* ¾ cup Poultry Rub
* 3 cups shredded cheddar cheese
* 12 slices bacon
* ½ cup store-bought barbecue sauce or Bacon-Flavored BBQ Sauce

Directions:
1. Flatten the chicken breasts with a meat mallet until they are half as thick as when you started.
2. Coat the chicken breasts on both sides with the rub. Set them on a sheet of wax or parchment paper so that there are no spaces between them and they form a large rectangle. Over each chicken breast, evenly spread ½ cup cheddar. Very carefully, roll the entire chicken rectangle into a tight log enclosed in the wax paper. Twist the ends of the wax paper to close and refrigerate the chicken log for 1 hour.
3. Preheat the smoker to 275°F.
4. On another sheet of wax paper, lay out the bacon slices so that there are no spaces between them. Unwrap the chicken log and set it on the edge of the bacon. Carefully roll the chicken on the bacon to make a bacon-wrapped chicken log. Leave the log on the wax paper.
5. Brush the bacon-wrapped log with the barbecue sauce.
6. Cut the wax paper to make two "handles" on each end for lifting the log and placing it in the smoker.

7. Set the chicken in the smoker and carefully remove the wax paper. Smoke for 1 hour 15 minutes, or until the internal temperature reaches 165°F.
8. Slice the log and serve warm.

Morocco Smoked Whole Chicken Recipe

Servings: 3
Cooking Time: 3 Hours

Ingredients:
* 1 teaspoon fresh cilantro
* 4 tablespoons olive oil
* 1 teaspoon garlic powder
* 1 tablespoon onion powder
* 1 teaspoon cumin
* 1 teaspoon paprika
* ½ teaspoon ground red pepper
* 1 tablespoon dry lemon zest
* Salt, to taste
* Other Ingredients:
* 1 whole chicken, about 2.5 pounds

Directions:
1. Combine all the rub ingredients in a small bowl for further use.
2. Preheat the smoker to 250 degrees F for 40 minutes by adding cherry wood chips.
3. Rinse the chicken and trim out the excess fat.
4. Tie the legs together using a kitchen string.
5. Now rub the spice blend over the chicken and then cover for a few hours.
6. Place the chicken on a baking rack and put it inside the smoker.
7. Cook until internal temperate reaches 165 degrees F, about 3 hours
8. Take out the chicken and let it sit for a few hours before serving.

Garlic Mustard Smoked Beef Tenderloin

Servings: 3
Cooking Time: 3 Hours 30 Minutes

Ingredients:

- 3 pounds beef tenderloin
- 2 sticks or cubes of butter
- 2 tablespoons black peppercorns
- 2 tablespoons white peppercorns
- 1 tablespoon sea salt
- 10 cloves fresh garlic, minced
- ⅓ cup parsley, chopped
- ½ cup rosemary, chopped
- 2 teaspoons English mustard
- 2 teaspoons honey
- 2 tablespoons of olive oil
- 6 ounces of Armagnac or brandy

Directions:

1. Combine all the basting Ingredients in a large pot and submerge the beef in it for 4 hours.
2. Afterward, take out the tenderloin from the basting mixture and let it sit at room temperature.
3. Mix the entire rub ingredient in a small bowl and rub it gently all over the beef tenderloin for fine coating.
4. Smoke on top most racks for half hour at 225 degrees F by adding apple wood chips.
5. Afterward, transfer it to the plate and rub 2 sticks of butter.
6. Seal it with aluminum foil and cook for 3 hours at 225°F.
7. Remove from smoker and immediately serve.
8. Enjoy.

Lemon Garlic Chicken Breast Recipe

Servings: 2
Cooking Time: 90 Minutes

Ingredients:

- 2-pound chicken breasts, boneless and skinless
- 4 cloves minced garlic
- 2-inches ginger, minced
- 4 lemons, juice only
- 4 tablespoons olive oil
- Salt, to taste
- Black pepper, to taste
- 1 teaspoon turmeric

Directions:

1. Take a bowl and combine salt, pepper, lemon juice, olive oil, turmeric, ginger, and garlic in a bowl.
2. Mix well and rub the chicken with the prepared mix.
3. Let the chicken marinate for 2 hours in the refrigerator.
4. Now preheat the smoker to 250 degrees F.
5. Add the cherry wood chip to the smoker and let the smoke release.
6. Place the chicken into the smoker.
7. Cook for 90 minutes or until the internal temperature reaches 165 degrees F.
8. Use the digital meat thermometer to measure the temperature.
9. Serve and enjoy.

Beef Sirloin

Servings: 4
Cooking Time: 4-5 Hours

Ingredients:

- 4 pounds beef sirloin
- Salt and black pepper, to taste
- 2 tablespoons vegetable oil
- 1 cup red wine
- 310 mL beef consommé
- 2 tablespoons butter

Directions:

1. Sprinkle meat with salt, pepper, and rub vegetable oil on top.
2. Afterward, put the meat in the electric smoker and cook for 4-5 hours at 220°F.
3. Meanwhile, take a saucepan and add butter.
4. Let it melt, and then pour in the red wine and let it cook until boil comes.
5. Add the beef consommé.
6. Once smooth and light, the sauce is ready. Turn off the heat.

7. Take out the beef sirloin from the smoker and let it stand at room temperature for 20 minutes.

8. Cut the meat and serve it by pouring sauce over the top.

Smoked Chicken Gumbo

Servings: 6 To 8
Cooking Time: 4 Hours

Ingredients:

- FOR THE RICE
- 1 tablespoon unsalted butter
- 1 tablespoon extra-virgin olive oil
- 1 cup diced yellow onions
- Flaked sea salt
- Freshly ground black pepper
- 2 cups long-grain white rice, or brown rice
- 1 tablespoon fresh thyme leaves, stripped and finely chopped
- 1 fresh bay leaf
- 4 cups chicken (or vegetable) stock
- FOR THE GUMBO
- ½ cup canola oil
- 3 pounds bone-in skin-on chicken thighs
- Flaked sea salt
- Freshly ground black pepper
- 8 ounces andouille sausage, thinly sliced
- 6 thick-cut smoked bacon slices
- 1 cup all-purpose flour
- 6 garlic cloves, finely chopped
- 1 cup diced yellow onion
- 1 cup diced celery heart
- 1 green bell pepper, trimmed, seeded, and diced
- 1 quart chicken (or vegetable) stock
- 12 okra, cut into ½-inch slices
- 6 Roma tomatoes, cored, quartered, and diced
- 1 tablespoon fresh thyme leaves
- 3 fresh or dried bay leaves
- Hot sauce, for serving

Directions:

1. TO MAKE THE RICE

2. Heat a large saucepan over medium-high heat and combine the butter, olive oil, and onion. Season with salt and pepper. Sauté for about 10 minutes, until the onion is golden brown.

3. Stir in the rice, thyme, and bay leaf, stirring to coat the rice in the butter and oil.

4. Add the chicken stock. Stir gently, cover the pan, and reduce the heat to low. Cook for 45 to 60 minutes, until the liquid is absorbed.

5. TO MAKE THE GUMBO

6. Preheat the electric smoker to 275°F. Ensure the drip tray is clean and in place. Seal the door.

7. Place the wood chips in the smoking tray or firebox, get a good smoke rolling, and seal the door.

8. Place a large cast iron casserole, such as a Dutch oven, or deep roasting pan on a smoking rack to preheat and pour in the canola oil.

9. Pat the chicken dry with a paper towel and season both sides of the chicken with salt and pepper. Arrange the chicken on smoking trays, skin-side up, leaving space between each piece. Insert a probe thermometer (if available) into the thickest part of the meat, not touching the bone. Set the target temperature for 165°F. Smoke for about 2 hours.

10. Add the sausage and bacon to the preheated casserole. Cook for about 45 minutes, or until lightly browned and the fat renders, turning the casserole 2 or 3 times. Stir in the flour, creating a roux.

11. Add the garlic, onion, celery, and green pepper. Cook for about 20 minutes, until tender.

12. Stir in the chicken stock to deglaze the pan, scraping up any browned bits from the bottom. Add the okra, tomatoes, thyme, and bay leaves. Stir to incorporate.

13. When the chicken is fully cooked, nestle it into the casserole on top of the other ingredients. Smoke for about 1 hour more, or until the okra is tender and the liquid has reduced to your desired consistency.

14. To finish, remove the chicken from the gumbo. Debone the chicken. Remove and discard the skin. Shred the meat into bite-size pieces and return the chicken to the gumbo. Season with salt and pepper.

15. Serve with a side of rice and a good Southern hot sauce.

Best Damn Holiday Turkey Breast

Servings: 6 To 8
Cooking Time: 15 Minutes

Ingredients:
- 6 to 8-pound bone-in whole turkey breast
- ½ cup (1 stick) butter, softened
- ¼ cup chopped fresh herbs (about 1 tablespoon each of rosemary, thyme, sage, and oregano)
- 1 tablespoon minced garlic
- 1 tablespoon coarse kosher salt
- 1 teaspoon black pepper

Directions:
1. Prepare the smoker's water pan according to the manufacturer's instructions and preheat the electric smoker to 250°F. While it heats, fill a medium bowl with water and add 3 or 4 handfuls of wood chips to soak.
2. Remove any turkey giblets, if your bird comes with them, then rinse and dry well. In a medium bowl, combine the butter with all the remaining ingredients and stir with a fork to combine. Rub the breast heavily on all sides with the butter-and-seasoning mixture; you'll use most if not all of it. Add some under any loose skin for even more flavor.
3. Set the turkey breast directly on a smoker rack, skin side up, and add a small handful of the soaked wood chips to the chip loading area. Keep adding more chips at least every 30 minutes. The turkey is done when it reaches an internal temperature of 165°F, about 3½ to 4½ hours depending on the size of your turkey breast.
4. Remove from smoker and loosely place a foil tent over the breast to cool for 15 to 30 minutes before slicing.

Spicy Baby Back Ribs

Servings: 6
Cooking Time: 6 Hours

Ingredients:
- 2 teaspoons salt
- 4 pounds slabs baby back ribs
- 1 teaspoon chili powder
- 1 teaspoon lemon pepper
- ½ teaspoon garlic pepper
- 1 teaspoon paprika
- 1 teaspoon black pepper
- 2 teaspoons lemon juice
- 2 teaspoons BBQ sauce

Directions:
1. Cut the baby back ribs into pieces.
2. Mix all the ingredients together in a bowl.
3. Rub the mixture on the baby back ribs.
4. Put the baby back ribs in the electric smoker at 225°F for 6 hours.
5. Serve and enjoy.

Mustard And Lime Flavored Brisket

Servings: 3
Cooking Time: 4 Hours 50 Minutes

Ingredients:
- 1 teaspoon paprika
- 1 teaspoon dried mustard
- ½ teaspoon thyme
- 2 teaspoons lime juice
- 1 teaspoon salt
- 3 pounds brisket

Directions:
1. Mix paprika, dried mustard, thyme, lime juice, and salt together.
2. Massage it all over the brisket for fine coating.
3. Let it marinate in the refrigerator for 2 hours.
4. Afterward, put the brisket in the electric smoker for cooking at 230°F for 4 hours 50 minutes.
5. Serve and enjoy.

Smoked Leg Of Lamb

Servings: 1
Cooking Time: 90 Minutes

Ingredients:
- 1 teaspoon coriander
- ½ teaspoon black pepper
- 1 teaspoon turmeric
- 2 teaspoons salt
- ½ teaspoon paprika
- 2 teaspoons vinegar

- 1 teaspoon onion powder
- 1 pound leg of lamb

Directions:

1. Mix the coriander, black pepper, turmeric, salt, paprika, vinegar, and onion powder in a large bowl.
2. Sprinkle the mixture all over the leg of lamb.
3. Rub well for fine coating.
4. Then put it in the smoker at 225°f for 90 minutes by adding apple wood chip for enhanced flavoring.
5. After 3 hours, remove it from the electric smoker.
6. Let stand at room temperature for 10 minutes.
7. After 10 minutes cut it into small pieces.
8. Enjoy!

Smoked Chicken Lollipops

Servings: 4

Cooking Time: 2 Hours

Ingredients:

- 2 pounds chicken drumsticks
- 8 garlic cloves, peeled
- 3 tablespoons sliced peeled fresh ginger
- 3 tablespoons fresh cilantro leaves, plus more for garnish
- 1 jalapeño pepper, trimmed, halved, and seeded
- ¼ cup rice wine vinegar
- 2 tablespoons fish sauce
- 2 tablespoons soy sauce
- 2 tablespoons ground paprika
- Flaked sea salt
- Freshly ground black pepper
- 4 limes, quartered, for serving

Directions:

1. To french the chicken, place your sharp knife about 1 inch below the knuckle bone and cut all the way around the bone, cutting through the skin and tendons. Push the meat down the bone toward the chicken drumstick and remove any excess skin or tendons. Trim the bone clean, as needed. Repeat with all the drumsticks.
2. In a food processor, combine the garlic, ginger, cilantro, jalapeño, vinegar, fish sauce, soy sauce, and paprika. Process until smooth. Transfer to a large food-grade plastic bag.

3. Add the chicken, remove as much of the air as possible from the bag, and seal it. Refrigerate for 24 hours to marinate, turning 2 or 3 times.
4. Preheat the electric smoker to 250°F. Ensure the drip tray is clean and in place. Seal the door.
5. Place the wood chips in the smoking tray or firebox, get a good smoke rolling, and seal the door.
6. Remove the drumsticks from the marinade, reserving the marinade in the refrigerator. Season the chicken with salt and pepper. Arrange the drumsticks on smoking trays, leaving space between each piece. Insert a probe thermometer (if available) into the thickest part of the meat, not touching the bone. Set the target temperature for 165°F. Smoke for about 30 minutes, then baste using the reserved marinade.
7. Smoke for 30 minutes more and baste again. Repeat smoking and basting about 2 times more, or until the chicken reaches an internal temperature of 165°F.
8. Remove the chicken lollipops from the smoker, baste, loosely tent with aluminum foil, and let rest for 10 minutes before serving with lime garnish.

Smoked Buffalo Chicken Meatballs

Servings: 4

Cooking Time: 90 Minutes

Ingredients:

- 2 pounds ground chicken
- 3 tablespoons cooked carrot, finely chopped
- 4 tablespoons celery, finely chopped
- 2 green onions, finely chopped
- ⅓ cup dry bread crumbs
- ⅓ teaspoon salt
- ⅓ teaspoon paprika
- ⅓ teaspoon brown sugar
- ⅓ teaspoon garlic powder
- ⅓ teaspoon ground black pepper
- ⅓ cup non-fat Greek yogurt
- ⅓ cup mayonnaise
- 2 tablespoon buttermilk
- ⅓ teaspoon seasoned salt
- ¼ teaspoon dill
- ½ teaspoon chili powder

- ¼ teaspoon granulated garlic
- ½ cup hot sauce
- ⅓ cup butter
- ⅓ teaspoon Worcestershire

Directions:

1. Combine celery, carrots, chicken, onions and bread crumbs along with salt, sugar, garlic, paprika, and pepper in a bowl.
2. Mix well to form the meatballs
3. Freeze at least for 30 minutes.
4. Combine the entire ranch dip ingredient in a bowl.
5. Refrigerate for about 20 minutes.
6. Preheat the smoker grill to 250 degrees F.
7. Meanwhile, place the hot sauce, butter and Worcestershire sauce in a pot and let it simmer on medium flame.
8. Layer meatball in a pan sheet and place the meatballs on the topmost rack and cook for about 30 minutes.
9. Turn the meatballs around and then cook for further 10 minutes.
10. Once the internal temperature reaches 165 degrees F, take out the meatballs and then toss them in the buffalo sauce glaze.
11. Return to the smoker and cook for 50 more minutes.
12. Serve it with ranch dip.

Cinnamon-cured Fire-smoked Chicken

Servings: 4
Cooking Time: 15 Minutes

Ingredients:

- 1 quart water
- ¼ cup salt
- ¼ cup firmly packed brown sugar
- 4 chicken breasts
- 1 onion, sliced
- 1 lemon, sliced
- 2 cinnamon sticks, halved
- 1 tablespoon ground cinnamon
- 1 tablespoon red pepper flakes
- 1 tablespoon seasoned salt

Directions:

1. In a large bowl, stir together the water, salt, and brown sugar until dissolved.
2. Add the chicken, onion, lemon, and cinnamon sticks. Cover the bowl with plastic wrap and refrigerate for 1 hour.
3. Preheat the smoker to 250°F with the apple or cherrywood.
4. Remove the chicken from the refrigerator and discard the marinade.
5. Sprinkle the chicken with the cinnamon, red pepper flakes, and seasoned salt. Place it on the smoker rack and smoke for about 1½ hours until the internal temperature reaches 165°F.

Spiced Citrus Duck With Shallots And Plums

Servings: 4
Cooking Time: 3 To 4 Hours

Ingredients:

- 2 tablespoons canola oil
- 1 duck, whole
- Flaked sea salt
- Freshly ground black pepper
- 4 mandarin oranges, halved, divided
- 8 thyme sprigs, divided
- 8 blue plums, halved and pitted
- 8 shallots, halved
- 4 star anise, whole
- 4 cloves, whole
- 2 cinnamon sticks, whole
- 1 (750-mL) bottle sauvignon blanc

Directions:

1. Preheat the electric smoker to 275°F. Ensure the drip tray is clean and in place. Seal the door. Coat a roasting pan with canola oil. Set aside.
2. Place the wood chips in the smoking tray or firebox, get a good smoke rolling, and seal the door.
3. Season the duck all over, inside and out, with salt and pepper. Stuff the cavity with 4 orange halves and 4 thyme sprigs. Set the duck in the prepared roasting pan, breast-side up.

4.   Arrange the plums, shallots, star anise, cloves, cinnamon sticks, remaining 4 orange halves, and remaining 4 thyme sprigs around the duck.

5.   Pour the white wine over the ingredients surrounding the duck. Season with salt and pepper.

6.   Place the roasting pan on a smoking tray. Insert a probe thermometer (if available) into the thickest part of the meat, not touching the bone. Set the target temperature for 165°F. Smoke for about 2 hours, opening the smoker occasionally to spoon the rendered liquids over the entire dish. Continue to smoke for 1 to 2 hours more, or until the internal temperature reaches 165°F.

7.   Remove the duck from the smoker, loosely tent it with aluminum foil, and let it rest for 20 minutes.

8.   Remove and discard the thyme, star anise, and cinnamon sticks. Serve the duck with a side of the plums and shallots.

Herbed Lemon Chicken Thighs

Servings: 4
Cooking Time: 15 Minutes

Ingredients:
- 4 bone-in, skin-on chicken thighs (about 2 pounds total)
- zest and juice of 2 lemons
- 2 tablespoons olive oil
- 1 tablespoon chopped fresh thyme
- 1 tablespoon chopped fresh oregano
- 2 teaspoons salt
- 1 teaspoon black pepper

Directions:
1.   Place the chicken thighs in a 1-gallon zip-top plastic bag. Add the remaining ingredients, seal, and refrigerate for 1 to 2 hours to let the flavors combine.

2.   Prepare the smoker's water pan according to the manufacturer's instructions and preheat the smoker to 225°F. While it heats, fill a medium bowl with water and add 3 or 4 handfuls of pecan wood chips to soak.

3.   Remove the chicken pieces from the bag and place them directly on a smoker rack. Add a small handful of the soaked pecan chips to the chip loading area, and keep adding more chips at least every 30 minutes. The

chicken is done when it reaches an internal temperature of 165°F, about 2 hours. Remove from the smoker and serve while hot.

Smoked Butter Chicken

Servings: 6 To 8
Cooking Time: 30 Minutes

Ingredients:
- 2 pounds boneless, skinless chicken breasts, cut into 1-inch pieces
- 5 tablespoons butter, divided
- 1 cup sour cream
- 1 tablespoon fresh-squeezed lemon juice
- 2 tablespoons chili powder, divided
- 2½ tablespoons garam masala, divided
- 2 tablespoons plus 2 teaspoons minced garlic (about 10 to 12 cloves)
- 1 tablespoon plus 2 teaspoons freshly grated ginger, divided
- 2 teaspoons coarse kosher salt, divided
- 1 medium onion, minced
- 1 jalapeño chile, seeded and minced
- 1 tablespoon sugar
- 1 teaspoon ground coriander
- 1 (28-ounce) can crushed tomatoes
- 1 tablespoon tomato paste
- ¾ cup heavy cream
- cooked rice and naan bread, for serving

Directions:
1.   Place the chicken breasts in a 1-gallon zip-top plastic bag. Melt 3 tablespoons of the butter and add to the bag along with the sour cream, lemon juice, 1 tablespoon chili powder, 1 tablespoon garam masala, 2 teaspoons garlic, 2 teaspoons ginger, and 1 teaspoon salt. Seal the bag and gently massage to combine the ingredients. Refrigerate for 1 to 3 hours to marinate the chicken.

2.   Prepare the smoker's water pan according to the manufacturer's instructions and preheat the smoker to 250°F. While it heats, fill a medium bowl with water and add 3 or 4 handfuls of pecan wood chips to soak.

3.   Pour the chicken and marinade into a 10-inch cast-iron skillet and place in the smoker, but don't add any

wood chips yet. Cook for 30 minutes, stirring after 15 minutes.

4. While the chicken is cooking, add the remaining 2 tablespoons butter and 2 tablespoons garlic to a medium skillet along with the onion and jalapeño. Cook on the stovetop over medium-high heat for 3 to 5 minutes, or until the onion is soft and translucent. Stir in the sugar, coriander, and remaining 1 tablespoon chili powder, 1½ tablespoons garam masala, 1 tablespoon ginger, and 1 teaspoon salt. Cook for 1 minute to release the flavors, then stir in the crushed tomatoes, tomato paste, and heavy cream. Bring to a boil, reduce the heat to low, and simmer for 5 minutes, stirring occasionally. Remove from the heat and carefully remove the cast-iron skillet from the smoker. Pour the sauce into the cast-iron skillet with the chicken and stir to combine. Return the cast-iron skillet to the smoker.

5. Close the smoker door and add a handful of the soaked pecan chips to the chip loading area. Add more chips and stir the chicken and sauce again in 30 minutes. The chicken is done when its internal temperature reaches 165°F, about 1 more hour (total cooking time about 1½ hours).

6. Remove the skillet from the smoker and serve the chicken and its sauce over rice, along with Indian naan bread.

Smoked Chicken Thighs With Wasabi-soy Marinade

Servings: 4
Cooking Time: 5 Hours

Ingredients:
- ¼ cup soy sauce, plus more for serving
- 2 tablespoons rice vinegar
- 1 tablespoon grated peeled fresh ginger
- 2 teaspoons wasabi paste, plus more for serving
- 2 teaspoons chili-garlic sauce
- 1 tablespoon sesame seeds
- 1 tablespoon minced garlic
- 3 tablespoons sesame oil, divided
- 2 pounds bone-in, skin-on chicken thighs

Directions:

1. In a container with a cover, mix together the soy sauce, vinegar, ginger, wasabi, chili-garlic sauce, sesame seeds, garlic, and 1 tablespoon sesame oil.

2. Add the chicken thighs and coat them completely. Cover the container and refrigerate for 4 hours.

3. Remove the chicken thighs from the marinade and pat them dry with paper towels. Let them rest for another 45 minutes to 1 hour at room temperature.

4. Preheat the smoker to 275°F.

5. Brush the chicken with the remaining 2 tablespoons sesame oil.

6. Place the chicken thighs in the smoker and smoke for 1 hour, or until the internal temperature reaches 165°F.

7. Serve warm, with some soy sauce and wasabi on the side for dipping.

Cajun Smoked Chicken Recipe

Servings: 5
Cooking Time: 4 Hours

Ingredients:
- 5 pounds whole chicken
- ½ cup of Cajun Spice Mix Seasoning, such as from Discovery

Directions:

1. Turn the chicken, breast side down.

2. Cut along the spine, and remove the backbone from the chicken.

3. Press the breast bit down so the chicken get flat.

4. Rub the chicken with the Cajun spice mix.

5. Place the chicken on a rack.

6. Place the thermometer into the chicken.

7. Place it in the electric smoker.

8. Fill the wood chip holder with cherry or apple wood chips.

9. Fill the water container with water.

10. Close the door of the smoker and set the temperature to 250 degrees F.

11. Cook until temperature reaches 165 degrees F, or about 4 hours.

12. Allow it to come to room temperature, then serve.

Balsamic Vinegar Chicken Breasts

Servings: 2
Cooking Time: 2 Hours

Ingredients:
- 4 tablespoons olive oil
- ½ cup balsamic vinegar
- 4 cloves garlic, minced
- 2 tablespoons basil, fresh
- 1 teaspoon red chili powder
- Salt and black pepper, to taste
- 2 pounds chicken breasts, boneless and skinless

Directions:
1. Take a zipper-lock plastic bag and combine all the ingredients except chicken.
2. Place the chicken in the bag and let it marinate in the refrigerators for 2 hours.
3. Now preheat the smoker for a few minutes at 250 degrees F and add cherry or apple wood chip to the smoker.
4. Place the chicken into the smoker once the smoke started to come out.
5. Cook until the internal temperature reaches 165 degrees F.
6. Use the digital meat thermometer to measure the temperature.
7. Serve and enjoy.

Beer-brined Smoked Chicken Legs

Servings: 4
Cooking Time: 3 Hours

Ingredients:
- 8 chicken drumsticks
- 1 ½ cups cold water
- 2 (12-ounce) bottles beer or ale
- ½ cup coarse salt
- ½ cup packed light brown sugar
- 1 tablespoon minced garlic
- 1 tablespoon Dijon mustard
- 2 teaspoons chopped fresh rosemary
- 3 tablespoons olive oil
- ¼ cup Poultry Rub

Directions:
1. Place the drumsticks in a large container that has a lid.
2. Fill a 1-gallon or larger pitcher with the water and beer. Stir in the salt and continue to stir until it's completely dissolved. Then stir in the brown sugar, making sure it's also dissolved. Mix in the garlic, mustard, and rosemary.
3. Pour the brine over the drumsticks, cover the container, and refrigerate for 2 hours 30 minutes.
4. Preheat the smoker to 275°F.
5. Rinse the drumsticks to get rid of the excess salt. Then pat them dry with paper towels. Brush them with the olive oil and rub with the poultry rub until they're coated all over.
6. Place the drumsticks in the smoker. Make sure the drip pan is in place under them. Smoke for 2 hours to 2 hours 30 minutes, or until the internal temperature reaches 165°F.
7. Serve warm.

APPETIZERS & DESSERTS RECIPES

Bacon-wrapped Stuffed Dates

Servings: 36
Cooking Time: 30 Minutes

Ingredients:
- 4 ounces cream cheese, softened
- 2 tablespoons finely chopped chives
- 36 pitted dates
- 1 pound sliced bacon (or 12 slices), each strip cut into thirds maple syrup, slightly warmed, for brushing and dipping
- 36 toothpicks (optional)

Directions:
1. Preheat the electric smoker to 275°F without using the water pan. While it heats, fill a medium bowl with water and add 3 or 4 handfuls of mesquite wood chips to soak.
2. In a medium bowl, combine the cream cheese and chives, mixing well. Gently slice into a date to separate the halves, without cutting them apart (essentially you are butterflying the date). Working with 2 small spoons, fill the date with a scoop of cream cheese mixture and gently press the halves back together. Wrap a slice of bacon around the stuffed date, beginning and ending with the bacon ends on the bottom; secure with a toothpick if needed. Repeat with the remaining dates.
3. Place the stuffed dates in a grill basket or 8 × 12-inch disposable foil pan that is sprayed with cooking spray and brush with warm maple syrup. Add a small handful of the soaked mesquite chips to the chip loading area. Every 15 minutes, turn over the dates and baste with maple syrup, then add more wood chips. Smoke for 40 to 45 minutes, or until the bacon is cooked and crispy.
4. Remove from the smoker and let cool for 10 minutes before serving. Serve warm or at room temperature, with additional warm maple syrup for dipping.

Smoked Almonds

Servings: 8
Cooking Time: 10 Minutes

Ingredients:
- 4 tablespoons (½ stick) unsalted butter
- 2 tablespoons salt
- 2 teaspoons freshly ground black pepper
- 2 pounds skin-on almonds

Directions:
1. Preheat the smoker to 225°F.
2. In a saucepan on the stovetop, melt the butter over medium heat. Stir in the salt and pepper.
3. Place the almonds in a bowl and pour the seasoned melted butter over them. Stir the nuts to coat.
4. With BBQ mitts, lay a sheet of aluminum foil over a cooking rack. Spread the almonds in one layer on the foil. Use more foil, if necessary, to make sure the almonds are in one layer.
5. Set the rack in the smoker and smoke the almonds for 2 hours 30 minutes, stirring the almonds halfway through to make sure they get evenly smoked.
6. Let the almonds rest for 30 minutes before serving.

Smoked Cheddar Cheese

Servings: 6
Cooking Time: 4 Hours

Ingredients:
- 3 (8-ounce) blocks aged cheddar cheese

Directions:
1. Preheat the smoker to 125°F.
2. Set the blocks of cheese away from the hottest part of the smoker. Smoke them for 1 hour.
3. Let the cheese cool to room temperature, then put them in separate zip-top bags and refrigerate for at least 4 hours before serving.

Baked Peach Cobbler

Servings: 4
Cooking Time: 3 Hours

Ingredients:

- 2 teaspoons melted butter
- 3 pounds sliced peaches
- ½ cup maple syrup
- 1 cup self-rising flour
- 3/4 tsp baking powder
- 1 pinch cinnamon
- 1 pinch salt
- ⅓ cup unsalted butter, cut into small cubes
- ⅓ cup white sugar
- 2 eggs
- ½ tsp vanilla

Directions:

1. Set the electric smoker temperature to 220 degrees F,and add cherry wood chips.
2. Coat a large heatproof pan with melted butter.
3. Take a bowl and toss peaches with maple syrup.
4. In a small bowl, combine flour, baking powder, salt and cinnamon, and set it aside.
5. In a separate bowl, mix butter along with sugar.
6. Then add eggs and the vanilla extract.
7. Combine the flour mixture with egg mixture.
8. Spoon this batter on top of peaches.
9. Cook in the electric smoker for 3 hours at 260 degrees F.
10. Once done serve.
11. Enjoy.

Chocolate Cobbler

Servings: 3
Cooking Time: 80 Minutes

Ingredients:

- 2 cups chocolate, chopped
- 1 cup whipped cream, (for a topping)
- Cobbler Topping Ingredients:
- 1.5 cups all-purpose flour
- 4 tablespoons sugar
- 1 teaspoon baking powder
- 5 tablespoons cocoa powder
- ½ cup sour cream

Directions:

1. Start the smoker and add wood chips and wait until the smoke is established.
2. Set temperature to 350 degrees F.
3. Meanwhile, take a separate medium bowl and mix together the sugar, flour, baking soda, and cocoa powder.
4. Add the sour cream.
5. Mix gently to form a dough.
6. Add chocolate pieces to a baking bowl and pour the dough mixture on top.
7. Place it inside smoker and cooks or 80 minutes or until top get brown and bubbling.
8. Serve with whipped cream if desired.

No-churn Smoked Peach Ice Cream

Servings: 6 To 8
Cooking Time: 15 Minutes

Ingredients:

- 4 peaches
- 1 (8-ounce) container unsweetened heavy whipping cream
- 1 (14-ounce) can sweetened condensed milk
- 2 teaspoons vanilla

Directions:

1. Preheat the electric smoker to 210°F without using the water pan. While it heats, fill a medium bowl with water and add 3 or 4 handfuls of maple wood chips to soak. Prepare a 9 × 13-inch foil pan by poking a dozen small holes with a sharp knife in the bottom and spray it lightly with cooking spray. The slits will allow the smoke to come up through the bottom of the pan.
2. Cut the peaches in half, remove the pits, and place in the prepared pan. Set the pan in the smoker and add a small handful of the soaked maple chips to the chip loading area. Add more wood chips at least every 30 minutes. Remove the peaches from the smoker after 1 hour and let them cool completely, or refrigerate overnight.
3. Using a blender or food processor, purée the cooled peaches until nearly smooth, with just a few small chunks left. In a large chilled bowl, whip the heavy cream into stiff peaks and then gently fold in the

sweetened condensed milk and vanilla with a spatula to keep the whipped cream from deflating. Gently fold in the peach purée until the peaches are almost fully incorporated—just a few large streaks of peach purée is ideal.

4.   Pour into a metal bread pan and place in the freezer for 4 to 6 hours, or until frozen through. Serve within a couple days. Remove from the freezer a few minutes before serving; however, this ice cream will melt faster than store-bought ice cream, so don't let it sit out too long before serving it.

Easy Pineapple Upside-down Cake

Servings: 8 To 10
Cooking Time: 15 Minutes

Ingredients:
*   1 (15.25-ounce) yellow cake mix or 2 (15-ounce) gluten-free yellow cake mixes
*   ½ to ¾ cup light brown sugar
*   1 (20-ounce) can pineapple rings, drained
*   1 (10-ounce) jar pitted maraschino cherries, drained

Directions:
1.   Preheat the electric smoker to 225°F without the water pan. While it heats, fill a medium bowl with water and add 1 or 2 handfuls of pecan or maple wood chips to soak.
2.   Prepare the cake batter according to the package instructions and set aside. Spray a 12-inch cast-iron skillet with cooking spray, coating well. Sprinkle the brown sugar into the bottom of the skillet to coat evenly. Arrange pineapple rings in a circle around the edge of the skillet and add another in the center. Place a cherry (without stem) in the center of each pineapple ring and add more cherries in between the rings. Carefully pour the prepared cake batter over the pineapple slices, being careful not to disturb the cherries.
3.   Place the skillet in the smoker and add a small handful of the soaked pecan chips to the chip loading area. Add more wood chips at least every 20 to 30 minutes. Smoke for 1½ to 2 hours, or until the cake is lightly browned.

4.   Remove the cake from the smoker and let it cool for 20 to 30 minutes. Run a butter knife around the inside edge of the skillet to loosen the cake. Then place a serving plate or cake stand upside down over the skillet and carefully invert the cake onto the plate. Serve warm or let cool for another 30 minutes to serve at room temperature.

Smoked Deviled Eggs

Servings: 4
Cooking Time: 50 Minutes

Ingredients:
*   6 large eggs
*   2 teaspoons salt, divided
*   2 teaspoons apple cider vinegar, divided
*   1 teaspoon olive oil
*   3 tablespoons mayonnaise
*   2 teaspoons Dijon mustard
*   1 teaspoon hot sauce
*   1 teaspoon garlic powder
*   1 teaspoon onion powder
*   1 teaspoon freshly ground black pepper
*   2 teaspoons smoked paprika

Directions:
1.   Preheat the smoker to 212°F.
2.   In a medium pot, combine the eggs with enough water to cover by 1 inch. Add 1 teaspoon salt and 1 teaspoon vinegar. Bring to a boil, then reduce to a simmer and cook for 10 minutes. Drain and cool the eggs under cold running water, then peel them.
3.   Set the eggs on a grill screen, place in the smoker, and smoke for 30 minutes.
4.   Transfer the eggs to a bowl and refrigerate to cool them down, about 30 minutes.
5.   Halve the eggs lengthwise. Pop the yolks into a bowl. Place the empty halves of the egg whites on a serving dish.
6.   Add the olive oil to the yolks and break them up with a fork until they are well mashed. Add the mayonnaise, mustard, hot sauce, garlic powder, onion powder, pepper, and remaining 1 teaspoon vinegar and 1 teaspoon salt. Blend the ingredients together until

they form a thick paste. If you want your deviled eggs to be creamier, add another 1 to 2 teaspoons mayonnaise.

7.   Fill each egg white half with about 1 tablespoon of the yolk mixture.

8.   Sprinkle the smoked paprika over the filling and serve.

Smoked Spicy Queso Dip

Servings: 4
Cooking Time: 15 Minutes

Ingredients:

- 2 tablespoons unsalted butter
- 1 medium red onion, diced
- 1 tablespoon minced garlic
- 1 jalapeño pepper, seeded and diced
- 1 pound Velveeta cheese, cut into 1-inch cubes
- ¾ cup drained canned diced tomatoes
- 1 teaspoon hot sauce
- Chips, for dipping

Directions:

1.   Preheat the smoker to 250°F and fill the water pan.

2.   In a skillet on the stovetop, heat the butter over medium heat. Add the onion and garlic and sauté for 5 to 7 minutes, until tender and translucent.

3.   Transfer the sautéed onion and garlic to a shallow aluminum baking dish or 12-inch cast-iron skillet and add the jalapeño and Velveeta. Stir it all up to make sure everything is mixed.

4.   Smoke the cheese mixture for 2 hours. As soon as the cheese starts to melt, stir in the diced tomatoes and hot sauce. After that, stir the queso every 30 minutes.

5.   Remove the pan from the smoker and stir the dip a final time until everything's smooth and evenly combined.

6.   Serve immediately with chips for dipping. If you'd like, you can also keep it heated in a slow cooker on the lowest setting, so it stays smooth and soft.

Cast-iron Triple Berry Crisp

Servings: 6 To 8
Cooking Time: 5 Minutes

Ingredients:

- 2 cups (6 ounces) fresh blueberries
- 1 cup (6 ounces) fresh blackberries
- 1 pound fresh strawberries (about 2 cups)
- ½ cup light brown sugar
- 2½ tablespoons cornstarch
- ¾ cup all-purpose flour (regular or gluten-free)
- ¾ cup rolled oats
- 1½ cups granulated sugar
- ½ cup (1 stick) butter, cut in thin slices

Directions:

1.   Preheat the electric smoker to 275°F without using the water pan. While it heats, fill a medium bowl with water and add 2 to 3 handfuls of maple wood chips to soak. Spray a 10-inch cast-iron skillet with cooking spray.

2.   Rinse the berries and spread on paper towels to dry. Cut the strawberries into pieces about the size of the blackberries. In a large bowl, gently combine the berries with the brown sugar and cornstarch. Pour into the prepared pan.

3.   In another bowl, combine the flour, oats, and granulated sugar. Pour the mixture over the berries, making sure to completely cover them. The better everything is covered, the less likely the filling will bubble over. Scatter slices of butter all over the top of the oat mixture.

4.   Place the pan in the smoker and add a small handful of the soaked maple chips to the chip loading area. Adding more chips at least every 20 minutes, smoke for 1½ to 2 hours, or until the top is lightly browned and crisp. Cool for 30 minutes before serving. Transfer any leftovers to a storage container, cover, and store in the refrigerator for up to one week

Barbecue Meatballs

Servings: 15 To 20
Cooking Time: 15 Minutes

Ingredients:

- 1 pound ground chicken
- ¼ cup bread crumbs (either regular or gluten-free)
- ½ teaspoon salt
- ½ teaspoon ground cumin
- ½ teaspoon chili powder

- ¼ teaspoon black pepper
- 4 cloves garlic, finely minced
- 1 tablespoon minced green onions (whites and greens)
- ¾ cup Tangy Smoked Barbecue Sauce (page 17), divided, plus more for serving if desired

Directions:

1. Preheat the electric smoker to 275°F without using the water pan. While it heats, fill a medium bowl with water and add 2 handfuls of hickory wood chips to soak.
2. In a large bowl, combine the ground chicken with the next 7 ingredients (bread crumbs through green onions) and ¼ cup of the barbecue sauce. Use your hands to gently mix everything together. The key to a moist and tender meatball is to not overwork it.
3. Using a large cookie scoop (1 to 2-tablespoon size), scoop out some of the chicken mixture and roll it gently into a ball; set aside. Continue forming meatballs with the rest of the mixture.
4. Spray a grill basket with cooking spray and place the meatballs in a single layer in the basket. Add a small handful of the soaked hickory chips to the chip loading area. Add more chips and baste the tops and sides with the remaining ½ cup barbecue sauce at least every 30 minutes. (There is no need to turn the meatballs while they cook.)
5. Smoke until the meatballs are fully cooked, about 1 hour. Serve warm on skewers or toothpicks, and offer more barbecue sauce for dipping, if you wish.

Blueberry Crumble

Servings: 4
Cooking Time: 3.5 Hours

Ingredients:

- 1 cup blueberries
- ¾ cup dark brown sugar
- ½ cup self-rising flour
- 2 teaspoons lemon zest, grated
- 2 tablespoons lemon juice
- 1.5 cups quick-cooking oats
- ⅓ cup all-purpose flour
- ½ cup packed brown sugar
- 2 teaspoons cinnamon

- ⅓ cup butter

Directions:

1. Place the washed the blueberries in a mixing bowl and add sugar, lemon zest, lemon juice, and flour.
2. Mix all the ingredients well.
3. Take an aluminum pan and coat it with oil spray.
4. Spoon the filling into the pan.
5. Then combine all the crumble ingredients in a separate bowl and pour over the blueberry mixture in the pan.
6. Cook in the electric smoker for 3.5 hours at 260 degrees F.
7. Once done, serve.

Rhubarb Cobbler

Servings: 3
Cooking Time: 3 Hours

Ingredients:

- 1 pound rhubarb, chopped
- ⅓ cup brown sugar
- Pinch of salt
- 1 teaspoon lemon juice
- 1 tablespoon lemon zest
- 2 teaspoons vanilla extract
- Cobbler Topping Ingredients:
- 1.5 cups all-purpose flour
- 4 tablespoons sugar
- 1 teaspoon baking powder
- ¼ tsp kosher salt
- 10 tablespoons unsalted butter
- ⅓ cup sour cream

Directions:

1. Start the electric smoker and add mild flavor wood chips and wait until the smoke is established.
2. Set temperature to 260 degrees F.
3. Take a medium bowl and mix cobbler topping ingredients including salt, flour, baking powder, and sugar
4. Add butter and sour cream.
5. Mix gently with the fork to form the smooth dough.
6. Take a small bowl and then mix chopped rhubarb, lemon juice, lemon zest, vanilla extract, and salt, and sugar.

7. Transfer this mixture to the desired baking dish.
8. Spoon the prepared dough on top.
9. Place it inside smoker and cooks for 3hours or until the top gets brown and bubbling.
10. Serve.

Bacon-wrapped Stuffed Jalapeños

Servings: 10
Cooking Time: 15 Minutes

Ingredients:
- 10 large jalapeño chiles
- 10 slices thick-cut bacon (about 1 pound)
- 8 ounces cream cheese, softened
- 1 pound breakfast sausage, crumbled, cooked, and drained
- ⅛ cup chopped fresh chives
- pinch of salt

Directions:
1. Preheat the electric smoker to 275°F without using the water pan. While it heats, fill a medium bowl with water and add 3 or 4 handfuls of mesquite wood chips to soak.
2. Cut the jalapeños in half lengthwise, leaving the stems attached but scooping out the seeds and most of the veins. Set aside. Cut the bacon slices in half so that you have 20 short pieces.
3. In a medium bowl, combine the cream cheese, cooked sausage, chives, and salt. Mix well. Working with 2 small spoons, fill a jalapeño half with 1 or 2 spoonfuls of the cream cheese mixture. Wrap a slice of bacon around the stuffed jalapeño, beginning and ending with the bacon ends on the bottom. Repeat with the remaining chiles.
4. Set the jalapeños, filling side up, in a grill basket or disposable foil pan that has been sprayed with cooking spray. Add a small handful of the soaked mesquite chips to the chip loading area and keep adding more chips at least every 15 minutes. Smoke for 40 to 45 minutes, or until the bacon is cooked and crispy.

5. Remove the peppers from the smoker and let cool for 10 minutes before serving. Serve warm or at room temperature.

Basque-style Cheesecake

Servings: 8
Cooking Time: 20 Minutes

Ingredients:
- 1 tablespoon softened butter, for the pan
- 3 (8-ounce) packages cream cheese, at room temperature
- 1 cup sugar
- ½ teaspoon salt
- 3 tablespoons all-purpose flour
- ½ teaspoon pure vanilla extract
- 4 extra-large eggs, at room temperature
- 1 ¼ cups heavy (whipping) cream

Directions:
1. Preheat a pellet smoker to 400°F.
2. Butter a 9-inch cake pan. Cut a sheet of parchment paper large enough to line the bottom and sides of the pan with a few extra inches. Butter the paper and press it into the pan, butter-side up, flattening any major creases. Trim away any excess paper from the sides until you have an inch or two of overhang.
3. In a bowl, combine the cream cheese, sugar, salt, and flour. Stir and smear together with a spatula until very smooth and creamy.
4. Whisk in the vanilla and 1 egg. Add the remaining 3 eggs, whisking each one in completely before adding the next. Pour in the heavy cream and mix until smooth.
5. Pour the batter into the prepared pan. Tap the pan against the counter to burst any air bubbles.
6. Bake the cake in the smoker for 40 minutes.
7. Increase the temperature to 425°F and cook for 10 minutes more, or until it's puffed, well browned, and nearly burned on the edges.
8. Remove the cheesecake and let it cool to room temperature. Lift it out onto a plate and peel back the parchment paper with a spatula. Refrigerate until thoroughly chilled, then serve.

Killer Stuffed Potato Skins

Servings: 8
Cooking Time: 20 Minutes

Ingredients:
- 4 large russet potatoes
- 2 tablespoons sour cream, plus more for topping
- 1 cup shredded Cheddar cheese, plus more for topping
- 4 slices bacon, cooked and crumbled
- 4 green onions (whites and greens), finely minced, plus more for topping
- ½ cup prepared guacamole
- salt and black pepper

Directions:
1. Pierce each potato several times with a fork. Wrap individually in paper towels and cook in the microwave for about 10 to 15 minutes, or until tender. (Alternatively, plan ahead and bake your potatoes in a 425°F oven for 50 minutes to 1 hour directly on the oven rack or a baking sheet. Turn potatoes every 20 minutes during baking.) Set aside to cool.
2. Prepare the smoker's water pan according to the manufacturer's instructions and preheat the smoker to 275°F. While it heats, fill a medium bowl with water and add 2 handfuls of hickory wood chips to soak.
3. When the potatoes are cool enough to handle, cut in half lengthwise and scoop out three-quarters of the insides from each half, leaving about ¼ inch of potato in the skin. In a medium bowl, use a fork to mash the potato flesh you've removed. Add the 2 tablespoons sour cream, 1 cup cheese, and salt and pepper to taste; mix well. Scoop the filling into the potato skins.
4. Top the stuffed potato skins with the crumbled bacon, green onions, and a little more cheese. Place directly on a smoker rack and add a small handful of the soaked hickory chips to the chip loading area. Add chips again after they've been smoking for 30 minutes. Smoke for 1 hour, or until the stuffing is hot and bubbly and the cheese is melted.
5. Top heated potatoes with sour cream, guacamole, and additional chopped green onions as desired.

Smoked Peanut Butter Cookies

Servings: 12
Cooking Time: 15 Minutes

Ingredients:
- 1 cup peanut butter (crunchy or creamy)
- 1 cup sugar, plus more for the cookie tops
- 1 egg

Directions:
1. Preheat the smoker to 275°F without using the water pan. While it heats, fill a medium bowl with water and add 1 or 2 handfuls of maple wood chips to soak. Line 2 disposable 8 × 12-inch foil pans with parchment paper and set aside.
2. In a medium bowl, combine the peanut butter, 1 cup sugar, and egg; mix well. Drop by tablespoonfuls onto the prepared pans. Dip a fork into sugar and press into the cookie tops twice, once in each direction, creating a crosshatch pattern.
3. Set the pans in the smoker and add a small handful of the soaked maple chips to the chip loading area. Adding more wood chips at least every 20 minutes, smoke for 45 minutes to 1 hour, or until the cookies are lightly browned and set on top. The cookies may still be a little soft, but they'll firm up as they cool.
4. After cooling completely, store in an airtight container at room temperature for up to one week.

Smoked Cheese

Servings: 1
Cooking Time: 5 Minutes

Ingredients:
- 1 pound Cheddar cheese

Directions:
1. Preheat the smoker to 190°F without using the water pan.
2. While it heats, cut the cheese into 1-inch slices. Fill a disposable foil pan with ice cubes and cover with a sheet of foil; this will keep the cheese cool enough that it won't melt. Arrange the cheese slices in a single layer on the foil.
3. Set the pan on the top rack of the smoker and add a handful of dry (not soaked) pecan wood chips to the chip

loading area. Check the ice level in the pan every 15 minutes, drain any melted water and add more ice as needed to keep the cheese cool. After 30 minutes of smoking, add more dry pecan chips and flip the cheese slices.

4. Remove the pan from the smoker after 1 hour. Transfer the cheese slices onto paper towels to absorb any excess oil. When completely cool, wrap the slices in several clean paper towels and place in a zip-top plastic bag. Refrigerate for 1 week before using to let the cheese mellow. Keep cheese wrapped in clean paper towels in a zip-top bag in the refrigerator for up to two weeks after smoking.

Smoked Salmon Spread

Servings: 6
Cooking Time: 1 Hour, 15 Minutes

Ingredients:
- 8 ounces cream cheese, at room temperature
- ¼ cup heavy (whipping) cream
- ½ cup chopped scallions
- 1 tablespoon minced capers (optional)
- 2 teaspoons chopped fresh dill
- 1 teaspoon garlic powder
- 1 teaspoon freshly ground black pepper
- 8 ounces Canadian-Style Smoked Salmon on Cedar, finely chopped

Directions:
1. In a large bowl, blend together the cream cheese and cream until smooth. Stir in the scallions, capers (if using), dill, garlic powder, and pepper. Add the salmon and stir to evenly distribute. Cover and refrigerate for 1 hour before serving.

Stuffed And Smoked French Toast

Servings: 3
Cooking Time: 15 Minutes

Ingredients:
- 6 (1-inch-thick) slices egg bread
- ½ cup whole milk
- 11 large eggs
- 1 ½ teaspoons cinnamon sugar
- 1 teaspoon pure vanilla extract
- 8 ounces cream cheese, at room temperature
- ½ cup canned apple pie filling
- ½ cup canned blueberry pie filling
- ½ cup canned cherry pie filling
- 1 tablespoon powdered sugar
- ½ cup maple syrup

Directions:
1. Preheat a pellet smoker to 275°F.
2. Place the slices of bread in the smoker for 10 minutes to dry them out a bit.
3. Increase the temperature to 350°F and place grill mats in the smoker.
4. In a large bowl, mix together the milk and eggs. Add the cinnamon sugar and vanilla and beat the mixture until it's frothy.
5. Spread the cream cheese on one side of each slice of bread. Reserving a little of each pie filling for serving, top 3 of the slices with the pie fillings (one type of filling per slice). Close up the sandwiches, setting the remaining 3 slices on top, cream cheese-side down.
6. Dip each sandwich completely in the egg mixture, letting them soak for about 5 seconds, then immediately place the sandwiches on the grill mat.
7. Smoke them for 5 to 7 minutes, until the bread is browned. Flip the sandwiches and cook for another 5 minutes.
8. To serve, top each sandwich with some of the reserved pie filling and sprinkle with the powdered sugar. Drizzle the maple syrup over it all and serve hot.

Cherry Crumble

Servings: 4
Cooking Time: 3 Hours

Ingredients:
- Filling Ingredients:
- 1 cup of cherries
- ¾ cup dark brown sugar
- 1 cup self-rising flour
- 1.5 cup quick oats
- ⅓ cup all-purpose flour
- ½ cup raisin

- ⅓ cup butter

Directions:

1. Place the washed cherries in a mixing bowl and add sugar and flour, and mix gently.
2. Take the aluminum pan and coat it with oil spray.
3. Spoon the flour filling into the aluminum pan.
4. Add oats, raisins, butter, and flour.
5. Mix well until it is lumpy in consistency.
6. Cook in an electric smoker or 3 hours at 260 degrees F.
7. Once it's done, serve.

Beef Jerky

Servings: X
Cooking Time: 30 Minutes

Ingredients:

- 3 pounds boneless beef bottom round
- 3 cups cold water
- 1 cup light brown sugar
- ¼ cup coarse kosher salt
- ⅛ cup prepared hot sauce
- ⅛ cup Worcestershire sauce
- 1 tablespoon garlic powder
- 1 tablespoon onion powder
- 2 teaspoons ground coriander
- 2 teaspoons black pepper
- 1 teaspoon mustard powder
- 1 teaspoon dried oregano
- 1 teaspoon ground sage
- ½ teaspoon dried thyme

Directions:

1. Place the beef in the freezer for about 30 minutes to make slicing easier. Then slice it in long, narrow strips about ⅛ to ¼ inch thick (or ask your butcher to do it for you).
2. In a large container or freezer-weight zip-top plastic bag (the 2-gallon size should be just right), gently mix all the remaining ingredients so that the salt and sugar are dissolved. Add the sliced beef, seal, and refrigerate for 24 hours to let the meat marinate. Every few hours, knead the bag or stir in the container to ensure that the beef is evenly coated with marinade.

3. Prepare the smoker's water pan according to the manufacturer's instructions, but substitute about half of the water with the marinade from the meat container. Preheat the smoker to 170°F. (If your smoker doesn't go down to 170°F, set it as low as it will go.) While it heats, fill a medium bowl with water and add a handful of hickory wood chips to soak.
4. Remove the beef strips from the remaining marinade and arrange them on a smoker racks in a single layer, trying to keep them from touching each other. Place a couple handfuls of the soaked hickory chips in the chip loading area. This is the only time you should add chips; otherwise the jerky might turn bitter. Since the meat is so thin, there is no need to turn or flip it during cooking.
5. The jerky will take from 4 to 6 hours to smoke, depending on your smoker's temperature and the water content of the beef. When done, the meat should be dried out but still a little pliable. Let cool completely, then seal in a zip-top plastic bag and store in the refrigerator for up to 2 weeks.

Poblano Salsa

Servings: 2
Cooking Time: 10 Minutes

Ingredients:

- 1 small onion, quartered
- 4 Roma tomatoes
- 3 jalapeño chiles
- 2 cloves garlic
- 3 poblano chiles
- 2 limes, juiced, or more as needed
- 2 teaspoons salt, or more as needed
- ½ cup chopped fresh cilantro leaves

Directions:

1. Prepare the smoker's water pan according to the manufacturer's instructions and preheat the smoker to 210°F. While it heats, fill a medium bowl with water and add 3 or 4 handfuls of pecan wood chips to soak.
2. Place the onion, tomatoes, jalapeños, garlic, and poblanos in a disposable foil pan. Set the pan in the smoker and add a small handful of the soaked pecan chips to the chip loading area. Keep adding more chips

at least every 30 minutes. Let the vegetables cook for 1 to 1½ hours, or until they are dark and tender.

3.   Remove the vegetables from the smoker and let cool. Cut the stems from the chiles and tomatoes and remove the liquid and seeds from the tomatoes. For a less-spicy salsa, seed and devein the chiles; or leave some whole to add spice.

4.   Transfer the onion, garlic, and chiles to the bowl of a food processor and pulse to start chopping them. Add the tomatoes, half of the lime juice, and 1 teaspoon of salt and process until the salsa has the desired degree of chunkiness. Add the cilantro and pulse once or twice to incorporate. Taste and adjust the salt and lime level juice as needed.

5.   Transfer the salsa to a container with a lid and refrigerate for several hours or overnight to let the flavors combine. The smokiness will mellow as the mixture sits in the refrigerator.

Smoked Coconut Macaroons

Servings: 12
Cooking Time: 15 Minutes

Ingredients:
- 4 cups sweetened flaked coconut
- 4 egg whites
- ½ cup canned sweetened coconut milk
- ½ teaspoon vanilla
- ¼ cup sugar

Directions:
1.   Preheat the smoker to 210°F without using the water pan. While it heats, fill a medium bowl with water and add 3 or 4 handfuls of maple wood chips to soak.

2.   Spread the coconut in an 8 × 12-inch disposable foil pan and place in the smoker. Add a small handful of the soaked maple chips to the chip loading area. Add more chips at least every 15 to 30 minutes, and stir the coconut every 15 minutes so that it smokes evenly. Remove from the smoker after 1 hour or when most of the coconut is golden brown and let cool.

3.   Line 2 disposable 8 × 12-inch foil pans or small baking sheets with parchment paper; set aside. Turn up the smoker heat to 275°F.

4.   In a large bowl, whisk the egg whites until frothy and add the smoked coconut, coconut milk, vanilla, and sugar. Stir well to combine. Drop by large tablespoonfuls onto the parchment paper. Place the pans in the smoker and add a small handful of chips to the chip loading area. Adding more wood chips at least every 20 minutes,

5.   Smoke for 30 to 45 minutes, or until the cookies are lightly browned and the tops are set.

6.   After cooling, store in an airtight container for up to one week.

Smoked Candied Nuts

Servings: 8
Cooking Time: 15 Minutes

Ingredients:
- ½ cup raw almonds
- 1 cup raw cashews
- 4 ½ cups raw hazelnuts
- 1 cup raw pecans
- 6 tablespoons unsalted butter
- 6 tablespoons dark brown sugar
- 1 teaspoon ground cinnamon
- 1 teaspoon coarse salt
- 1 tablespoon dark rum

Directions:
1.   Preheat the smoker to 225°F.
2.   Spread the nuts evenly in a shallow baking dish.
3.   Smoke the nuts for 1 hour 30 minutes.
4.   Take out the pan, stir the nuts around, and return to the smoker for another 1 hour 30 minutes. Check them in the last 30 minutes to make sure they don't get too dark.

5.   About 15 minutes before the nuts are done, in a saucepan on the stovetop, melt the butter over medium heat. Stir in the brown sugar, cinnamon, and salt until well combined. Add the rum and keep stirring for 5 to 7 minutes as the mixture thickens.

6.   Take the nuts out of the smoker and place them in a bowl. Pour the sugar/butter mixture over them and stir to coat the nuts with the glaze.

7.   Serve warm or let cool to room temperature.

Smoked Pineapple Chocolate Upside-down Cake

Servings: 8
Cooking Time: 20 Minutes

Ingredients:

- 1 (15.25-ounce) box double-fudge chocolate cake mix
- ⅓ cup vegetable oil
- 3 large eggs
- 1 ¼ cups pineapple juice
- ⅓ cup unsalted butter
- 1 ⅓ cups packed light brown sugar
- 7 pineapple rings, canned or cored fresh
- 8 maraschino cherries

Directions:

1. Preheat a pellet smoker to 350°F.
2. Follow the directions on the cake box to make the batter, using the vegetable oil and eggs as directed but substituting the pineapple juice for water.
3. In a 12-inch cast-iron skillet on the stovetop, melt the butter over medium heat. As soon as the butter is melted, sprinkle the brown sugar over it.
4. Set the pineapple rings in the butter and sugar in a circle with one in the middle. Then put one cherry in the center of each ring, pressing them down a little. Pour the cake batter over the pineapple and cherries.
5. Set the skillet on the grill grate in the smoker and smoke for 25 minutes.
6. To make sure it bakes evenly, rotate the pan a half turn and smoke for another 25 minutes. Like all cakes, you'll know it's done when you stick a toothpick or knife blade into it and it comes out clean.
7. Run a knife around the side of the skillet to loosen the cake. Place a big serving plate or cutting board upside-down on the pan. Then flip everything over to release the cake, but leave the skillet in place. Let the cake rest—with the pan still on top of it—for 5 minutes to set the pineapple and sugar.
8. Remove the skillet and serve the cake warm or cool.

Smoked Bacon-wrapped Cheese Sandwiches

Servings: 2
Cooking Time: 30 Minutes

Ingredients:

- 4 (1-inch-thick) slices bread
- 6 slices pepper Jack cheese
- 1 teaspoon cayenne pepper
- 16 slices bacon
- 1 tablespoon Pork Rub

Directions:

1. Preheat the smoker to 250°F.
2. Place the bread in the smoker and cook for 10 minutes. This will remove moisture and keep the sandwich from getting soggy. Let the bread cool for 10 minutes.
3. For each sandwich, place 3 slices of cheese between 2 slices of bread. On a sheet of wax paper, arrange 4 slices of bacon side by side, overlapping by about ¼ inch. Set a cheese sandwich on the bacon, 1 ½ inches in from one of the ends of the bacon. Fold that bacon over the end of the sandwich. With your fingers on the 1 ½ inch line of bacon, flip the sandwich over, then flip it forward again and the bacon will wrap around one side of the sandwich.
4. Now, to finishing wrapping the sandwich, repeat the arranging of 4 slices of bacon on the wax paper. Set the sandwich over the bacon so that the bacon will wrap the exposed sides and repeat the flipping steps above.
5. Repeat to make the second sandwich.
6. Sprinkle the bacon with the pork rub.
7. Smoke the bacon-wrapped sandwiches for 1 hour, or until the bacon has browned.
8. To serve, cut the sandwiches into quarters.

Smoked Nuts

Servings: 2 To 3
Cooking Time: 5 Minutes

Ingredients:

- 2 to 3 cups raw, shelled nuts (walnuts, pecans, cashews, or other nuts of your choice)

Directions:

1. Preheat the smoker to 210°F without using the water pan. While it heats, fill a medium bowl with water and add 3 or 4 handfuls of maple wood chips to soak.
2. Spread the nuts in a disposable 9 × 13-inch foil pan and set in the smoker. Add a small handful of the soaked maple chips to the chip loading area, and keep adding more chips at least every 30 minutes. Stir every 30 minutes until all the nuts are smoked, about 1 to 1½ hours.
3. Remove the pan from the smoker and let the nuts cool to room temperature before serving or using them in a recipe. You can store the smoked nuts in an airtight container for up to 3 weeks.

Smoked No-bake Chocolate Oatmeal Coconut Cookies

Servings: 24
Cooking Time: 20 Minutes

Ingredients:

- 2½ cups quick-cooking rolled oats
- 1 cup sweetened flaked coconut
- 1 cup chopped nuts
- 2 cups sugar
- 6 tablespoons (¾ stick) butter
- ½ cup unsweetened cocoa powder
- ½ cup evaporated milk
- 1 teaspoon vanilla

Directions:

1. Preheat the smoker to 210°F without using the water pan. While it heats, fill a medium bowl with water and add 1 or 2 handfuls of maple wood chips to soak.
2. Spread the oats, coconut, and nuts evenly in an 8 × 12-inch disposable foil pan. Place in the smoker and add a small handful of the soaked maple chips to the chip loading area. Add more chips at least every 15 to 30 minutes, and stir the oat mixture every 15 minutes so that everything smokes evenly. Remove from the smoker after 1 hour and let cool.
3. In a large stockpot, combine the sugar, butter, cocoa powder, and evaporated milk. Bring to a rolling boil on the stovetop over high heat and boil for exactly 1 minute. Remove from the heat and stir in the vanilla and the smoked oat mixture, combining well.
4. Drop the cookies by the spoonful onto wax or parchment paper. Let cool completely to firm up. Store in an airtight container at room temperature for up to one week.

FISH & SEAFOOD RECIPES

Smoked Salmon Pasta With Lemon And Dill

Servings: 4

Cooking Time: 3 Hours 20 Minutes

Ingredients:

- FOR THE SALMON
- 1 (1-pound) skin-on salmon fillet
- 2 tablespoons coarse salt
- 2 tablespoons chopped fresh dill
- 1 tablespoon light brown sugar
- 2 teaspoons grated lemon zest
- 1 teaspoon freshly ground black pepper
- FOR THE PASTA AND SAUCE
- 1 pound fettuccine or linguine
- 4 tablespoons (½ stick) unsalted butter
- 1 teaspoon minced garlic
- 1 teaspoon paprika
- 6 tablespoons white wine
- 2 cups heavy (whipping) cream
- 1 tablespoon chopped fresh dill

Directions:

1. TO MAKE THE SALMON
2. Preheat the smoker to 225°F.
3. With needle-nose pliers or fish tweezers, remove any pin bones from the fillet.
4. In a bowl, mix together the salt, dill, brown sugar, lemon zest, and pepper. Rub the mixture into the flesh side of the salmon. Wrap the fillet tightly in plastic and refrigerate for 3 hours.
5. Unwrap the salmon and pat it dry with paper towels.
6. Smoke the salmon for 40 minutes, or until the internal temperature reaches 145°F.
7. Let the salmon rest while you prepare the pasta and sauce.
8. TO MAKE THE PASTA AND SAUCE
9. Cook the pasta according to the package directions.
10. In a large saucepan on the stovetop, melt the butter over medium-high heat. Add the garlic and sauté for 1 minute. Stir in the paprika and then the wine. Cook for 5 minutes to reduce, then add the cream. Cook over low heat, stirring occasionally, for about 7 minutes, or until the sauce gets a little thicker.
11. Meanwhile, cut the salmon into chunks.
12. When the sauce has reduced, stir the salmon in very gently.
13. Serve the salmon sauce over the pasta and sprinkle the chopped dill over the top.

Simple Seasoned Crab Legs

Servings: 4

Cooking Time: 5 Minutes

Ingredients:

- 1½ pounds precooked crab legs (thawed if frozen)
- ¼ cup Old Bay Seasoning
- melted butter, for serving

Directions:

1. Prepare the smoker's water pan according to the manufacturer's instructions and preheat the smoker to 275°F. While it heats, fill a medium bowl with water and add 1 handful of beech wood chips to soak.
2. Place the crab legs in a 2-gallon zip-top plastic bag along with the Old Bay. Seal completely and shake vigorously to completely coat the crab legs. Let sit for at least 10 minutes to make sure the crabmeat is fully flavored with the seasoning.
3. Transfer the crab legs to a grill basket and place in the smoker. Add a small handful of the soaked beech chips to the smoker's chip loading area, and add more chips after 15 minutes. Smoke for 20 minutes, or until the crab is hot. Serve with melted butter for dipping.

Silky Scrambled Eggs With Smoked Salmon

Servings: 4

Cooking Time: 30 Minutes

Ingredients:

- 2 tablespoons unsalted butter
- 1 pound sockeye salmon, cut into 1-inch strips

- Flaked sea salt
- Freshly ground black pepper
- 1 lemon, halved
- 12 large eggs, lightly beaten
- 1 cup heavy (whipping) cream
- 2 tablespoons chopped fresh chives, plus more for garnish
- 1 loaf crusty artisan bread, cut into 8 slices on a 45-degree angle
- ¼ cup Greek yogurt, whipped

Directions:

1. Preheat the electric smoker to 275°F. Ensure the drip tray is clean and in place. Seal the door.
2. Place the wood chips in the smoking tray or firebox, get a good smoke rolling, and seal the door.
3. Place a large cast iron skillet on a smoking rack to preheat, and drop in the butter to melt.
4. Season the salmon fillets on all sides with salt and pepper. Place the fillets on the smoking racks, leaving space between them. Squeeze the lemon halves over the fillets. Smoke for about 30 minutes, or until the salmon turns an opaque bright pink color. Salmon can be enjoyed rare, medium-rare, or fully cooked—use the opacity to judge doneness.
5. In a large bowl, whisk together the eggs, cream, and chives. Season with salt and pepper. Pour the egg mixture into the skillet. Smoke until the eggs are still partially liquid and creamy, stirring occasionally with a wooden spoon. Remove the skillet from the smoker, but continue to stir, using the pan's residual heat to finish cooking the eggs to your desired consistency.
6. Place the bread slices on smoking racks, leaving space between them. Smoke for about 5 minutes, or until warm.
7. Spoon the eggs over the toasted bread. Top with slices of salmon and garnish with a dollop of yogurt and more chives, if desired.

Salmon With Stone-ground Mustard And Tarragon

Servings: 4
Cooking Time: 30 Minutes

Ingredients:

- ¼ cup mayonnaise
- 2 tablespoons stone-ground mustard
- 2 tarragon sprigs, leaves stripped and finely sliced, plus more for garnish
- Grated zest of 1 lemon, plus juice of 1 lemon, plus 1 lemon, quartered, for serving
- 4 (8-ounce) salmon fillets, skin removed and deboned
- Flaked sea salt
- Freshly ground black pepper

Directions:

1. Preheat the electric smoker to 275°F. Ensure the drip tray is clean and in place. Seal the door.
2. Place the wood chips in the smoking tray or firebox, get a good smoke rolling, and seal the door.
3. In a large bowl, whisk together the mayonnaise, mustard, tarragon, lemon zest, and half the lemon juice.
4. Season the salmon on both sides with salt and pepper. Top each fillet with the mayonnaise mixture. Place the fillets on smoking racks, leaving space between each one. Drizzle with the remaining lemon juice. Smoke for 20 to 30 minutes, until lightly browned. Total smoking time will depend on your desired doneness and the thickness of the fillets. Test for doneness by sliding a paring knife into the thickest part of a fillet and leaving it there for 5 seconds. Remove the knife and gently touch the flat side to your lower lip—if the knife is warm, the salmon is fully cooked.
5. Top with a sprinkle of tarragon. Serve with lemon wedges for squeezing.

Cajun Salmon Blts

Servings: 4
Cooking Time: 20 Minutes

Ingredients:

- 1 tablespoon onion powder
- 1 tablespoon paprika
- 2 teaspoons dried thyme
- 2 teaspoons garlic powder
- 2 teaspoons dried oregano
- 1 teaspoon coarse kosher salt
- ½ teaspoon cayenne pepper

- ½ teaspoon black pepper
- ⅓ cup mayonnaise
- ⅓ cup Smoked Walnut Pesto (page 105)
- 4 (4 to 6-ounce) salmon fillets, about 1 pound total weight (skin removed)
- 2 tablespoons olive oil
- 4 hearty rolls (such as ciabatta rolls)
- 8 slices hickory-smoked bacon, cooked
- 4 Romaine lettuce leaves
- 4 tomato slices

Directions:

1. Prepare the smoker's water pan according to the manufacturer's instructions and preheat the smoker to 275°F. While it heats, fill a medium bowl with water and add 3 or 4 handfuls of beech wood chips to soak.

2. In a small bowl, combine the onion powder, paprika, thyme, garlic powder, oregano, salt, cayenne, and black pepper; set aside. In a separate bowl, combine the mayonnaise and the walnut pesto. Cover and refrigerate until ready to use.

3. Using paper towels, pat the salmon pieces dry. Rub each with a drizzle of olive oil and generously sprinkle with the dry seasoning mix. Store any leftover seasoning mix in an airtight container.

4. Prepare a foil pan by poking a dozen small holes in the bottom with a sharp knife and then lightly spraying it with cooking spray. The holes allow the smoke to penetrate the bottom of the fish without the need to flip the fish since it's delicate and might fall apart if flipped. Lay the fish in the pan and place in the smoker. Add a small handful of the soaked beech chips to the chip loading area, and keep adding more chips at least every 15 minutes. Smoke for 30 to 40 minutes, or until the thickest part of the fish reaches an internal temperature of 145°F.

5. Place each smoked salmon piece on a hearty roll generously spread with pesto mayonnaise. Top with 2 slices of bacon, a lettuce leaf, and a tomato slice.

Lemon Pepper Bacon-wrapped Trout

Servings: 4
Cooking Time: 15 Minutes

Ingredients:
- 4 trout fillets
- 1 tablespoon freshly ground black pepper
- 2 teaspoons salt
- 4 to 8 bacon slices, partially cooked
- Juice of 1 lemon
- Chopped fresh parsley leaves, for garnish

Directions:

1. Preheat the smoker to 200°F with alder, apple, or cherrywood.

2. Generously season the fillets with the salt and pepper before wrapping each with 1 or 2 bacon slices, depending on the size of the fish. Wrap the bacon tightly and secure the ends as tightly as possible.

3. Squeeze lemon juice on all sides of the fillets, and head to the smoker.

4. Place the fish in the smoker and smoke for 2 to 2½ hours until the fish reaches an internal temperature of 160°F. The flesh should be soft yet flaky when gently pressed with a fork.

5. Sprinkle with parsley and serve warm.

Smoked Halibut With Mango-pineapple Salsa

Servings: 4
Cooking Time: 1 Hour

Ingredients:
- 4 halibut fillets, rinsed and patted dry with a paper towel
- 2 tablespoons extra-virgin olive oil, plus more for garnish
- Flaked sea salt
- Freshly ground black pepper
- 2 cups diced pineapple
- 2 cups diced mango
- 1 red bell pepper, trimmed, seeded, and diced
- ¼ cup diced red onion
- 1 chile pepper, trimmed, seeded, and diced
- 1 cup fresh cilantro leaves, finely sliced
- Grated zest of 2 limes, plus juice of 2 limes

Directions:

1.   Preheat the electric smoker to 275°F. Ensure the drip tray is clean and in place. Seal the door.

2.   Place the wood chips in the smoking tray or firebox, get a good smoke rolling, and seal the door.

3.   Brush the halibut with 2 tablespoons of the olive oil and season it on all sides with salt and pepper. Gently place the fish on smoking racks, leaving space between each fillet. Smoke until the fish is opaque, for 10 to 15 minutes. Halibut can be enjoyed rare, medium-rare, or fully cooked—use the opacity to judge doneness.

4.   In a large bowl, combine the pineapple, mango, red bell pepper, onion, chile pepper, and cilantro. Add the lime zest and lime juice. Season with salt and pepper and gently stir to combine. Refrigerate until needed.

5.   Serve the halibut fillets topped with the salsa. Season with salt, pepper, and a drizzle of olive oil.

Smoked Shrimp With Garlic And Rosemary

Servings: 4
Cooking Time: 30 Minutes

Ingredients:

- 2 tablespoons extra-virgin olive oil, plus more for brushing
- 2 tablespoons unsalted butter
- 1 baguette loaf, cut into ½-inch-thick slices on an angle
- Flaked sea salt
- Freshly ground black pepper
- 4 garlic cloves, finely sliced
- 4 rosemary sprigs
- 2 pounds shrimp, shelled, deveined, rinsed, and patted dry with a paper towel
- Grated zest of 1 lemon, plus juice of 1 lemon

Directions:

1.   Preheat the electric smoker to 275°F. Ensure the drip tray is clean and in place. Seal the door.

2.   Place the wood chips in the smoking tray or firebox, get a good smoke rolling, and seal the door.

3.   Place a large cast iron skillet on a smoking rack to preheat, then pour in 2 tablespoons of the olive oil and add the butter to melt.

4.   Brush the baguette slices with olive oil, season with salt and pepper, and arrange them on the smoking racks with space between each slice.

5.   In the skillet, combine the garlic and rosemary. Toss to coat with the oil and butter, season with salt and pepper, and smoke for 15 minutes.

6.   Add the shrimp and lemon zest. Toss to coat and season with salt and pepper. Smoke for about 15 minutes, until the flesh turns slightly pink. Turn and smoke the shrimp for 15 minutes more.

7.   Remove and discard the rosemary. Drizzle the shrimp with lemon juice. Serve with the smoked baguette slices.

Honey Mustard Halibut Fillets

Servings: 6
Cooking Time: 6 Hours

Ingredients:

- ⅓ cup kosher salt
- 1 cup brown sugar
- 4 tablespoons cumin
- 1 tablespoon dried bay leaves, crushed
- ½ gallon water
- Other Ingredients:
- 6 halibut fillets
- 1 cup honey mustard rub

Directions:

1.   Combine and mix well all the brine ingredients in a large bowl and place the fish in it for 2 hours. Next, pat dry the fish and let it dry. Season the fish with the mustard rub and massage gently for fine coating.

2.   Place the fish on a rack inside the smoker and cook for 6 hours at 225 degrees F.

3.   The internal temperature of fish should be about 150°F at the end of cooking.

4.   Serve and enjoy.

Cast Iron Lemon Sole In Brown Butter

Servings: 2
Cooking Time: 30 Minutes

Ingredients:

- 3 tablespoons unsalted butter
- 2 Dover or lemon sole, filleted and skin removed
- ½ cup all-purpose flour
- Flaked sea salt
- Freshly ground black pepper
- Grated zest of 1 lemon, plus 1 lemon, quartered, for serving

Directions:

1. Preheat the electric smoker to 275°F. Ensure the drip tray is clean and in place. Seal the door.
2. Place the wood chips in the smoking tray or firebox, get a good smoke rolling, and seal the door.
3. Place a cast iron skillet on a smoking rack to preheat, then drop in the butter to melt and brown.
4. Lightly coat the sole fillets on both sides with flour, knocking off any excess. Season with salt and pepper.
5. Once the butter has lightly browned, gently place the fillets into the skillet. Top each fillet with lemon zest. Smoke for 15 minutes. Turn the fillets over and smoke for 15 minutes more.
6. Top each fillet with a spoonful of the browned butter and serve with lemon wedges for squeezing.

Teriyaki Shrimp Skewers

Servings: 4
Cooking Time: 30 Minutes

Ingredients:

- 24 large raw shrimp (21 to 25 per pound), thawed if frozen, peeled, and deveined
- 1 pineapple, trimmed, peeled, quartered lengthwise, cored, and cut into large dice
- 4 cilantro sprigs, leaves stripped and finely sliced, plus more for garnish
- 4 garlic cloves, minced
- 4 scallions, trimmed and finely sliced on a 45-degree angle
- ¼ cup soy sauce
- 2 tablespoons fish sauce
- Grated zest of 2 limes, plus juice of 2 limes
- 2 tablespoons dark brown sugar
- 1 tablespoon finely grated fresh ginger
- 1 teaspoon sesame oil
- Flaked sea salt
- Freshly ground black pepper

Directions:

1. Alternate 3 shrimp with 3 pineapple chunks on each of 8 bamboo skewers that have been soaked in water.
2. In a large bowl, whisk together the cilantro, garlic, scallions, soy sauce, fish sauce, lime zest, lime juice, sugar, ginger, and sesame oil. Transfer to a large food-grade plastic bag and add the skewers. Remove as much air as possible from the bag and seal it. Refrigerate for 4 hours, turning the bag 2 or 3 times.
3. Remove the skewers, reserving the marinade in the refrigerator.
4. Preheat the electric smoker to 275°F. Ensure the drip tray is clean and in place. Seal the door.
5. Place the wood chips in the smoking tray or firebox, get a good smoke rolling, and seal the door.
6. Place the skewers on smoking racks, leaving space between each one. Season with salt and pepper. Smoke for 10 minutes. Brush the shrimp and pineapple with the reserved marinade.
7. Smoke for about 20 minutes more, until the shrimp are fully cooked, pink, and firm.

Classic Smoke Trout

Servings: 2
Cooking Time: 4 Hours

Ingredients:

- 3 cups water
- 1-2 cups dark-brown sugar
- 1 cup of coarse salt
- 4 pounds of trout, backbone and pin bones removed
- 2 tablespoons vegetable oil for the grill basket

Directions:

1. First, make the brine by mixing all the brine Ingredients: in a large pot.
2. Submerge the fish in the brine for a few hours.

3. Then pat dry the fish and drizzle oil all over the fish.

4. Heat the smoker and add the wood chips.

5. Fill the water pan with water.

6. Wait until the smoke started to come out.

7. Place a dripping pan beneath the grill grate to get all the drippings.

8. Soak the wood in water and then add to coals.

9. Smoke the fish for 4 hours at 225 degrees F, then serve.

Simple Salt & Pepper Smoked Salmon

Servings: 2

Cooking Time: 2 Hours

Ingredients:

- 2 pounds fresh salmon fillets
- 4 tablespoons melted butter
- 2 tablespoons lemon juice
- Salt and pepper

Directions:

1. Preheat the smoker to 225 degrees F.

2. Add wood chips to begin the smoke.

3. Now brush the butter over the fillets.

4. Pour lemon juice over the fillets.

5. Sprinkle the generous amount of pepper and salt to taste.

6. Place salmon into the electric smoker.

7. Cook for 2 hours.

8. Once the fillets temperature reaches 150 degrees Fahrenheit, it's done.

9. Serve and enjoy.

Seafood Scampi

Servings: 4

Cooking Time: 20 Minutes

Ingredients:

- 1 cup (2 sticks) butter
- 8 to 10 cloves garlic, finely minced
- ½ pound fresh scallops
- ½ pound crab meat
- ½ pound raw shrimp (31–40 size), peeled and deveined

- pinch of salt
- 1 pound dry spaghetti or angel hair pasta
- 3 tablespoons finely chopped fresh parsley

Directions:

1. Prepare the smoker's water pan according to the manufacturer's instructions and preheat the smoker to 275°F. While it heats, fill a medium bowl with water and add 3 or 4 handfuls of beech wood chips to soak.

2. In a small saucepan, gently warm the garlic and butter until melted. Alternatively, you can heat it in the microwave for 20 to 30 seconds in a microwave-safe bowl. Then pour the butter into an 8 × 12-inch foil pan. Add the garlic and a pinch of salt and stir to combine, then add the fresh seafood. Turn the seafood once or twice to coat with the garlic butter.

3. Place the pan in the smoker and add a small handful of the soaked beech chips to the chip loading area. Adding more chips at least every 15 minutes, smoke for 30 to 40 minutes, or until the seafood is fully cooked.

4. When the seafood is almost done, cook the pasta according to the package directions. Drain and toss with the smoked shellfish and garlic butter. Stir in the fresh parsley.

Pan-roasted Trout Bruschetta

Servings: 4

Cooking Time: 1 Hour

Ingredients:

- 2 rainbow trout, whole, cleaned and rinsed
- Flaked sea salt
- Freshly ground black pepper
- 2 cups mixed heirloom cherry tomatoes, halved lengthwise
- 1 cup ground cherries (or grapes or blackberries)
- 4 scallions, trimmed and thinly sliced on an angle
- 1 loaf country bread, cut into 8 slices on a 45-degree angle
- 8 slices provolone cheese
- 2 tablespoons extra-virgin olive oil, for drizzling

Directions:

1. Preheat the electric smoker to 225°F. Ensure the drip tray is clean and in place. Seal the door.

2. Place the wood chips in the smoking tray or firebox, get a good smoke rolling, and seal the door.

3. Season the trout inside and out with salt and pepper. Gently place the trout on the smoking rack, leaving space between them. Smoke for 1 hour, or until the flesh turns opaque. Trout can be enjoyed rare, medium-rare, or fully cooked—use the opacity to judge doneness.

4. In a large bowl, combine the tomatoes, cherries, and scallions. Season with salt and pepper.

5. Remove the trout from the smoker and let it cool slightly.

6. Arrange the bread slices on smoking racks, leaving space between them. Top each piece of bread with a slice of provolone. Smoke the bread for 3 to 5 minutes, or until the cheese is just melted. Remove from the heat.

7. Using a fork, gently flake the trout off the bones and combine it with the bruschetta mixture.

8. Top the smoked cheesy bread with the bruschetta and drizzle with the olive oil. Season with salt and pepper, if desired.

Pineapple Maple Glaze Fish In The Smoker

Servings: 6
Cooking Time: 6 Hours

Ingredients:
- 6 pounds fresh salmon
- ⅓ cup maple syrup
- ½ cup pineapple juice
- Brine Ingredients:
- ½ gallon water
- ⅓ cup sea salt (non-iodized)
- 1 cup pineapple juice
- ¼ cup brown sugar
- 3 tablespoons Worcestershire sauce
- 2 tablespoons garlic salt

Directions:
1. Prepare the brine by mixing all the brine ingredients in a large pot. Submerge the fish in it for 2 hours. Next, pat dry the fish and let it dry.

2. Preheat the smoker to 225 degrees F.

3. Place the dry salmon inside the smoker once the smoker starts to build.

4. Place the fish in the smoker and cook it for 6 hours.

5. Now mix ½ cup pineapple juice with maple syrup and baste the fish every 30 minutes, while cooking.

6. Add soaked wood chip if the smoke is not enough.

7. Serve it once done.

Spicy Smoked Tuna Tacos

Servings: 4
Cooking Time: 5 Hours

Ingredients:
- 3 tablespoons Fish Rub
- 2 tablespoons olive oil
- 1 tablespoon minced garlic
- Salt
- Freshly cracked black pepper
- 2 (5-ounce) tuna steaks, about 1 ¼ inches thick
- 1 tablespoon red pepper flakes
- 1 (14-ounce) bag coleslaw mix
- 1 cup cubed fresh pineapple
- 1 ½ cups poppy seed dressing
- 4 (8-inch) flour tortillas
- 1 cup cilantro-lime dressing
- 2 limes, cut into quarters

Directions:
1. In a small bowl, combine the fish rub, olive oil, garlic, and salt and pepper to taste. Rub both sides of the steaks with the mixture. Place the tuna in a plastic zip-top bag and refrigerate for 5 hours.

2. Preheat the smoker to 250°F.

3. Take the tuna out of the bag and sprinkle the red pepper flakes on both sides.

4. Smoke the tuna for about 1 hour, or until the internal temperature reaches 140°F.

5. Meanwhile, in a large bowl, toss together the slaw mix, pineapple, and poppy seed dressing.

6. Wrap the tortillas in aluminum foil and place them on a smoker rack to keep them warm.

7. Place the cooked tuna on a cutting board and cut it into ½-inch slices.

8. For each taco, add a couple tablespoons of coleslaw, a couple slices of grilled tuna, and then another couple tablespoons of coleslaw. Drizzle the cilantro-lime dressing over the taco.

9. Serve warm with limes for squeezing.

Smoked Tuna

Servings: 2
Cooking Time: 90 Minutes

Ingredients:

- 2 pounds tuna steaks
- 2 tablespoons soy sauce
- 6-10 cups warm water
- ½ cup salt
- Dip Ingredients:
- ½ cup mayonnaise
- 2 ounces cream cheese
- ½ cup red onion, diced
- ⅓ cup fresh parsley, chopped
- 3 tablespoons lemon juice
- ½ tablespoon garlic powder
- ⅓ teaspoon black pepper
- Salt, to taste
- ½ tablespoon hot sauce

Directions:

1. Prepare brine by combining the entire brine ingredient in a pot.
2. Soak the tuna in the brine overnight.
3. Water should be enough to cover the tune well.
4. Afterward, rinse under tap water.
5. Pat dry the tuna with the paper towel, and then let it sit at room temperate to get dry.
6. Rinse, dry, and lightly coat with soy sauce.
7. Preheat the smoker and cook the tuna inside a smoker at 250 degrees F for 90 minutes.
8. Meanwhile, prepare the sauce by mixing together the entire dip ingredient in a small bowl.
9. Remove the tuna from smoker and let it get cold. Chop the tuna if desired.
10. Add chopped tuna to the dip and let it sit in a refrigerator for a few minutes.
11. Then serve.

Smoked Mussels With Garlic Butter

Servings: 2
Cooking Time: 25 Minutes

Ingredients:

- 2 pounds frozen mussels in the shell
- 8 tablespoons (1 stick) unsalted butter
- 1 tablespoon minced garlic
- 1 teaspoon dried oregano
- 1 teaspoon salt
- 1 teaspoon freshly ground black pepper

Directions:

1. Thaw the mussels in the fridge or in a plastic bag in a big bowl of water.
2. Preheat the smoker to 275°F.
3. Remove the top shell, leaving the mussel in the bottom shell. Arrange the mussels on wire racks or grill mats.
4. Transfer the mussel-topped wire rack or mat to the smoker and smoke for 10 minutes.
5. Meanwhile, in a saucepan on the stovetop, melt the butter over low heat. Add the garlic, oregano, salt, and pepper and simmer for 5 minutes over medium heat.
6. Spoon the butter mixture onto the mussels and smoke for another 10 minutes, so that they baste in their shells.
7. Remove the mussels from the smoker and serve immediately.

Smoked Scallops Gratinée

Servings: 4
Cooking Time: 1 Hour

Ingredients:

- FOR THE MORNAY SAUCE
- 2 tablespoons unsalted butter
- 2 tablespoons all-purpose flour
- 1 cup whole milk, cold
- 1 cup finely grated Gruyère cheese
- 1 large egg yolk
- Flaked sea salt
- Freshly ground black pepper
- FOR THE SCALLOPS
- 8 sea scallops on the half shell, side muscle removed
- 1 cup finely grated Gruyère cheese
- 2 parsley sprigs, leaves stripped and minced
- 2 lemons, quartered lengthwise

Directions:

1. TO MAKE THE MORNAY SAUCE

2. On the stovetop, in a saucepan over medium heat, melt the butter and cook it until fragrant. Whisk in the flour to combine.

3. Pour the cold milk into the roux. Reduce the heat to low. Whisk to combine and cook for 10 minutes, whisking occasionally. Remove the pan from the heat and whisk in the cheese to combine. Let it cool slightly.

4. Whisk in the egg yolk. Season with salt and pepper.

5. TO MAKE THE SCALLOPS

6. Preheat the electric smoker to 275°F. Ensure the drip tray is clean and in place. Seal the door.

7. Place the wood chips in the smoking tray or firebox, get a good smoke rolling, and seal the door.

8. Arrange the scallops on the half shell and top each with a heavy dollop of Mornay sauce.

9. Place the scallop shells on smoking racks, leaving space between each shell. Smoke for 20 to 30 minutes, until golden brown.

10. Garnish with Gruyère cheese and parsley and serve with lemon wedges for squeezing.

Smoked Halibut With King And Oyster Mushrooms

Servings: 4
Cooking Time: 1 Hour

Ingredients:

- 2 tablespoons extra-virgin olive oil, plus more for garnish
- 2 tablespoons unsalted butter
- 4 (8-ounce) Alaskan halibut fillets, trimmed, checked for bones, and skin removed
- Flaked sea salt
- Freshly ground black pepper
- 8 oyster mushrooms, trimmed and torn lengthwise
- 4 chanterelle mushrooms, trimmed and torn lengthwise
- 4 king mushrooms, trimmed and finely sliced lengthwise
- 2 thyme sprigs, leaves stripped
- 2 lemons, quartered

Directions:

1. Preheat the electric smoker to 275°F. Ensure the drip tray is clean and in place. Seal the door.

2. Place the wood chips in the smoking tray or firebox, get a good smoke rolling, and seal the door.

3. Place a large cast iron skillet on a smoking rack to preheat, then add the butter to melt.

4. Brush the halibut with 2 tablespoons of the olive oil and season it on all sides with salt and pepper. Gently place the fish on smoking racks, leaving space between the fillets. Smoke until the flesh is opaque, about 10 to 15 minutes. Halibut can be enjoyed rare, medium-rare, or fully cooked—use the opacity to judge doneness.

5. In the skillet, combine the oyster mushrooms, chanterelle mushrooms, king mushrooms, and thyme. Toss to coat in the oil and butter and season with salt and pepper. Smoke for 30 minutes. Gently toss the mushrooms.

6. Remove the halibut from the smoker and let it rest, uncovered, for 5 minutes.

7. Serve the halibut topped with the mushrooms and a drizzle of olive oil, and with the lemon wedges on the side for squeezing.

Maple-walnut Salmon

Servings: 4
Cooking Time: 30 Minutes

Ingredients:

- 4 (8-ounce) salmon fillets, trimmed, skin removed, and checked for bones
- Flaked sea salt
- Freshly ground black pepper
- Grated zest of 2 lemons, plus juice of 2 lemons, plus 1 lemon, quartered, for serving
- 1 cup walnuts, finely chopped
- 1 cup pure maple syrup

Directions:

1. Preheat the electric smoker to 275°F. Ensure the drip tray is clean and in place. Seal the door.

2. Place the wood chips in the smoking tray or firebox, get a good smoke rolling, and seal the door.

3. Season the salmon fillets on both sides with salt and pepper. Top each with lemon zest.

4. On a piece of parchment paper, arrange the chopped walnuts.

5. Brush each fillet with maple syrup and press the fillets into the walnuts. Place the fillets on a maple plank. Drizzle with lemon juice. Place the plank on a smoking rack. Smoke for 20 to 30 minutes, until the salmon is lightly browned and crispy.

6. Serve with lemon wedges for squeezing.

Smoky Oysters

Servings: 1
Cooking Time: 30 To 40 Minutes

Ingredients:

- 1 dozen raw oysters, shucked, oysters left in the bottom shell, top shell discarded
- ½ cup (1 stick) butter, at room temperature
- ¼ cup grated Parmesan cheese
- 2 garlic cloves, minced
- 3 tablespoons chopped fresh parsley leaves
- 2 tablespoons hot sauce
- 1 teaspoon paprika, or cayenne pepper

Directions:

1. Heat the smoker to 225°F to 250°F with the apple, cherry, or oak wood.

2. Slide a knife under each oyster to loosen it.

3. In a small bowl, blend the butter, Parmesan, garlic, parsley, hot sauce, and paprika. Top each oyster with 1 tablespoon of the butter mixture. Place the oysters in the smoker and smoke for 15 to 20 minutes. Serve immediately.

Smoked Fish In A Brine

Servings: 5
Cooking Time: 5 Hours

Ingredients:

- 5 pounds of fish fillets
- BRINE Ingredients:
- 1 gallon water
- 2 cups canning salt
- ⅔ cup brown sugar

Directions:

1. Combine sugar, water, and salt in a large pot.

2. Split the fish into two halves and then soaks in the brine overnight.

3. Prepare the electric smoker and then use apple wood chip to create smoke.

4. Place the fish for cooking inside the smoker and let it cook for 5 hours at 225 degrees F.

5. The time depends on the temperature of how hot the smoker gets.

Smoked Whole Red Snapper

Servings: 4
Cooking Time: 20 Minutes

Ingredients:

- 2 tablespoons unsalted butter, at room temperature
- 3 tablespoons olive oil, divided
- 2 teaspoons Fish Rub
- 1 teaspoon minced garlic
- ½ teaspoon dried tarragon
- 1 (4- to 5-pound) whole red snapper, gutted and cleaned
- 5 lime slices (¼ inch thick)
- 1 scallion, coarsely chopped

Directions:

1. Preheat the smoker to 160°F.

2. In a bowl, combine the butter, 2 tablespoons olive oil, the fish rub, garlic, and tarragon and mix them well. Rub the mixture all over the fish, including the inside. Place the lime slices and the chopped scallions in the belly cavity.

3. Coat a smoker rack with the remaining 1 tablespoon olive oil. Place the fish on a wire rack and set it in the smoker. (Or in a pellet smoker, just put the fish on the grates.) Smoke the fish for 1 hour.

4. Increase the smoker temperature to 225°F. Smoke the fish for another 2 hours to 2 hours 20 minutes, or until the internal temperature reaches 145°F.

5. Transfer the fish to a cutting board and let it rest for 5 minutes. Then you can fillet it or serve it in pieces.

Bacon-wrapped Chinook Salmon

Servings: 4
Cooking Time: 1 Hour

Ingredients:
- 1 tablespoon extra-virgin olive oil
- 4 tablespoons unsalted butter
- 4 (8-ounce) Chinook salmon fillets, trimmed
- 2 rosemary sprigs, leaves stripped and minced
- Flaked sea salt
- Freshly ground black pepper
- 12 bacon slices
- 2 lemons, halved

Directions:
1. Preheat the electric smoker to 275°F. Ensure the drip tray is clean and in place. Seal the door.
2. Place the wood chips in the smoking tray or firebox, get a good smoke rolling, and seal the door.
3. Place a large cast iron skillet on a smoking rack to preheat, then pour in the olive oil and add the butter to melt.
4. Season the salmon fillets on all sides with the rosemary, salt, and pepper.
5. Firmly (but not too tightly) wrap each fillet with 3 bacon slices, overlapping them, allowing the ends to be exposed. Roll the prepared fillets in the browned butter, then place them on a smoking rack, leaving space between each fillet. Smoke for 30 to 45 minutes, or until the salmon flesh is bright pink and opaque, and the bacon is cooked. Salmon can be enjoyed rare, medium-rare, or fully cooked—use the opacity to judge doneness.
6. Serve with lemon halves for squeezing.

Canadian-style Smoked Salmon On Cedar

Servings: 6
Cooking Time: 5 Hours

Ingredients:
- 1 ½ cups maple sugar
- ½ cup coarse salt
- 2 tablespoons Fish Rub
- 1 tablespoon freshly ground black pepper
- 2 teaspoons grated lemon zest
- 2 (1 ½- to 2-pound) skin-on salmon fillets
- ¾ cup maple syrup, divided
- 2 untreated cedar planks
- 2 teaspoons chopped fresh parsley

Directions:
1. In a bowl, mix together the maple sugar, salt, fish rub, pepper, and lemon zest. Season the salmon on both sides with the mixture, then drizzle ½ cup maple syrup over the flesh side of each fillet.
2. Wrap the fillets in plastic wrap and refrigerate for 4 hours.
3. Rinse the fish under cold water to remove the rub. Pat dry with paper towels and let the fillets air-dry in a cool place for 1 hour.
4. At the same time, soak the cedar planks for 1 hour.
5. Preheat the smoker to 250°F.
6. Set the planks inside the smoker. Wait until they start to crack or smoke a little, then take them out, using your BBQ mitts. Place the fish on the planks skin-side down, then return the fish-topped planks to the smoker.
7. Smoke the fish for 25 minutes.
8. Baste the fillets lightly with the remaining ¼ cup maple syrup and continue to smoke for another 15 minutes, or until the internal temperature reaches 140°F.
9. Let the salmon rest for 10 minutes, then garnish with the parsley and serve.

Country Cajun Catfish

Servings: 2 To 4
Cooking Time: 10 Minutes

Ingredients:
- 1 cup salt
- 4 to 6 catfish fillets
- 2 tablespoons Cajun seasoning
- 2 teaspoons freshly ground black pepper
- 2 teaspoons ground nutmeg
- 1 teaspoon ground allspice
- ¼ cup sriracha
- Tartar sauce, for serving

Directions:
1. In a shallow dish, make a simple brine by dissolving the salt in just enough water to cover the fish. This will help keep the fish from drying out during the smoking

process. Submerge the catfish, cover the dish, and refrigerate for at least 4 hours.

2.   Preheat the smoker to 200°F with the alder, apple, cherry, or oak wood.

3.   Remove the fish from the brine. Rinse it, pat it dry, and discard the liquid.

4.   In a small bowl, stir together the Cajun seasoning, pepper, nutmeg, and allspice. Sprinkle this on both sides of the fish.

5.   Drizzle with the Sriracha.

6.   Place the fish on the smoker grate and smoke for 2 to 2½ hours until the internal temperature reaches 145°F.

7.   Serve with tartar sauce.

Smoked Crab Legs

Servings: 4

Cooking Time: 5 Minutes

Ingredients:

- 10 pounds king crab legs
- 2 cups (4 sticks) unsalted butter
- 1 tablespoon minced garlic
- 1 tablespoon Seafood Seasoning
- 2 tablespoons chopped fresh cilantro
- 2 or 3 lemons or limes, cut into wedges

Directions:

1.   If the crab legs were frozen, thaw them completely in the refrigerator.

2.   Preheat the smoker to 275°F.

3.   In a saucepan on the stovetop, melt the butter over low heat. Add the garlic just as the butter melts, then stir in the seafood seasoning and cilantro and simmer for 90 seconds.

4.   Brush the crab legs with the seasoned butter. Smoke them for 25 minutes, brushing them with the seasoned butter twice throughout and once again when you remove them.

5.   Serve immediately with lemon wedges and the remaining seasoned butter for dipping.

Peppercorn Tuna Steaks

Servings: 2 To 4

Cooking Time: 10 Minutes

Ingredients:

- ¼ cup salt
- 2 pounds yellowfin tuna
- ¼ cup Dijon mustard
- Freshly ground black pepper
- 2 tablespoons peppercorns

Directions:

1.   In a container large enough to hold the brine and tuna, dissolve the salt in just enough warm water to cover the fish.

2.   Place the tuna in the brine, cover, and refrigerate for 8 hours or overnight.

3.   Preheat the smoker to 250°F with the apple, cherry, or oak wood.

4.   Remove the tuna from the brine and pat dry. Do not rinse the tuna. Place it on a grill pan.

5.   Spread the Dijon mustard all over the tuna, season with pepper, and sprinkle with the peppercorns.

6.   Place the tuna in the smoker and smoke for about 1 hour, or until it reaches an internal temperature of 125°F.

Bacon-wrapped Smoked Scallops

Servings: 6

Cooking Time: 1 Hour 30 Minutes

Ingredients:

- ½ cup olive oil
- 2 tablespoons fresh lime juice
- 2 teaspoons minced garlic
- 2 teaspoons chopped fresh cilantro
- 1 teaspoon salt
- 1 teaspoon freshly ground black pepper
- 24 sea scallops (about 2 pounds)
- 24 slices bacon
- 1 lemon, cut into wedges

Directions:

1.   In a bowl, mix together the olive oil, lime juice, garlic, cilantro, salt, and pepper. Add the scallops and toss to coat them completely. Cover the bowl and refrigerate for about 1 hour.

2.   Preheat the smoker to 225°F. If using wooden skewers, soak them in water for at least 30 minutes.

3.   Wrap a scallop with a piece of bacon, going around twice, and run a skewer through it. Repeat with the

remaining scallops and bacon so that each skewer has 4 scallops on it.

4. Transfer the marinade to a small saucepan on the stovetop over medium heat and boil for 5 minutes, then set it aside.

5. Smoke the skewers, turning frequently, for 45 minutes to 1 hour, or until the internal temperature reaches 145°F. Each time you turn the skewers, brush them with the reserved marinade.

6. Serve immediately with the lemon wedges.

Succulent Salmon Nuggets

Servings: 4 To 6
Cooking Time: 20 Minutes

Ingredients:
- 3 cups firmly packed brown sugar
- 1 cup salt
- 1 tablespoon dry minced onion
- 2 teaspoons chipotle seasoning
- 2 teaspoons freshly ground black pepper
- 1 garlic clove, minced
- 1 to 2 pounds salmon fillets, cut into bite-size chunks

Directions:
1. In a large bowl, stir together the brown sugar, salt, onion, chipotle seasoning, pepper, and garlic.

2. Place the salmon in a large, shallow marinating dish and pour the dry marinade over the fish. Cover and refrigerate overnight.

3. Preheat the smoker to 180°F with the alder wood.

4. Rinse the salmon chunks thoroughly to remove the salt. Place them on a grill rack and put them into the smoker. Smoke for 1 to 2 hours. Remove from the heat when the internal temperature is 130°F to 140°F.

Smoked Littleneck Clams

Servings: 4
Cooking Time: 1 Hour

Ingredients:
- 2 shallots, very thinly sliced
- 2 flat-leaf parsley sprigs
- 2 fresh bay leaves
- 1 cup water
- 1 cup vodka
- 10 peppercorns, whole
- Flaked sea salt
- Freshly ground black pepper
- 10 pounds littleneck clams, rinsed twice (note: discard any clams that do not close when tapped—see tip)

Directions:
1. Preheat the electric smoker to 275°F. Ensure the drip tray is clean and in place. Seal the door.

2. Place the wood chips in the smoking tray or firebox, get a good smoke rolling, and seal the door.

3. Place a cast iron pan with a lid on a smoking rack to preheat.

4. In a large bowl, stir together the shallots, parsley, bay leaves, water, vodka, and peppercorns. Add the mixture to the pan. Season with salt and pepper. Smoke for 20 minutes, stirring occasionally.

5. Add the clams to the pan, cover the pan, and smoke for 8 to 10 minutes, until the clams open. Remove the lid and smoke the clams for 4 to 5 minutes more. Discard any clams that have not opened.

6. Serve the clams with the sauce. Taste and season with salt and pepper.

Smoked Shrimp And Scallops

Servings: 3 Or 4
Cooking Time: 15 Minutes

Ingredients:
- ½ cup granulated sugar
- ¼ cup firmly packed brown sugar
- 2 garlic cloves, finely minced
- 1 tablespoon hot chili powder
- 1 tablespoon salt
- 2 teaspoons ground coriander
- 2 teaspoons freshly ground black pepper
- 1 teaspoon ground white pepper
- 1 teaspoon cayenne pepper
- 1 teaspoon ground ginger
- 1 pound jumbo shrimp, peeled, deveined, and tails removed
- 1 pound sea scallops

- Cocktail sauce, lemon wedges, and saltine crackers, for serving

Directions:
1. Preheat the smoker to 200°F with the cherry, mesquite, oak, or pecan wood.
2. In a small bowl, mix together the granulated sugar, brown sugar, garlic, chili powder, salt, coriander, black pepper, white pepper, cayenne, and ginger to make a rub.
3. Place the shrimp in a large bowl and the scallops in a separate bowl (or use gallon-size resealable plastic bags).
4. Pour half the rub over the shrimp and half over the scallops. Using your hands, make sure everything is well coated.
5. The scallops will take a little longer to cook so place them on a grill pan in a single layer and into the smoker for about 10 minutes.
6. Add the shrimp to the smoker and continue to smoke everything for 15 more minutes.
7. Remove from the heat and serve with cocktail sauce, lemon wedges, and crackers.

Smoked Ahi Tuna With Sesame And Wasabi

Servings: 4
Cooking Time: 2 Hours

Ingredients:
- FOR THE SMOKED TUNA
- 2 tablespoons coarse salt
- 1 tablespoon light brown sugar
- 1 teaspoon freshly ground black pepper
- 4 (6-ounce) ahi tuna steaks
- 2 tablespoons olive oil
- ¼ cup Seafood Seasoning
- 1 tablespoon toasted sesame seeds, for serving
- FOR THE WASABI SAUCE
- ¾ cup mayonnaise
- 1 tablespoon fresh lime juice
- 1 teaspoon sesame oil
- 2 teaspoons minced garlic
- 1 teaspoon wasabi powder or paste

Directions:

1. TO SMOKE THE TUNA
2. In a small bowl, mix together the salt, brown sugar, and pepper. Rub the mixture into the tuna. Wrap the steaks in plastic and refrigerate for 2 hours.
3. Preheat the smoker to 200°F.
4. Wipe the dry brine off the tuna. Brush the tuna with the olive oil, then sprinkle the seafood seasoning on both sides of the steaks.
5. Smoke the tuna for about 1 hour, or until the internal temperature reaches 125°F for medium-rare or 140°F for medium.
6. TO MAKE THE WASABI SAUCE
7. Meanwhile, in a bowl, blend together the mayonnaise, lime juice, sesame oil, garlic, and wasabi. Refrigerate the sauce until serving time.
8. When the tuna steaks are done, lightly sprinkle them with the sesame seeds. Let them rest for 5 minutes, then serve them with the wasabi sauce on the side.

Smoked Eel

Servings: 2
Cooking Time: 3 Hours

Ingredients:
- 10 cups warm water
- 1-½ cup salt
- ½ cup brown sugar
- 4 lemons, halved
- 2 sprigs fresh thyme
- Other Ingredients:
- 2 fillets whole eel, cleaned and washed

Directions:
1. First, prepare the brine by mixing all the brine ingredients in a large pot, and place eel in it for 10 hours. Next day, pat dry the eel and let it dry.
2. Now, preheat the electric smoker to 235 degrees F and add wood chips.
3. Smoke the eel for about 3 hours.
4. Once the skins get crisp, the eel is ready to be served.
5. Enjoy.

Smoked Catfish Recipe

Servings: 5
Cooking Time: 5 Hours

Ingredients:

- 3 tablespoons paprika
- ½ teaspoon salt
- 2 tablespoons garlic powder
- 2 tablespoons onion powder
- ⅓ tablespoon dried thyme
- ⅓ tablespoon cayenne
- Other Ingredients:
- 5 fresh catfish fillets, about 1 pound each
- 4 tablespoons butter, soften

Directions:

1. Mix all rub ingredients in a small bowl.
2. Lightly rub the fillets with butter.
3. Sprinkle the generous amount of rub onto fillets.
4. Preheat the smoker to 225 degrees F,and add wood chips.
5. Once the smoker starts to smoke, place the fish inside the smoker.
6. Cook for 5 hours.
7. Then serve.

Smoke And Ice Oysters

Servings: 2
Cooking Time: 30 Minutes

Ingredients:

- 12 fresh oysters, divided
- Grated zest of 2 limes, plus juice of 2 limes
- 2 mint sprigs, leaves stripped and finely sliced
- 1 tablespoon finely grated fresh ginger
- 1 tablespoon wildflower honey
- ¼ cup champagne or other sparkling white wine

Directions:

1. Store oysters on ice in the refrigerator (see tip). Shuck just before preparing: Find the seam where the shell halves come together. Wearing protective gloves, gently work a knife into the crack, twisting left and right until the shells separate. Free the muscle from the shell using a paring knife. Preserve the juices in their half shell and return them to the ice.

2. Preheat the electric smoker to 275°F. Ensure the drip tray is clean and in place. Seal the door.

3. Place the wood chips in the smoking tray or firebox, get a good smoke rolling, and seal the door.

4. In a small bowl, whisk together the lime zest, lime juice, mint, ginger, honey, and champagne. Top the oysters in their shells with the marinade.

5. Place 6 oysters on a smoking rack, leaving space between them, and smoke for 10 to 15 minutes.

6. Serve the remaining 6 raw oysters on a bed of crushed ice and serve the smoked oysters in a cast iron skillet.

Brown Sugar Salmon

Servings: 4
Cooking Time: 15 Minutes

Ingredients:

- 4 (6-ounce) salmon fillets, skin removed
- 2 tablespoons light brown sugar
- ½ teaspoon coarse kosher salt
- ½ teaspoon black pepper
- zest of 1 large lemon
- 1 tablespoon chopped fresh dill
- ¼ cup real maple syrup
- ¼ cup yellow mustard

Directions:

1. Prepare the smoker's water pan according to the manufacturer's instructions and preheat the smoker to 225°F. While it heats, fill a medium bowl with water and add 3 or 4 handfuls of maple wood chips to soak.

2. Check the salmon fillets for any small bones and place on a cutting board or tray. In a small bowl, combine the brown sugar, salt, and pepper. Rub the mixture over the tops and sides of the salmon fillets.

3. Transfer the fillets onto a large piece of parchment paper and carefully place in the smoker. Add a small handful of the soaked maple chips to the chip loading area, and keep adding more chips at least every 30 minutes.

4. While the salmon begins to smoke, prepare the maple glaze. In a small bowl, combine the lemon juice and zest, dill, maple syrup, and mustard, whisking to

mix well. Brush the salmon with the glaze every 30 minutes.

5.   Smoke for 1 to 1½ hours, or until the thickest part of the fish reaches an internal temperature of 145°F. Remove from the smoker and serve immediately.

Smoked Lobster

Servings: 4
Cooking Time: 20 Minutes

Ingredients:
- 8 (5-ounce) lobster tails
- 8 tablespoons (1 stick) unsalted butter
- 2 tablespoons minced garlic
- 2 teaspoons salt
- 1 teaspoon freshly ground black pepper
- 1 teaspoon dried oregano
- 1 lemon, cut into wedges

Directions:
1.   If the lobster tails are frozen, slowly thaw them out in the refrigerator (this may take a whole day). Then remove them from the refrigerator and let them come almost to room temperature.
2.   In a saucepan on the stovetop, melt the butter over low heat. Add the garlic, salt, pepper, and oregano and simmer for 2 minutes. Remove from the heat and set aside.
3.   Preheat the smoker to 225°F. If using wooden skewers, soak them in water for at least 30 minutes.
4.   Using kitchen scissors, cut through the lobster shell along the back, starting near the top, where the head used to be, to just before the fin. Then gently open the lobster tail, just a little, to expose the meat. Be careful not to break the back of the shell.
5.   Push a skewer through the center of each lobster, from the head end toward the tail. It should poke out below the fin. This keeps the lobster tail from curling up.
6.   Brush the meat side of the tails with the butter mixture. Place the lobsters shell-side down in the smoker and smoke for 30 minutes, or the internal temperature reaches 135°F. Baste with the butter mixture every 10 minutes.
7.   Serve immediately with the lemon wedges.

Maple-glazed Salmon

Servings: 10 To 12
Cooking Time: 15 Minutes

Ingredients:
- 2 cups firmly packed brown sugar
- ½ cup salt
- ¼ cup maple syrup
- 3 ounces crab boil seasoning
- 1 (3- to 5-pound) whole salmon fillet
- Chopped fresh parsley leaves, for garnish
- Cream cheese, for serving

Directions:
1.   In a medium bowl, mix the brown sugar, salt, maple syrup, and crab boil into a paste. Rub the paste all over the salmon and place the salmon in a shallow dish. Cover and refrigerate for a minimum of 8 hours or overnight.
2.   Remove the salmon from the refrigerator and let it sit for 1 hour to take the chill off.
3.   Preheat the smoker to 250°F with the alder wood. Cedar planks work great, especially if you are smoking smaller fillets.
4.   Place the salmon on the smoker rack (or cedar plank) and smoke for 1 to 2 hours. The target temperature is 145°F. It's done when it flakes easily with a fork.
5.   Remove from the heat, sprinkle with parsley, and serve with cream cheese.

Smoked Cod With Citrus And Olives

Servings: 2
Cooking Time: 1 Hour

Ingredients:
- 1¼ tablespoons extra-virgin olive oil, divided
- 1 tablespoon unsalted butter
- 2 (1-pound) cod fillets, trimmed
- Flaked sea salt
- Freshly ground black pepper
- Grated zest of 1 lemon, plus juice of 1 lemon
- 2 cups Pinot Grigio
- 1 cup mixed olives, pitted and halved
- 1 cayenne chile pepper, stemmed and finely sliced

- 4 flat-leaf parsley sprigs, finely chopped, plus more for garnish

Directions:

1. Preheat the electric smoker to 275°F. Ensure the drip tray is clean and in place. Seal the door.

2. Place the wood chips in the smoking tray or firebox, get a good smoke rolling, and seal the door.

3. Place a large cast iron skillet on a smoking rack to preheat, then pour in 1 tablespoon of the olive oil and add the butter to melt.

4. Season the cod on both sides with salt, pepper, and lemon zest. Place the cod in the skillet, flesh-side down. Smoke for about 15 minutes, until golden brown.

5. Remove the cod from the skillet and place it flesh-side up on a smoking rack above the skillet.

6. Stir the wine into the skillet to deglaze the pan, scraping up any browned bits from the bottom. Add the olives, the remaining ¼ tablespoon of olive oil, and the chile pepper. Taste and season with salt and pepper, as needed.

7. Smoke the cod and the pan sauce for 15 minutes more.

8. Return the cod to the skillet, flesh-side up. Smoke for about 10 minutes more, until the fish is fully cooked.

9. Top with parsley. Serve in a shallow bowl with the wine and olive sauce and a squeeze of fresh lemon juice.

Jerk Tilapia

Servings: 4
Cooking Time: 20 Minutes

Ingredients:

- 5 cloves garlic
- 1 small onion
- 3 jalapeño chiles, seeded (leave seeds to make it spicier)
- 3 teaspoons ground ginger
- 3 tablespoons light brown sugar
- 3 teaspoons dried thyme
- 2 teaspoons salt
- 2 teaspoons ground cinnamon
- 1 teaspoon black pepper
- 1 teaspoon ground allspice
- ¼ teaspoon cayenne pepper

- 4 (4 to 6-ounce) tilapia fillets
- ¼ cup olive oil
- 1 cup sliced carrots
- 1 bunch green onions, whole
- 2 tablespoons whole allspice

Directions:

1. In a blender or food processor bowl, combine the first 11 ingredients (garlic through ground allspice) and purée well. Place the fish pieces in a large zip-top plastic bag, then add the puréed mixture and the olive oil. Seal and gently press the bag to coat the fish pieces with the marinade. Let marinate for 30 minutes to 1 hour in the refrigerator.

2. Prepare the smoker's water pan according to the manufacturer's instructions and preheat the smoker to 225°F. While it heats, fill a medium bowl with water and add 3 or 4 handfuls of pecan wood chips and the whole allspice to soak.

3. Prepare a 9 × 13-inch foil pan by poking a dozen small holes with a sharp knife in the bottom and spray with non-stick cooking spray. Spread the carrots and green onions across the bottom of the pan, arrange the fish pieces on top, and put the pan in the smoker. Add a small handful of the soaked pecan chips and allspice to the chip loading area, and keep adding more chips at least every 15 minutes. Smoke for 45 minutes, or until the temperature reaches 145°F in the thickest part of the fish.

Scuppernong Lobster

Servings: 4
Cooking Time: 40 Minutes

Ingredients:

- 1 bunch scuppernong grapes (or muscadines)
- 4 tablespoons butter, melted
- 1 teaspoon freshly ground black pepper
- 1 teaspoon sea salt
- 4 lobster tails, split down the middle on top of the shell

Directions:

1. In a saucepan over high heat, put the scuppernongs and add enough water to cover them. Bring to a boil and cook for about 5 minutes until the grapes are soft or

begin to split. Drain in a fine-mesh strainer, then mash through the strainer into a bowl. You should be left with juice and pulp. Discard the skin and seeds.

2.   Stir in the butter, pepper, and salt.

3.   Season the tails with the spiced-pulp blend. Reserve any unused pulp to baste during cooking.

4.   Preheat the smoker to 225°F with the alder or oak wood.

5.   Place the lobster tails in the smoker and smoke for 45 minutes to 1 hour until the internal temperature reaches 130°F to 140°F. Start checking after about 30 minutes, and baste the tails whenever you open the smoker to check them, and again when you remove them from the heat.

Smoked Shrimp With Spicy Peanut Sauce

Servings: 4
Cooking Time: 40 Minutes

Ingredients:

- ½ cup sesame oil, divided
- ¼ cup soy sauce
- 1 tablespoon minced garlic
- 1 teaspoon ground ginger
- 1 teaspoon freshly ground black pepper
- 24 jumbo shrimp (about 1 ½ pounds), peeled and deveined, tails left on
- 1 cup Spicy Peanut Sauce

Directions:

1.   In a bowl, mix ¼ cup sesame oil, the soy sauce, garlic, ginger, and black pepper. Add the shrimp to the marinade and toss to coat completely. Cover the bowl and refrigerate for 30 minutes.

2.   Preheat the smoker to 275°F. If using wooden skewers, soak them in water for at least 30 minutes.

3.   To thread the shrimp onto skewers, hold the shrimp horizontally and run the skewer through one side, just below the head end, and out through the other side, just above the tail. Thread 4 shrimp onto each skewer.

4.   In a saucepan on the stovetop, warm the peanut sauce over low heat.

5.   Smoke the skewers for 10 minutes.

6.   Baste the shrimp with the remaining ¼ cup sesame oil and smoke for another 5 minutes.

7.   Remove the skewers and baste with the spicy peanut sauce. Return them to the smoker and smoke for 10 more minutes.

8.   Serve warm.

Smoked Lobster Tails

Servings: 4
Cooking Time: 25 Minutes

Ingredients:

- 4 tablespoons (½ stick) butter, melted
- Juice of 1 lemon
- 3 teaspoons freshly ground black pepper
- 3 teaspoons ground white pepper
- 2 teaspoons red pepper flakes
- 1 garlic clove, minced
- 1 tablespoon lemon-pepper seasoning
- 4 lobster tails, split at the top of the shell

Directions:

1.   Preheat the smoker to 225°F with the alder or oak wood.

2.   In a small bowl, stir together the butter, lemon juice, black and white peppers, red pepper flakes, garlic, and lemon-pepper seasoning.

3.   Baste the lobster tails with the seasoned butter and place them on a smoker rack. Smoke for about 30 minutes, then baste again. Continue to smoke for about 30 minutes more, or until the internal temperature reaches 130°F to 140°F.

4.   Remove from the heat and baste again. You may need to microwave the lemon butter between bastings to keep it hot. Serve the lobster tails warm.

Smoked Sea Bass

Servings: 4
Cooking Time: 3 Hours 45 Minutes

Ingredients:

- 2 cups water
- ½ cup coarse salt
- ¼ cup packed light brown sugar
- 3 cups ice

- ½ cup white wine
- 1 tablespoon fresh lime juice
- 1 tablespoon minced garlic
- 1 tablespoon coarsely ground black pepper
- 2 (1-pound) skin-on striped bass fillets
- ¼ cup olive oil
- 2 teaspoons smoked paprika

Directions:

1. In medium pot, bring the water almost to a boil. Add the salt and brown sugar and stir until the salt and sugar are dissolved. Remove from the heat and cool the brine down by adding the ice. Add the wine, lime juice, garlic, and pepper to the brine. Refrigerate the pot of brine until it is cold.

2. Use fish tweezers or needle-nose pliers to remove any bones from the bass fillets.

3. Place the fillets in a 2-gallon zip-top bag and pour the brine over them. Put the bag in a bowl (in case of leaks) and refrigerate for 3 hours.

4. Remove the fish from the brine and pat dry with paper towels. Brush both sides of the fillets with the olive oil, then sprinkle with the smoked paprika.

5. Let the fillets come up to room temperature for about 30 minutes.

6. Preheat the smoker to 200°F.

7. Smoke the fillets for 1 hour 45 minutes, or until the internal temperature reaches 140°F. Check after 1 hour 15 minutes to be safe and avoid overcooking.

8. Let the fillets rest for 5 minutes before serving.

Smoked Halibut

Servings: 4
Cooking Time: 4 Hours 30 Minutes

Ingredients:

- 1 tablespoon coarse salt
- 1 tablespoon granulated garlic
- 2 teaspoons freshly ground black pepper
- 2 (1-pound) skin-on halibut fillets
- 2 teaspoons olive oil
- 2 tablespoons Fish Rub

Directions:

1. In a small bowl, mix together the salt, granulated garlic, and pepper. Rub the mixture into the flesh side of the fillets. Tightly wrap each fillet in plastic and refrigerate for 4 hours.

2. Preheat the smoker to 225°F.

3. Pat the fish dry with paper towels. Brush both sides of the fillets with the olive oil. Generously sprinkle the fish rub on the flesh side. Let it come to room temperature for about 15 minutes.

4. Set the fillets skin-side down in the smoker and smoke for about 2 hours, or until the internal temperature reaches 145°F. Serve immediately.

Smoked Seafood Salad

Servings: 6
Cooking Time: 30 Minutes

Ingredients:

- ¾ cup olive oil, divided
- 4 tablespoons fresh lime juice, divided
- 2 tablespoons Seafood Seasoning
- 2 tablespoons minced garlic
- 1 pound jumbo shrimp, peeled and deveined
- 2 tablespoons honey
- 1 teaspoon grated lime zest
- ½ teaspoon salt
- ½ teaspoon freshly ground black pepper
- 24 ounces salad greens, such as mesclun
- 2 Smoked Lobster tails, cut into bite-size pieces

Directions:

1. In a bowl, mix together ½ cup olive oil, 2 tablespoons lime juice, the seafood seasoning, and garlic. Add the shrimp to the marinade and coat them completely. Refrigerate for 30 minutes.

2. Preheat the smoker to 275°F. If using wooden skewers, soak them in water for at least 30 minutes.

3. To thread the shrimp onto skewers, hold the shrimp horizontally and run the skewer through one side, just below the head end, and out through the other side, just above the tail. Thread 4 shrimp onto each skewer. Reserve the marinade.

4. Smoke the shrimp for 10 minutes.

5. Baste the shrimp with the marinade, then return to the smoker for another 15 minutes. Take them out and let them rest for 10 minutes, then chop into bite-size pieces.

6. In a medium bowl, whisk together the remaining ¼ cup olive oil, 2 tablespoons lime juice, the honey, lime zest, salt, and pepper.

7. Place the salad greens in a large serving bowl. Scatter the shrimp and lobster over the leaves. Whisk the dressing again, pour it over the greens, and serve.

Crab-stuffed Tomato

Servings: 8
Cooking Time: 20 Minutes

Ingredients:

* 1 pound fresh lump crabmeat
* 2 cups panko bread crumbs
* 1 cup chopped scallions, white and green parts
* 2 large eggs, beaten
* ½ cup (1 stick) butter, melted
* ¼ cup freshly squeezed lemon juice
* 1 teaspoon salt
* ½ teaspoon freshly ground black pepper
* 8 large tomatoes, hollowed out, leaving enough flesh all around and on the bottom to form a shell

Directions:

1. Preheat the smoker to 200°F with the oak wood (which I recommend for both tomato and crab).

2. In a large bowl, stir together the crabmeat, bread crumbs, scallions, eggs, butter, lemon juice, salt, and pepper.

3. Stuff the tomatoes with the crab mixture and place them on a grill pan. Place the pan in the smoker and smoke for about 45 minutes.

Cumin-lime Shrimp Skewers

Servings: 4 Or 5
Cooking Time: 20 Minutes

Ingredients:

* 1 pound raw shrimp (31–40 size), peeled and deveined
* 8 wooden skewers
* 2 teaspoons coarse kosher salt
* 2 teaspoons ground cumin
* 2 teaspoons garlic powder
* zest of 3 limes

Directions:

1. Prepare the smoker's water pan according to the manufacturer's instructions and preheat the smoker to 275°F. While it heats, fill a medium bowl with water and add a handful of beech chips to soak.

2. Thread 5 or 6 shrimp onto each skewer and set aside. In a small bowl, combine the salt, cumin, garlic powder, and lime zest. Rub the mixture evenly over the shrimp.

3. Prepare a 9 × 13-inch foil pan by poking a dozen small holes with a sharp knife in the bottom and spray with cooking spray. Arrange the shrimp skewers in the pan and place in the smoker. Add a small handful of the soaked beech chips to the chip loading area, and add more chips after 15 minutes. Smoke for 30 minutes, or until the shrimp are fully cooked.

Bacon-wrapped Crab-stuffed Shrimp

Servings: 1
Cooking Time: 35 Minutes

Ingredients:

* 2 cups panko bread crumbs
* ½ cup (1 stick) butter, melted
* 1 small onion, finely chopped
* Juice of 1 lemon
* 1 teaspoon salt
* 1 teaspoon freshly ground black pepper
* 2 (6-ounce) cans precooked lump crabmeat
* 1 dozen jumbo shrimp, peeled and deveined (tails on), butterflied
* 1 pound bacon

Directions:

1. Preheat the smoker to 200°F with mesquite or pecan wood.

2. In a small bowl, stir together the bread crumbs, butter, onion, lemon juice, salt, pepper, and crabmeat. Using a large melon baller, scoop some of the mixture and place it in the center of each shrimp.

3. Wrap each stuffed shrimp with 1 bacon slice and secure the ends as tightly as possible, tucking them in. Place the shrimp on a grill pan and head to the smoker.

4. Place the shrimp in the smoker and smoke for 20 to 30 minutes until the shrimp are tender and pink.

Sugared Sea Bass

Servings: 6 To 8
Cooking Time: 10 Minutes

Ingredients:

- 4 cups buttermilk
- ½ cup granulated sugar
- ¼ cup salt
- 2 bay leaves, crumbled
- 1 tablespoon ground cloves
- 2 teaspoons dried thyme
- 2 teaspoons dried basil
- 1½ teaspoons freshly ground black pepper
- 8 to 10 head-on sea bass
- ½ cup firmly packed brown sugar
- 1 lemon, thinly sliced
- ¼ cup chopped fresh parsley leaves

Directions:

1.   In a large bowl, combine the buttermilk, granulated sugar, salt, bay leaves, cloves, thyme, basil, and pepper to make a brine. Transfer to a container large enough to hold the brine and bass, or divide among multiple containers. Submerge the bass, cover the container, and refrigerate overnight.

2.   Preheat the smoker to 200°F with the alder or oak wood.

3.   Remove the fish and discard the brine.

4.   Pat the fish dry and sprinkle it on both sides with the brown sugar.

5.   Place the lemon slices on top of the fish. Sprinkle with the parsley. Place the fish in a single layer on a grill pan and into the smoker for 2½ to 3 hours until the internal temperature reaches 140°F.

Driftwood Yellow Perch Curry With Naan

Servings: 4
Cooking Time: 1 Hour

Ingredients:

- ¼ cup extra-virgin coconut oil
- 4 cardamom pods
- 4 garlic cloves, finely chopped
- 2 tablespoons finely grated peeled fresh ginger
- 1½ tablespoons coriander seeds, whole
- 1 cinnamon stick, whole
- ½ teaspoon chili powder
- ½ teaspoon ground turmeric
- 1 teaspoon ground cumin
- ¼ teaspoon ground cinnamon
- ¼ teaspoon ground cloves
- ¼ teaspoon ground nutmeg
- 12 fresh curry leaves
- 2 shallots, thinly sliced
- 2 Roma tomatoes, cored and cut into thin wedges
- 2 fresh green cayenne chile peppers, stemmed and halved lengthwise
- 2 fresh lemongrass stalks, trimmed and cut into thin rounds
- 2 pounds yellow perch fillets, skin removed
- Flaked sea salt
- Freshly ground black pepper
- 1 cup water
- 1 cup coconut milk
- 1 tablespoon fresh cilantro leaves, for garnish

Directions:

1.   Preheat the electric smoker to 275°F. Ensure the drip tray is clean and in place. Seal the door.

2.   Place the wood chips in the smoking tray or firebox, get a good smoke rolling, and seal the door.

3.   Place a large cast iron skillet on a smoking rack to preheat, then pour in the coconut oil to melt.

4.   Use a mortar and pestle to combine the cardamom pods, garlic, ginger, coriander seeds, and cinnamon stick. Grind into a smooth paste. If a mortar and pestle are not available, fold the ingredients in parchment paper and crush them using a heavy pan. Add the paste to the skillet and smoke for 20 minutes, gently tossing and stirring occasionally.

5.   In a small bowl, whisk together the chili powder, turmeric, cumin, ground cinnamon, cloves, and nutmeg. Set aside.

6.   Add the curry leaves, shallots, tomatoes, chile peppers, and lemongrass to the skillet. Smoke for 20 minutes.

7.   Season the perch on all sides with salt, pepper, and the dry spice mixture. Gently place the fish on smoking racks, leaving space between the fillets. Smoke until the

flesh is opaque, for 10 to 15 minutes. Total smoking time will depend on your desired doneness and the size of the fish.

8. Stir the water into the skillet to deglaze it, scraping up any browned bits from the bottom. Add the coconut milk. Smoke for 15 to 20 minutes more, or until the sauce is reduced to your desired consistency. Taste the sauce and season with salt and pepper, as needed.

9. Add the perch fillets and cilantro to the skillet and serve.

Smoked Grouper

Servings: 4
Cooking Time: 40 Minutes

Ingredients:

- 1 tablespoon coarse salt
- 1 teaspoon freshly ground black pepper
- 1 teaspoon light brown sugar
- 1 (1-pound) grouper fillet
- 2 teaspoons olive oil
- 1 tablespoon Fish Rub

Directions:

1. In a bowl, mix together the salt, pepper, and brown sugar. Rub it into both sides of the fillet, then wrap the fillet in plastic and refrigerate for 30 minutes.

2. Preheat the smoker to 225°F.

3. Rub off the remaining brine from the fillet with paper towels. Brush both sides of the fish with the olive oil, then sprinkle with the fish rub.

4. Smoke the fillet for 30 minutes, or until the internal temperature reaches 145°F.

5. Let the fish rest for 5 minutes before serving.

Smoked Salmon

Servings: 5
Cooking Time: 5 Hours

Ingredients:

- 5 pounds salmon, trout or char
- 1 ½ cup of maple syrup for basting
- BRINE Ingredients:
- 1 quart cold water
- ⅓ cup Diamond Crystal kosher salt

- 1 cup brown sugar

Directions:

1. Combine brine ingredients in a large bowl and place fish in for 2 hours. Next, pat dry the fish and let it dry. Place the fish on a rack and smoke the fish at 225 degrees F for 5 hours.

2. After one hour of cooking, baste the chicken with the maple syrup repeat every one hour.

3. The internal temperature of fish should be about 140°F to 150 degrees F.

4. The smoked fish is ready to be served. Enjoy.

Smoked Fish With The Delicious Dip

Servings: 6
Cooking Time: 6 Hours

Ingredients:

- 1 quart cold water
- ⅓ cup salt
- 1 cup brown sugar
- ½ cup soy sauce
- ½ cup of vinegar
- ½ cup almond milk
- 6 ounces cream cheese, softened
- ⅓ cup finely minced onion
- ½ stalk celery, finely chopped
- 1 tablespoon minced fresh parsley
- ½ teaspoon lemon juice
- 1 teaspoon Worcestershire sauce
- Cayenne pepper, to taste
- Salt and black pepper to taste
- Other Ingredients:
- 6 pounds of fish fillet

Directions:

1. Combine the brine ingredients in a large bowl and place the fish in the brine for 2 hours.

2. Next, blend all the sauce ingredients in a blender to make a smooth paste.

3. Next, pat dries the fish with paper towel. Place the fish on a topmost rack of the smoker and smoke the fish at 225 degrees F for 6 hours.

4. The internal temperature of fish should be about 150°F once done the cooking.

5. Enjoy warm served with prepared sauce.

Smoked Seafood Pizza

Servings: 4
Cooking Time: 40 Minutes

Ingredients:

- 2 tablespoons olive oil
- 2 tablespoons minced garlic
- 1 teaspoon chopped fresh cilantro
- 1 teaspoon coarse salt
- 1 teaspoon freshly ground black pepper
- 1 ½ pounds large shrimp, peeled and deveined
- ½ cup cornmeal
- 1 pound pizza dough, store-bought or your favorite recipe
- 2 cups store-bought Alfredo sauce
- 1 teaspoon red pepper flakes
- 8 ounces mozzarella cheese, shredded
- 4 ounces Parmesan cheese, grated

Directions:

1. Preheat a pellet smoker to 450°F. Then set a pizza stone in the center of the smoker to preheat.
2. In a large zip-top bag, mix together the olive oil, garlic, cilantro, salt, and pepper. Add the shrimp and make sure they are completely coated in the mixture. Refrigerate for 30 minutes.
3. Place a perforated BBQ skillet on the grate of the smoker and let it preheat.
4. If you have a pizza pan, spread the dough onto it. If you only have a pizza peel, sprinkle it with cornmeal and then place the stretched dough on it. Ladle the alfredo sauce on it. Place the shrimp on the sauce. Sprinkle the red pepper flakes, followed by the mozzarella and the Parmesan cheese, over the shrimp.
5. Carefully slide the pizza off the peel or pan and onto a pizza stone. Smoke the pizza for 15 to 20 minutes, until the crust is crisp and the sauce is bubbling.
6. Serve immediately.

Citrus And Garlic Scallops

Servings: 3 Or 4
Cooking Time: 10 Minutes

Ingredients:

- 2 to 3 pounds fresh scallops
- 1 tablespoon freshly squeezed lemon juice
- 1 tablespoon freshly squeezed orange juice
- 1 tablespoon freshly ground black pepper
- 2 teaspoons salt
- 1 garlic clove, minced
- Zest of 1 orange, lemon, or lime

Directions:

1. Preheat the smoker to 200°F with the cherrywood.
2. In a large bowl, gently stir the scallops with the lemon and orange juices.
3. Season with the pepper, salt, and garlic. Place the scallops on a grill pan or on skewers and put them into the smoker. Smoke for 30 to 40 minutes. The scallops will turn translucent. As with most seafood, scallops cook faster than you think, so watch them carefully to avoid overcooking.
4. Sprinkle the zest over the scallops before serving warm.

Smoked Snapper "ceviche"

Servings: 4
Cooking Time: 1 Hour

Ingredients:

- 2 pounds red snapper fillets, cleaned, skinned, rinsed, and diced
- Flaked sea salt
- Freshly ground black pepper
- ½ cup finely diced red onion
- Grated zest of 2 limes, plus juice of 2 limes, plus 1 lime, quartered, for serving
- 3 tablespoons fresh cilantro leaves, finely sliced
- 1 tablespoon finely grated fresh ginger
- 1 jalapeño pepper, trimmed, seeded, and finely sliced
- 2 ripe peaches, rinsed and thinly sliced

Directions:

1. Preheat the electric smoker to 225°F. Ensure the drip tray is clean and in place. Seal the door.
2. Place the wood chips in the smoking tray or firebox, get a good smoke rolling, and seal the door.
3. Season the snapper fillets on both sides with salt and pepper. Place the fillets on smoking racks, leaving space between them. Smoke for 1 hour, or until the snapper

flesh is opaque. Snapper can be enjoyed rare, medium-rare, or fully cooked—use the opacity to judge doneness.

4.   In a large bowl, gently combine the onion, lime zest, lime juice, cilantro, ginger, and jalapeño.

5.   Remove the snapper from the smoker and let it cool slightly. Using a fork, gently flake the snapper. Add it to the onion mixture and gently stir to combine. Refrigerate for 1 hour.

6.   Taste and season with salt and pepper, as needed. Serve the ceviche on peach slices with lime wedges on the side for squeezing. You can eat this dish open-faced or you can curl the peach slice around the filling like a taco!

Smoked Mussels

Servings: 2
Cooking Time: 30 Minutes

Ingredients:
- 1 fennel bulb, halved lengthwise, cored and thinly sliced
- 2 shallots, finely diced
- 1 red chile pepper, very thinly sliced
- 4 garlic cloves, minced
- 2 thyme sprigs, leaves stripped
- 1 fresh bay leaf
- 2 tablespoons extra-virgin olive oil, plus more for brushing
- Flaked sea salt
- Freshly ground black pepper
- 1 baguette loaf, cut on a 45-degree angle into 6 slices of your desired thickness
- 2 cups sauvignon blanc
- 1 cup 35 percent whipping cream
- 3 pounds mussels, cleaned and beards removed (note: discard any mussels that do not close when tapped—see tip)

Directions:
1.   Preheat the electric smoker to 275°F. Ensure the drip tray is clean and in place. Seal the door.

2.   Place the wood chips in the smoking tray or firebox, get a good smoke rolling, and seal the door.

3.   Place a cast iron pan with a lid on a smoking rack to preheat.

4.   In a large bowl, combine the fennel, shallots, red chile pepper, garlic, thyme, and bay leaf. Drizzle with 2 tablespoons of the olive oil and toss to coat. Transfer the mixture to the preheated pan, season with salt and pepper, and smoke uncovered for 20 minutes, tossing occasionally.

5.   Brush one side of the baguette slices with olive oil. Season the oiled side with salt and pepper.

6.   Stir the white wine into the pan to deglaze it, scraping up any browned bits from the bottom. Add the cream.

7.   Arrange the baguette slices on smoking racks, oiled-side up, leaving space between each slice. Smoke for 10 minutes.

8.   Add the mussels to the pan, cover the pan, and smoke for 8 to 10 minutes, until the mussels open. Discard any mussels that do not open. Remove and discard the bay leaf.

9.   Taste and season with salt and pepper, as needed. Serve with the crusty smoked bread.

Chesapeake Bay Crab Cakes With Remoulade Sauce

Servings: 4
Cooking Time: 1 Hour

Ingredients:
- FOR THE REMOULADE SAUCE
- 2 cups mayonnaise
- ½ cup dill pickles, diced
- ½ cup bread-and-butter pickles, diced
- 1 shallot, diced
- 2 tablespoons capers, roughly chopped
- 2 tablespoons fresh flat-leaf parsley leaves, very thinly sliced
- 1 tablespoon Dijon mustard
- Grated zest of 1 lemon, plus juice of 1 lemon
- 1 teaspoon paprika
- Flaked sea salt
- Freshly ground black pepper
- FOR THE CRAB CAKES
- 4 tablespoons unsalted butter
- 12 ounces lump crabmeat
- ¼ cup mayonnaise, lightly whipped

- 2 scallions, trimmed and finely sliced on the bias
- 1 large egg
- ½ cup bread crumbs, plus more as necessary to adjust the texture
- 1 tablespoon fresh flat-leaf parsley leaves
- 1 teaspoon Dijon mustard
- 1 teaspoon Worcestershire sauce
- Grated zest of 1 lemon, plus juice of 1 lemon, plus more lemon wedges, for serving
- Flaked sea salt
- Freshly ground black pepper

Directions:

1. TO MAKE THE REMOULADE SAUCE
2. In a medium bowl, gently fold together the mayonnaise, dill pickles, bread-and-butter pickles, shallot, capers, parsley, mustard, lemon zest, lemon juice, and paprika. Taste and season with salt and pepper. Refrigerate until needed. Taste again and reseason with salt and pepper, as needed.
3. TO MAKE THE CRAB CAKES
4. Preheat the electric smoker to 275°F. Ensure the drip tray is clean and in place. Seal the door.
5. Place the wood chips in the smoking tray or firebox, get a good smoke rolling, and seal the door.
6. Place a large cast iron skillet on a smoking rack to preheat, then drop in half the butter to melt.
7. In a large bowl, gently fold together the crabmeat, mayonnaise, remaining butter, scallions, egg, bread crumbs, parsley, mustard, Worcestershire sauce, lemon zest, and lemon juice. Season with salt and pepper. Divide the mixture into 4 or 8 portions, depending on the size of cakes you prefer. Gently press and form each portion into a patty. Season with salt and pepper.
8. Place the crab cakes in the skillet and smoke 4 large cakes for 18 to 20 minutes, or 8 small cakes for 12 to 14 minutes. Turn the cakes over and smoke for another 20 minutes for big cakes or 14 minutes for small cakes.
9. Serve topped with the remoulade and lemon wedges on the side.

VEGETABLES & SIDES RECIPES

Seasoned Spicy Broccoli

Servings: 4
Cooking Time: 5 Minutes

Ingredients:

- 1 head broccoli, trimmed and cut into florets
- 2 tablespoons olive oil
- 2 teaspoons seasoned salt
- 1 teaspoon red pepper flakes

Directions:

1. Prepare the smoker's water pan according to the manufacturer's instructions and preheat the smoker to 230°F. While it heats, fill a medium bowl with water and add 3 or 4 handfuls of hickory chips to soak.
2. Place the broccoli in a grill basket in a single layer. Drizzle olive oil over the top and sprinkle with the seasoned salt and red pepper, then toss gently to coat.
3. Set the grill basket in the smoker and add a small handful of the soaked hickory chips to the chip loading area. Adding more chips at least every 20 minutes, cook for 1 to 1½ hours, or until the broccoli is just slightly tender but still has some bite to it.

Smoked Cabbage

Servings: 4
Cooking Time: 10 Minutes

Ingredients:

- 1 head cabbage, cored completely
- 4 tablespoons butter
- 2 tablespoons rendered bacon fat, or 2 more tablespoons butter, melted
- 1 chicken bouillon cube
- 1 teaspoon freshly ground black pepper
- 1 garlic clove, minced

Directions:

1. Preheat the smoker to 240°F with the apple, maple, or oak wood.
2. Fill the hole left by coring the cabbage with the butter, bacon fat, bouillon cube, pepper, and garlic.
3. Wrap the cabbage in aluminum foil, two-thirds of the way up the sides to protect the outer leaves, leaving the top open to allow the smoke flavor to permeate the cabbage. Place the cabbage on the grill rack and smoke for about 2 hours.
4. Unwrap and enjoy as a side dish.

Smoked Potatoes And Onions

Servings: 8
Cooking Time: 20 Minutes

Ingredients:

- 2 pounds baby red potatoes
- 2 large sweet onions, such as Vidalia or Walla Walla
- 6 tablespoons olive oil
- 1 tablespoon minced garlic
- 1 tablespoon ground rosemary
- 1 tablespoon coarse salt
- 1 tablespoon coarsely ground black pepper
- 2 tablespoons chopped fresh parsley
- 4 ounces Parmesan cheese, grated

Directions:

1. Preheat the smoker to 250°F.
2. Scrub the potatoes and cut them in half. Pat them dry with paper towels.
3. Thinly slice the onions and place them on the bottom of a shallow baking dish. Place a layer of potatoes over the onions.
4. In a small bowl, mix together the olive oil, garlic, rosemary, salt, and pepper. Brush the potatoes with the seasoned oil.
5. Set the pan in the smoker and smoke for 2 hours, or until the potatoes are fork-tender.
6. Take the potatoes out of the smoker, sprinkle them with the parsley, and toss to combine everything. Let rest for 5 minutes.
7. Sprinkle the Parmesan over the pan. Toss again, transfer to a serving dish, and it's good to go.

Potato Torte Inside A Smoker

Servings: 6
Cooking Time: 90 Minutes

Ingredients:

- 6 potatoes, scrubbed but not skinned
- 3 tablespoons olive oil
- Salt and black pepper to taste
- 3 tablespoons fresh rosemary, chopped

Directions:

1. Preheat the smoker at 220 degrees F for 40 minutes by adding a wood chip of apple flavor.
2. Sprayed a heavy skillet with oil and then set aside for further use.
3. Take a mandolin and thinly slice the potatoes.
4. Place the potatoes in the skillet. As you add the slices, brush the potatoes with olive oil and sprinkle salt and pepper along with the rosemary.
5. Cook inside the smoker until start to sizzle for about an hour.
6. Carefully invert the torte on a flat plate.
7. Return the torte to the cooking skillet and place in the smoker for additional cooking for 30 minutes.
8. Then serve.

Eggplant In An Electric Smoker

Servings: 2
Cooking Time: 1-2 Hours

Ingredients:

- 3 cloves garlic, minced
- 4 tablespoons balsamic vinegar
- Salt and pepper, to taste
- 4 eggplants
- 3 tablespoons olive oil

Directions:

1. Preheat the smoke for 60 minutes by adding apple-flavor wood chips at 250 degrees F.
2. Cut the eggplant into round, thick circles.
3. Marinate the eggplant in a mixture of garlic, vinegar, salt, and pepper.
4. Let it marinate for 30 minutes.
5. Transfer the eggplant to the bowl and coat it with olive oil.

6. Smoke inside the preheated electric smoker for 1-2 hours.
7. Once it's done, serve.

Potato Bacon Bites

Servings: 5 Or 6
Cooking Time: 15 Minutes

Ingredients:

- 6 small red potatoes, or baby Dutch yellow potatoes
- ¾ cup (1½ sticks) butter, cut into 12 (tablespoon-size) slices
- 1 tablespoon chili powder
- 1 tablespoon garlic powder
- 2 teaspoons salt
- 2 teaspoons freshly ground black pepper
- 8 bacon slices, cooked and crumbled
- ½ cup chopped scallions, white and green parts
- 1 cup shredded Cheddar cheese
- 1 tablespoon dried parsley
- Sour cream, for serving

Directions:

1. Prick the potatoes with a fork and microwave on high power for 2 to 3 minutes. They should still be firm. Remove and let them cool.
2. Halve the cooled potatoes and scoop out the centers, leaving enough potato to keep the sides and bottom intact. Discard the extra potato or save for another use.
3. Place a pat of butter in the center of each potato shell.
4. In a small bowl, stir together the chili powder, garlic powder, salt, pepper, bacon, and scallion. Top each potato with some of this mixture and sprinkle on the Cheddar. Place the potatoes on a smoker rack and smoke for about 1½ hours until tender.
5. Sprinkle with the parsley and serve with sour cream.

Smoked Tofu And Vegetables

Servings: 4
Cooking Time: 2 Hours 15 Minutes

Ingredients:

- 1 (16-ounce) block firm or extra-firm tofu
- ½ cup soy sauce

- ½ cup sesame oil
- 4 scallions, chopped
- 2 tablespoons minced garlic
- 1 teaspoon ground ginger
- 8 ounces baby corn, preferably fresh (but canned or frozen okay)
- 8 ounces snow peas
- 1 tablespoon salt
- 2 teaspoons freshly ground black pepper
- 1 teaspoon red pepper flakes
- 1 tablespoon sesame seeds

Directions:

1. Set the block of tofu on a cutting board. Place another cutting board on top, then stack two dinner plates on it. Leave the tofu to press for 40 minutes, draining off the water as needed. Once pressed, cut the block into ½-inch-thick slices and place in a shallow baking dish.

2. In a small bowl, mix together the soy sauce, sesame oil, scallions, garlic, and ginger. Spoon half of the marinade over the tofu, coating all sides.

3. Arrange the baby corn and snow pea pods in a separate baking dish. Add the remaining marinade and toss to coat them.

4. Cover both baking dishes and refrigerate for 1 hour.

5. Take the dishes out of the fridge and let them sit on the counter, still covered, for about 30 minutes.

6. Preheat the smoker to 225°F and fill the water pan.

7. Arrange the tofu, baby corn, and snow peas on a grill screen. Sprinkle the vegetables with the salt, black pepper, and pepper flakes.

8. Set the grill racks in the smoker. Smoke for 1 hour 30 minutes.

9. Cut the tofu slices into chunks and put in a serving bowl. Scatter the baby corn and snow peas over the tofu. Sprinkle the sesame seeds on top. Gently mix and serve immediately.

Mixed Vegetable Skewers

Servings: 10
Cooking Time: 15 Minutes

Ingredients:

- 2 zucchini, sliced in ½-inch rounds
- 2 yellow summer squash, sliced in ½-inch rounds
- 1 red onion, cut in large chunks
- 4 bell peppers (any color), seeded and cut in large chunks
- 1 pint (about 2 cups) container grape tomatoes
- 10 wooden skewers
- 2 tablespoons olive oil
- 2 tablespoons seasoned salt

Directions:

1. Prepare the smoker's water pan according to the manufacturer's instructions and preheat the smoker to 250°F. While it heats, fill a medium bowl with water and add 3 or 4 handfuls of hickory chips to soak.

2. Thread the cut vegetables onto the skewers, alternating types and ending each skewer with a grape tomato. For easy handling, leave a couple inches on the dull end of the skewer free of vegetables. Drizzle on olive oil and sprinkle liberally with seasoned salt, making sure to coat all sides of the vegetables.

3. Arrange the skewers on the smoker racks and add a small handful of the soaked hickory chips to the chip loading area. Adding more chips at least every 20 minutes, cook for 1 to 1½ hours, or until the vegetables are just slightly tender but still have some bite to them.

Potatoes Inside Smoker

Servings: 2
Cooking Time: 2 Hours

Ingredients:

- ⅓ cup olive oil
- 4 large potatoes
- Salt and pepper, to taste
- 1 tablespoon onion powder
- 1 teaspoon garlic powder
- 1 teaspoon dried thyme

Directions:

1. Preheat the electric smoker for two hours at 200 degrees by adding mild or any other wood chips.

2. Cut the potatoes in half and then brush with the generous amount of olive oil.

3. Now sprinkle salt, onion powder, garlic powder, dried thyme, and pepper on top.

4. Smoke for 2 hours at 225 degrees F.

5. Then, serve and enjoy.

Smoked Potato Salad With Bacon

Servings: 4

Cooking Time: 30 Minutes

Ingredients:

- FOR THE POTATO SALAD
- 1 ½ pounds red potatoes or other small potatoes
- ¼ cup olive oil
- 2 teaspoons garlic powder
- 1 teaspoon dried oregano
- 1 tablespoon coarse salt
- 1 teaspoon freshly ground black pepper
- 6 slices bacon
- 1 celery stalk, diced
- 1 cup finely chopped red onion
- FOR THE DRESSING
- 1 ½ cups mayonnaise
- 2 tablespoons apple cider vinegar
- 2 tablespoons whole-grain mustard
- 1 tablespoon granulated sugar
- 1 teaspoon celery seed
- 1 teaspoon garlic powder
- 1 teaspoon paprika
- 1 teaspoon salt
- 1 teaspoon freshly ground black pepper

Directions:

1. TO MAKE THE POTATO SALAD
2. Preheat the smoker to 275°F.
3. Scrub the potatoes under cold water and dry them with paper towels.
4. In a small bowl, mix together the olive oil, garlic powder, oregano, salt, and pepper. Brush the potatoes with some of the mixture.
5. Set the potatoes in the smoker. Arrange the bacon on a wire rack or grill screen and set on a rack above the potatoes. Smoke for 35 minutes, or until the bacon is crisp. Remove the bacon and chop into small pieces.
6. Brush the potatoes with the rest of the olive oil mixture and smoke for 5 more minutes, or until the potatoes are fork-tender and their internal temperature reaches 210°F.
7. Let the potatoes rest for 20 minutes.
8. Cut the potatoes into chunks and place them in a large bowl. Sprinkle the chopped bacon, celery, and onion over the potatoes.
9. TO MAKE THE DRESSING
10. In a small bowl, whisk together the mayonnaise, vinegar, mustard, sugar, celery seed, garlic powder, paprika, salt, and pepper.
11. Pour the dressing over the vegetables and stir to combine. Cover the bowl and refrigerate for 30 minutes before serving.

Herb-roasted Potatoes With Goose Fat

Servings: 8

Cooking Time: 2 Hours

Ingredients:

- Coarse sea salt
- 5 pounds russet potatoes, scrubbed with skins left on
- 3 fresh bay leaves
- 8 ounces goose (or duck) fat
- 12 garlic cloves, unpeeled
- Flaked sea salt
- Freshly ground black pepper
- 3 thyme sprigs, leaves stripped and finely chopped
- 3 rosemary sprigs, leaves stripped

Directions:

1. Fill a large stockpot with cold water until it's three-fourths full. Generously season the water with coarse sea salt and add the potatoes and bay leaves. Place the pot over high heat and bring the water to a boil. Reduce the heat to medium and cook for about 45 minutes, or until the potatoes are tender. Remove the potatoes from the water and let them cool slightly.
2. Using a paring knife, gently peel the potatoes. Quarter them lengthwise.
3. Preheat the electric smoker to 275°F. Ensure the drip tray is clean and in place. Seal the door.
4. Place the wood chips in the smoking tray or firebox, get a good smoke rolling, and seal the door.
5. Put a large baking sheet on a smoking rack to preheat, then place the goose fat on it to melt.

6. Arrange the potatoes and garlic on the baking sheet, season with flaked sea salt and pepper, and toss to coat. Smoke for 1 hour. Remove the baking sheet from the smoker and gently turn the potatoes.

7. Add the thyme and rosemary. Return the pan to the smoker and smoke for 1 hour more, until the potatoes are golden brown, turning 2 or 3 times. Remove and discard the herbs. Finish with flaked sea salt.

Smoked Artichokes

Servings: 8
Cooking Time: 5 Minutes

Ingredients:
- ¼ cup olive oil
- 1 garlic clove, minced
- 1 teaspoon salt
- Juice of 1 lemon
- 4 artichokes, stemmed and halved lengthwise

Directions:
1. Preheat the smoker to 225°F with the hickory or maple wood.
2. In a small bowl, whisk together the olive oil, garlic, salt, and lemon juice.
3. Brush the artichoke halves with the seasoned olive oil. Place them directly on the smoker's grate and smoke for about 2 hours. The artichoke bottoms should look and feel tender when poked with a fork.

Corn On The Cob With Smoked Pesto Butter

Servings: 4
Cooking Time: 20 Minutes

Ingredients:
- 4 ears of corn, husks attached
- 1 cup coarse kosher salt
- ½ cup (1 stick) butter, softened
- 1½ tablespoons Smoked Walnut Pesto (page 105)

Directions:
1. Prepare the corn by peeling back the husks and removing the silks, then pulling the husks back up over the corn. Fill a large bucket or a sink with cool water, add the salt, and stir to combine. Soak the corn in the salted water for 2 to 3 hours.

2. Prepare the smoker's water pan according to the manufacturer's instructions and preheat the smoker to 275°F. While it heats, fill a medium bowl with water and add 3 or 4 handfuls of chips to soak.

3. Remove the corn from the salt water, shaking off the excess. Place the ears directly on a smoker rack. Add a small handful of the soaked wood chips to the chip loading area, and keep adding more chips at least every 15 minutes. Smoke until tender, about 1 to 1½ hours.

4. Meanwhile, in a small bowl combine the butter and the Smoked Walnut Pesto, using a fork to blend them together. Set the pesto butter in the refrigerator to chill.

5. Remove the corn from the smoker. When it's cool enough to handle, remove the husks. Serve the corn with smoked pesto butter on the side.

Smoked Mac 'n' Cheese

Servings: 6 To 8
Cooking Time: 20 Minutes

Ingredients:
- FOR THE MAC 'N' CHEESE
- 4 tablespoons (½ stick) unsalted butter
- ¼ cup all-purpose flour
- 3 cups whole milk
- 8 ounces cream cheese, in chunks
- 1 teaspoon salt
- ½ teaspoon freshly ground black pepper
- ½ cup shredded sharp cheddar cheese
- ½ cup shredded Gouda cheese
- ¼ cup shredded Parmesan cheese
- 1 pound elbow macaroni, cooked according to package directions
- FOR THE TOPPING
- 2 cups fine dried bread crumbs or panko
- 8 tablespoons (1 stick) unsalted butter, melted
- 1 teaspoon dried thyme
- 1 teaspoon dried rosemary
- 1 teaspoon poultry seasoning

Directions:
1. TO MAKE THE MAC 'N' CHEESE
2. Preheat the smoker to 225°F.

3. In a large saucepan on the stovetop, melt the butter over low heat. Whisk in the flour, increase the heat to medium, and cook for 2 minutes. Whisk in the milk and bring to a boil, then remove from the heat.

4. Stir in the cream cheese, salt, and pepper until smooth. Mix in the cheddar, Gouda, and Parmesan.

5. Spread the cooked macaroni in a 9 ½-by-11-by-2-inch roasting pan. Pour the cheese sauce over the macaroni, then gently fold it together until all the pasta is well coated.

6. TO MAKE THE TOPPING

7. In a large bowl, combine the bread crumbs, melted butter, thyme, rosemary, and poultry seasoning. Sprinkle the bread crumb mixture over the pasta.

8. Smoke the mac 'n' cheese for 50 minutes.

9. Serve warm.

Sautéed Brussels Sprouts With Pancetta

Servings: 8
Cooking Time: 2 Hours

Ingredients:
- 1 tablespoon extra-virgin olive oil
- 1 tablespoon unsalted butter
- 1 pound pancetta, cut into ½-inch pieces
- 4 shallots, trimmed and finely sliced
- 2 pounds Brussels sprouts, trimmed and halved
- Flaked sea salt
- Freshly ground black pepper

Directions:
1. Preheat the electric smoker to 275°F. Ensure the drip tray is clean and in place. Seal the door.

2. Place the wood chips in the smoking tray or firebox, get a good smoke rolling, and seal the door.

3. Place a large cast iron casserole, such as a Dutch oven, on a smoking rack to preheat, then pour in the olive oil and add the butter to melt.

4. Add the pancetta and shallots to the casserole and smoke for 1 hour, or until golden brown, tossing occasionally.

5. Add the Brussels sprouts to the casserole and season with salt and pepper. Smoke for 1 hour, or until golden brown. Cool slightly before serving.

Smoked Corn

Servings: 8
Cooking Time: 2-3 Hours

Ingredients:
- 8 ears of corn
- ½ cup mayo
- ½ cup sour cream
- 1 handful fresh cilantro, chopped
- 2 teaspoons paprika
- 1 teaspoon cumin
- Salt to taste
- Black pepper to taste
- 3 ounces spicy chipotle cream cheese, shredded
- 2 limes, sliced

Directions:
1. Preheat the smoker to 225 degrees F for 2 hours.

2. Next, husk the corn and remove the silk.

3. Arrange the corn inside the smoker by tightly tying the husks together.

4. Smoke for 2-3 hours.

5. Combine the remaining listed ingredient in a small bowl.

6. Serve it with smoked corn.

Smoked Onion Bombs

Servings: 4
Cooking Time: 15 Minutes

Ingredients:
- 4 large Vidalia onions, peeled
- ½ cup (1 stick) butter, divided 4 chicken bouillon cubes
- ½ cup grated Parmesan cheese
- 1 teaspoon freshly ground black pepper

Directions:
1. Preheat the smoker to 225°F with the maple or mesquite wood.

2. Angle a sharp knife into the onion from the top and cut all the way around, removing the top and creating a

deep well in the onion. Repeat with the remaining onions. Save the onion tops.

3.   Tear off four pieces of aluminum foil, each about 8 inches square. Place each onion on a sheet of foil. Press 2 tablespoons of butter into the well of each onion and top with a bouillon cube.

4.   In a small bowl, mix the Parmesan and pepper. Put about 2 tablespoons of the mixture in each onion well.

5.   Replace the onion tops tightly (cutting as necessary to fit) and wrap the foil up the sides, but leave the top of the packet open to allow the smoke flavor to permeate the onions.

6.   Smoke the onions for about 2 hours, until tender.

Smoked Tomatoes

Servings: 2
Cooking Time: 60 Minutes

Ingredients:
* 10 plum tomatoes
* Salt and pepper, to taste
* Thyme to taste

Directions:
1.   Preheat the smoker to 225 degrees F by adding hickory smoker chips.
2.   Remember to soak the wood chips in water for 60 minutes before adding to the smoker.
3.   Season the tomatoes with listed ingredients.
4.   Layer the tomatoes on a rack or baking pan and then cook inside the smoker for 60 minutes.
5.   Serve as a side dish.
6.   Enjoy.

Smoked Coleslaw

Servings: 10 To 12
Cooking Time: 10 Minutes

Ingredients:
* 1 head cabbage, shredded
* 1 carrot, shredded
* ¼ cup sugar
* ½ teaspoon salt
* ½ teaspoon freshly ground black pepper
* ¼ cup white vinegar
* 1 cup heavy (whipping) cream (do not whip)
* 1 teaspoon paprika

Directions:
1.   Preheat the smoker to 175°F with the maple wood.
2.   Spread the cabbage and carrot in a shallow aluminum foil pan. Place the pan in the smoker and smoke the vegetables for 30 minutes. Remove from the smoker and transfer the vegetables to a large bowl.
3.   Stir in the sugar, salt, pepper, vinegar, and heavy cream to combine. Refrigerate for 1 hour before serving.
4.   Sprinkle with paprika.

Lemon & Garlic Asparagus

Servings: 1
Cooking Time: 1.5 Hours

Ingredients:
* 2 cups asparagus
* Oil spray, for greasing
* Salt and pepper, to taste
* 2 tablespoons butter
* 2 garlic cloves, minced
* 1 lemon

Directions:
1.   Prepare the electric smoker for 2 hours at 200 degrees F with a mild or any other wood chips.
2.   Trim and cut the asparagus into a 1-inch length.
3.   Put the asparagus in hot boiling water for one minute and then drain the water.
4.   Pat dry the vegetable with the paper towel.
5.   Toss the asparagus with the salt, pepper, and oil it with cooking spray.
6.   Set the temperature of the electric smoker to 250 degrees F and cooks the asparagus for 1.5 hours.
7.   Just before when the asparagus is ready to serve, melt the butter in a separate saucepan and add garlic.
8.   Do not fry the garlic.
9.   Once the asparagus is cooked to its perfection, transfer it to the serving tray and then top it off with butter dressing.
10.   Serve with the lemon squeeze on top.
11.   Enjoy.

Savoy Cabbage Slaw

Servings: 8

Cooking Time: 10 To 15 Minutes

Ingredients:

- 6 tablespoons apple cider vinegar
- 2 tablespoons wildflower honey
- 2 tablespoons extra-virgin olive oil
- 2 tablespoons mayonnaise
- 1 tablespoon sriracha
- 1 tablespoon Dijon mustard
- 1 tablespoon celery seed
- 8 cups finely shredded Savoy cabbage
- 2 Fuji apples, cored and cut into matchsticks
- 2 scallions, trimmed and thinly sliced on an angle
- Grated zest of 1 lemon, plus juice of 1 lemon
- Flaked sea salt
- Freshly ground black pepper

Directions:

1. In a large bowl, whisk together the vinegar, honey, olive oil, mayonnaise, sriracha, mustard, and celery seed until smooth and combined.

2. Add the cabbage, apples, scallions, lemon zest, and lemon juice. Toss to coat well in the dressing. Cover with plastic wrap and refrigerate for 1 hour. Toss again before serving. Season with salt and pepper to taste.

Smoky Creamed Spinach

Servings: 8

Cooking Time: 20 Minutes

Ingredients:

- 1 pound spinach leaves, stemmed
- ¼ cup olive oil
- 1 teaspoon garlic powder
- 1 teaspoon salt
- 1 teaspoon freshly ground black pepper
- 6 tablespoons unsalted butter
- 1 teaspoon cayenne pepper
- 1 teaspoon grated nutmeg
- 1 cup heavy (whipping) cream
- 4 ounces cream cheese, cut into chunks
- ½ cup shredded Gouda cheese

Directions:

1. Preheat the smoker to 275°F.

2. Rinse the spinach leaves and pat dry with paper towels. Set in a bowl.

3. In a small bowl, mix together the olive oil with the garlic powder, salt, and pepper. Add the seasoned oil to the spinach and toss to coat all the leaves.

4. Place the spinach in a perforated BBQ skillet (ideally nonstick) and smoke for 10 minutes. Remove and chop up.

5. In a large saucepan on the stovetop, heat the butter over medium heat. Stir in the cayenne and nutmeg. Pour in the heavy cream and cook, stirring, for about 7 minutes, or until it thickens. Add the cream cheese and stir until it's blended. Add the chopped spinach and Gouda and stir to combine.

6. Serve immediately.

Butternut Squash Bread Pudding

Servings: 8

Cooking Time: 2 To 3 Hours

Ingredients:

- 1 pound bacon slices, cut into ½-inch pieces
- 6 large eggs, lightly beaten
- 2 cups heavy (whipping) cream
- 3 thyme sprigs, leaves stripped and finely chopped
- Flaked sea salt
- Freshly ground black pepper
- 1 large butternut squash, peeled, halved lengthwise, seeded, and diced (see tip)
- 3 leeks, white parts only, quartered lengthwise and thinly sliced
- 1 baguette loaf, diced
- 2 cups finely grated Parmesan cheese

Directions:

1. Preheat the electric smoker to 275°F. Ensure the drip tray is clean and in place. Seal the door.

2. Place the wood chips in the smoking tray or firebox, get a good smoke rolling, and seal the door.

3. Place a large cast iron casserole on a smoking rack to preheat. Smoke the bacon in the casserole for 30 minutes, or until golden brown, tossing occasionally. Spoon off and discard the excess fat.

4. In a large bowl, combine the eggs, heavy cream, and thyme leaves. Season with salt and pepper. Whisk to combine. Set aside.

5. Add the butternut squash and leeks to the skillet. Season with salt and pepper. Smoke for 30 minutes.

6. Add the bread cubes to the skillet and gently fold them into the squash and leeks.

7. Pour the egg mixture evenly over the skillet ingredients. Top with the Parmesan cheese and season with salt and pepper (keep in mind the Parmesan is quite salty). Smoke for 1 hour, or until golden brown and fully set. Let cool slightly before serving.

Smoked Bacon-wrapped Onion Rings

Servings: 16
Cooking Time: 20 Minutes

Ingredients:

- 2 large onions, peeled and sliced ½ inch thick (about 4 slices from each onion)
- ¼ cup hot sauce
- 4 tablespoons butter, melted
- 1 pound bacon
- 1 tablespoon cayenne pepper
- 1 tablespoon sugar

Directions:

1. Preheat the smoker to 250°F with the hickory, maple, or mesquite wood.

2. Separate the onion rings and remove the smaller internal rings to save for another use. I recommend leaving two rings intact on each to keep them sturdy. You should get about eight rings out of one large onion, two out of each slice.

3. In a small shallow bowl, mix together the hot sauce and melted butter.

4. Dip the onion rings in the butter–hot sauce mixture.

5. Wrap each onion ring tightly with a bacon slice.

6. In another small bowl, stir together the cayenne and sugar. Coat the bacon-wrapped rings well with this mixture. Secure the rings with toothpicks or place them on skewers.

7. Place the onion rings on a grill mat and smoke for about 1½ hours until the bacon is done and beyond "chewy" to bite through.

Bacon

Servings: 2½
Cooking Time: 15 Minutes

Ingredients:

- 4 pounds pork belly
- ¼ cup course kosher salt
- ¼ cup light brown sugar
- 5 cloves garlic, smashed
- 4 whole dried bay leaves
- 2 tablespoons coarse black pepper
- 2 teaspoons pink curing salt (page 88)

Directions:

1. Cut the pork belly into 1-pound sections. Combine all the seasonings in a large bowl and mix well. Divide the seasoning blend into 4 portions and rub a portion over each pork belly, covering all areas well. Place each pork belly in a 1-gallon zip-top plastic bag. (Each belly needs its own separate bag, or it won't get enough seasoning and you'll end up with something that's more like Canadian bacon.) Refrigerate the bags for 1 week, turning them over daily and rubbing the meat through the plastic to make sure it's evenly covered with seasonings.

2. After 7 days, prepare the smoker's water pan according to the manufacturer's instructions and preheat the smoker to 200°F. While it heats, fill a medium bowl with water and add 3 or 4 handfuls of mesquite or hickory wood chips to soak.

3. Remove the pork pieces from the bags, rinse under cold water, and pat dry using paper towels. Arrange in the smoker with plenty of space around each piece, and add a handful of wood chips to the chip loading area. Smoke the pork for about 2 hours, or until it reaches an internal temperature of 150°F. The goal isn't to cook the bacon but to impart a strong smoke flavor, so keep the temperature low and the smoke level high. Add wood chips every 30 minutes.

4. Remove the bacon from the smoker and let cool. Then remove the remaining top layer of fat and slice the bacon as thick or thin as you like. Freeze any that you aren't going to use within a week, arranging the slices in a single layer in zip-top plastic freezer bags.

5. To use, cook the bacon as you normally would. I like to cook mine in a 425°F oven for about 20 minutes, or until crispy.

Side Dish Smoked Cabbage

Servings: 2
Cooking Time: 2 Hours

Ingredients:
- 2 large cups cabbage
- 3 tablespoons steak seasoning
- 1 stick butter
- 1 vegetable bouillon cube

Directions:
1. Preheat the smoker, then add the hickory wood chips.
2. Wash the cabbage well and then slice the cabbage.
3. Put the cabbage into a tinfoil pan and place a stick of the butter on top.
4. Then sprinkle the crushed vegetable bouillon cube.
5. Sprinkle the steak seasoning at the end.
6. Wrap it in the tin foil leaving a top slightly open.
7. Once the smoke started to build, place the tin foil pan into the smoker and cook it for 2 hours at 250 degrees F.
8. Once it's done, serve.

Balsamic Glazed Potatoes And Carrots

Servings: 3
Cooking Time: 2 Hours

Ingredients:
- 1 pound sweet potatoes
- ½ pound Yukon gold potatoes
- 4 ounces baby carrots
- ½ cup extra-virgin olive oil
- Salt and pepper to taste
- ½ cup balsamic vinegar

Directions:
1. Preheat the electric smoker to 225 degrees F by adding mild or any other wood chips.
2. Peel, wash, and cut all the potatoes into 2–inch chunks.
3. Combine potato chunks with baby carrot and then drizzle olive oil on the top.
4. Season it with salt and pepper.
5. Stir well to combine ingredients well.
6. Place the ingredients in a large rack and smoker it for 1- 2 hours.
7. Once potatoes are tender, drizzle balsamic vinegar on top.
8. Enjoy.

Easy Green Chile Corn Bread

Servings: 4 To 6
Cooking Time: 15 Minutes

Ingredients:
- 1 (12-ounce) package cornbread mix
- 1 (4-ounce) can diced green chiles (hot or mild)
- 2 tablespoons mayonnaise

Directions:
1. Prepare the smoker's water pan according to the manufacturer's instructions and preheat the smoker to 230°F. While it heats, fill a medium bowl with water and add 3 or 4 handfuls of hickory wood chips to soak.
2. Mix the cornbread according to the package instructions. Stir the chiles and mayonnaise into the batter.
3. Spray an 8-inch cast-iron skillet with cooking spray, coating it well. Pour the cornbread batter into the skillet and place in the smoker. Add a small handful of the soaked hickory chips to the chip loading area, and keep adding more chips at least every 20 to 30 minutes.
4. Smoke for 1½ to 2 hours, or until the cornbread is lightly browned and a toothpick inserted in the middle comes out clean. Cool slightly before serving.

Cast-iron Baked Beans

Servings: 4

Cooking Time: 5 Minutes

Ingredients:

- 2 (31-ounce) cans pork and beans
- 8 slices bacon, cooked and roughly chopped, divided
- ¼ cup light brown sugar
- ½ cup Tangy Barbecue Sauce (page 17)
- 2 tablespoons Basic Barbecue Rub (page 19)
- 2 teaspoons Worcestershire sauce
- 1 jalapeño chile, halved and seeded (additional sliced jalapeño chile for serving, if desired)

Directions:

1. Prepare the smoker's water pan according to the manufacturer's instructions and preheat the smoker to 275°F. While it heats, fill a medium bowl with water and add 3 or 4 handfuls of wood chips to soak.

2. In a 10-quart cast-iron pot, combine the beans, half of the cooked bacon, and all the remaining ingredients. Leaving the pot uncovered, place in the smoker and add a small handful of the soaked wood chips to the chip loading area. Adding more chips and stirring the beans at least every 15 minutes, smoke for about 1 hour. To serve, top with the remaining bacon and a couple jalapeño slices, if desired.

Garlic-rosemary Potato Wedges

Servings: 6 To 8

Cooking Time: 15 Minutes

Ingredients:

- 4 to 6 large russet potatoes, cut into wedges
- ¼ cup olive oil
- 2 garlic cloves, minced
- 2 tablespoons chopped fresh rosemary leaves, or 1 tablespoon dried rosemary
- 2 teaspoons salt
- 1 teaspoon freshly ground black pepper
- 1 teaspoon sugar
- 1 teaspoon onion powder

Directions:

1. Preheat the smoker to 250°F with the maple or pecan wood.

2. In a large bowl, toss the potatoes with the olive oil to coat them well.

3. In a small bowl, stir together the garlic, rosemary, salt, pepper, sugar, and onion powder. Sprinkle this mixture on all sides of the potato wedges. Transfer the seasoned wedges to a grill pan and put it into the smoker.

4. Cook for about 1½ hours until a fork cuts through the wedges easily.

Smoked Corn Salsa

Servings: 6

Cooking Time: 25 Minutes

Ingredients:

- 6 ears corn, husked
- 4 tablespoons olive oil, divided
- 2 tablespoons garlic powder
- 1 tablespoon salt
- 1 tablespoon freshly ground black pepper
- 1 tablespoon minced garlic
- 12 large mushrooms, sliced
- 1 teaspoon fresh thyme, or dried
- Juice of 1 lime

Directions:

1. Preheat the smoker to 275°F.

2. Remove any silk from the corn. Brush the corn with 2 tablespoons olive oil. In a small bowl, mix together the garlic powder, salt, and pepper. Sprinkle the mixture over the corn.

3. Smoke the corn for 35 minutes, or until slightly browned and tender.

4. Let the corn cool for about 10 minutes.

5. In a large skillet on the stovetop, heat the remaining 2 tablespoons olive oil and the minced garlic over medium heat. Add the mushrooms and sauté for 4 minutes. Stir in the thyme and sauté for 1 more minute, or until the mushrooms are soft and juicy.

6. Cut the kernels off the cobs (I recommend using a knife with a serrated edge) into a bowl. Add the mushrooms and their juices. Pour the lime juice over the ingredients and mix it all up.

7. Serve immediately or cover and refrigerate to serve chilled.

Simple Smoked Asparagus

Servings: 4

Cooking Time: 5 Minutes

Ingredients:

- 1 bunch asparagus (about 1 pound), trimmed
- 2 tablespoons olive oil
- 1 teaspoon chopped garlic (about 2 cloves)
- large pinch of coarse kosher salt
- ⅛ teaspoon black pepper

Directions:

1. Prepare the smoker's water pan according to the manufacturer's instructions and preheat the smoker to 230°F. While it heats, fill a medium bowl with water and add 3 or 4 handfuls of pecan chips to soak.

2. Place the asparagus in a grill basket in a single layer. Drizzle olive oil over the top and sprinkle with the garlic, salt, and pepper. Toss gently to coat on all sides. Put the basket in the smoker and add a small handful of the soaked pecan chips to the chip loading area. Adding more chips at least every 20 minutes, cook for 1 to 1½ hours, or until the asparagus is just slightly tender but still has some bite to it.

Smoked Fingerling Potatoes With Shallots

Servings: 8

Cooking Time: 2 Hours

Ingredients:

- Coarse sea salt
- 2 pounds fingerling potatoes, rinsed
- 2 fresh bay leaves
- 2 tablespoons extra-virgin olive oil
- 2 tablespoons unsalted butter
- 8 shallots, trimmed and quartered lengthwise
- Flaked sea salt
- Freshly ground black pepper
- 2 parsley sprigs, leaves stripped and minced

Directions:

1. Fill a large stockpot with cold water until it's three-fourths full. Generously season the water with coarse sea salt and add the potatoes and bay leaves. Place the pot over high heat and bring the water to a boil. Reduce the heat to medium and cook for about 30 minutes, or until the potatoes are tender. Remove the potatoes from the water and let them cool slightly. Halve the potatoes.

2. Preheat the electric smoker to 250°F. Ensure the drip tray is clean and in place. Seal the door.

3. Place the wood chips in the smoking tray or firebox, get a good smoke rolling, and seal the door.

4. Place a large cast iron skillet on a smoking rack to preheat, then pour in the olive oil and add the butter to melt.

5. Add the potatoes and shallots to the skillet. Season with salt and pepper and toss to coat. Smoke the vegetables for about 45 to 60 minutes, until golden brown, tossing occasionally.

6. Top with fresh parsley and flaked sea salt to taste.

Sicilian-style Smoked Eggplant Salad

Servings: 4

Cooking Time: 30 Minutes

Ingredients:

- 2 large eggplants
- ½ cup olive oil, plus 2 tablespoons
- ¼ cup balsamic vinegar
- 4 teaspoons coarse salt
- 1 tablespoon granulated garlic
- 2 teaspoons red pepper flakes
- 1 teaspoon dried oregano
- 1 small red onion, diced
- 1 tablespoon minced garlic
- 1 red bell pepper, diced
- 2 plum tomatoes, diced
- 2 bay leaves
- ½ cup diced Sicilian olives
- 1 tablespoon chopped fresh basil
- 2 tablespoons pine nuts

Directions:

1. Preheat the smoker to 225°F.

2. Cut the eggplant into 1-inch cubes and place them in a large bowl.

3. In a medium bowl, mix together ½ cup olive oil, the vinegar, salt, granulated garlic, red pepper flakes, and oregano. Pour the oil mixture over the cubed eggplant and toss to coat. Cover the bowl and let it rest for 15 minutes.

4. Arrange the eggplant cubes on a grill screen and set them in the smoker. Smoke for 45 minutes.

5. About 20 minutes before the eggplant is done, in a large skillet on the stovetop, heat the remaining 2 tablespoons oil over medium-high heat. Add the onion and cook for 2 minutes. Add the minced garlic and bell pepper and sauté for another 3 minutes. Add the tomatoes and bay leaves and cook for another 15 minutes, stirring every few minutes, until the liquid is mostly reduced, just a little saucy.

6. Remove the eggplant from the smoker and transfer it to a large bowl. Sprinkle in the olives, basil, and pine nuts.

7. Discard the bay leaves and spoon the onion/pepper/tomato mixture over the eggplant. Mix it together gently.

8. Serve the salad hot or keep it covered and serve warm.

Bacon-wrapped Asparagus

Servings: 4
Cooking Time: 30 Minutes

Ingredients:
- 12 slices bacon
- 1 teaspoon salt
- 1 teaspoon freshly ground black pepper
- 1 teaspoon garlic powder
- 24 thin asparagus spears, tough ends trimmed

Directions:
1. Preheat the smoker to 275°F.
2. Lay the bacon on a wire rack or grill screen (or directly on the smoker rack, perpendicular to the grate) and smoke for 30 minutes.
3. Meanwhile, in a small bowl, mix together the salt, pepper, and garlic powder. Sprinkle it over the asparagus.
4. Take the partially cooked bacon out of the smoker (leave the smoker on).

5. Let the bacon cool for 5 minutes. Wrap 1 bacon slice around 2 spears of seasoned asparagus, starting at the bottom of the stalks. You can use a toothpick to make the bacon stay in place if needed.
6. Place the bacon-wrapped asparagus on the cooking rack and smoke for 1 hour 30 minutes, or until the bacon is nicely crisped (but not overly so).
7. Serve warm.

Spicy Black Beans

Servings: 8
Cooking Time: 2 Hours

Ingredients:
- 1 tablespoon extra-virgin olive oil
- 1 tablespoon unsalted butter
- 1 yellow onion, diced
- 1 jalapeño pepper, trimmed, seeded, diced, plus more for additional heat
- 3 garlic cloves, minced
- Flaked sea salt
- Freshly ground black pepper
- 6 cups black turtle beans (see tip)
- 3 fresh bay leaves
- 2 cups chicken (or vegetable) stock

Directions:
1. Preheat the electric smoker to 250°F. Ensure the drip tray is clean and in place. Seal the door.
2. Place the wood chips in the smoking tray or firebox, get a good smoke rolling, and seal the door.
3. Place a large cast iron casserole, such as a Dutch oven, on a smoking rack to preheat, then pour in the olive oil and add the butter to melt.
4. Add the onion, jalapeño, and garlic to the casserole. Season with salt and pepper and toss to coat with the oil and butter. Smoke for 30 minutes.
5. Using a heatproof spatula, stir in the beans, bay leaves, and chicken stock. Smoke for 90 minutes, or until soft. Taste and season with more jalapeño, salt, and pepper, as needed.

Loaded Hasselback Potatoes

Servings: 4
Cooking Time: 20 Minutes

Ingredients:

- 4 russet potatoes, cut Hasselback style (slice into the potato, all the way across, making your cuts about ¼ inch apart and being careful not to cut all the way through the bottom of the potato; see tip)
- 1 cup olive oil, divided
- 2 teaspoons salt
- 2 teaspoons freshly ground black pepper
- 1 small onion, sliced
- 2 jalapeño peppers, seeded and thinly sliced
- 2 cherry peppers, sliced
- 4 ounces block Cheddar cheese, thickly sliced
- 8 bacon slices, cooked and crumbled

Directions:

1. Preheat the smoker to 250°F with the hickory wood.
2. Place the potatoes on a grill pan. Drizzle ½ cup of olive oil over the potatoes and sprinkle with the salt and pepper. Place the pan in the smoker and smoke for about 1 hour.
3. Remove the potatoes from the smoker and place some onion, jalapeños, cherry peppers, Cheddar slices, and crumbled bacon in between each potato slice and on top.
4. Pour the remaining ½ cup of olive oil over all. Return the potatoes to the smoker for 30 to 40 minutes or so, until the potatoes are tender in a squeeze test.
5. Serve with sour cream, if desired.

Pan-roasted Asparagus

Servings: 4
Cooking Time: 20 To 30 Minutes

Ingredients:

- 1 tablespoon extra-virgin olive oil
- 1 tablespoon unsalted butter
- 1 pound fresh asparagus, woody ends trimmed (see tip)
- 4 shallots, trimmed and quartered
- Flaked sea salt
- Freshly ground black pepper
- 1 lemon, halved and seeded, for serving
- 1 cup sliced almonds

Directions:

1. Preheat the electric smoker to 275°F. Ensure the drip tray is clean and in place. Seal the door.
2. Place the wood chips in the smoking tray or firebox, get a good smoke rolling, and seal the door.
3. Place a large cast iron skillet on a smoking rack to preheat, then pour in the olive oil and add the butter to melt.
4. Add the asparagus and shallots to the skillet. Season with salt and pepper and toss to coat in the oil and butter and seasoning. Place the lemon halves in the skillet, cut-side down. Smoke for 20 minutes, tossing once during smoking.
5. To serve, add a squeeze or two from the charred lemons and top with the almonds.

Smoked Cauliflower Steaks

Servings: 4
Cooking Time: 10 Minutes

Ingredients:

- 2 heads cauliflower, leaves removed
- ¼ cup olive oil
- ¼ cup A1 Sauce, or Heinz 57 Steak Sauce, plus more for serving
- 2 garlic cloves, minced
- 2 teaspoons salt
- 2 teaspoons freshly ground black pepper

Directions:

1. Preheat the smoker to 250°F with the maple wood.
2. Trim the base off each cauliflower. Save the excess cauliflower florets for another use.
3. Carefully slice each head of cauliflower from top to bottom through the base into 2 thick slices.
4. In a small bowl, stir together the olive oil, steak sauce, garlic, salt and pepper. Brush both sides of the "steaks" with the mixture and let them marinate on the counter for about 10 minutes to absorb the flavors.
5. Place the cauliflower directly on a grill rack. Smoke for 45 minutes to 1 hour until tender.
6. Serve with additional steak sauce.

Smoked Asparagus

Servings: 4 Or 5
Cooking Time: 10 Minutes

Ingredients:

- 2 tablespoons butter, melted
- 2 garlic cloves, minced
- 2 tablespoons freshly squeezed lemon juice
- 1 tablespoon capers
- 1 tablespoon onion powder
- 1 teaspoon salt
- ½ teaspoon freshly ground black pepper
- 1 pound asparagus (about 18 to 20 stalks), woody ends snapped off

Directions:

1. Preheat the smoker to 240°F with the maple wood.
2. In a small bowl, stir together the butter, garlic, lemon juice, capers, onion powder, salt, and pepper.
3. Place the asparagus in a grill pan and drizzle with the seasoned butter. Put the pan in the smoker and smoke for about 1 hour until tender.

Smoked Spaghetti Squash

Servings: 4
Cooking Time: 10 Minutes

Ingredients:

- 1 spaghetti squash, ends trimmed, halved lengthwise, seeds and pulp discarded
- 2 tablespoons olive oil
- 2 teaspoons salt
- 2 teaspoons freshly ground black pepper

Directions:

1. Preheat the smoker to 275°F with the cherry or maple wood.
2. Rub the cut sides of the squash generously with the olive oil and sprinkle with the salt and pepper. Place the squash, cut-sides down, on a grill pan and smoke for 2½ to 3 hours until the flesh pulls apart into strands easily.
3. Discard the skins and serve the squash as a side dish, or use in place of pasta with marinara or Alfredo sauce.

Basque Piperade

Servings: 4
Cooking Time: 2 Hours

Ingredients:

- 2 tablespoons extra-virgin olive oil
- 4 garlic cloves, thinly sliced
- 1 yellow onion, thinly sliced
- 1 red bell pepper, cored, seeded, and sliced
- 1 yellow bell pepper, cored, seeded, and sliced
- 1 green bell pepper, cored, seeded, and sliced
- Paprika
- Flaked sea salt
- Freshly ground black pepper
- 1 cup white wine
- 4 Roma tomatoes, cored and quartered lengthwise
- 2 basil sprigs, leaves stripped and thinly sliced

Directions:

1. Preheat the electric smoker to 250°F. Ensure the drip tray is clean and in place. Seal the door.
2. Place the wood chips in the smoking tray or firebox, get a good smoke rolling, and seal the door.
3. Place a large cast iron skillet on a smoking rack to preheat, then pour in the olive oil.
4. Add the garlic, onion, and the red, yellow, and green bell peppers to the skillet. Season with paprika, salt, and pepper to taste, and toss to coat. Smoke for 60 minutes.
5. Stir in the white wine to deglaze the skillet, scraping up any browned bits from the bottom.
6. Add the tomatoes to the skillet and return it to the smoker. Smoke for 20 to 30 minutes, until slightly browned. Top with the basil and a sprinkle of sea salt.

Smoked Southern Baked Beans

Servings: 12
Cooking Time: 2 Hours

Ingredients:

- 3 tablespoons extra-virgin olive oil
- 1 pound bacon, cut into thin slices
- 8 cups navy beans (see tip)
- 4 cups beef stock
- 2 cups diced Roma tomatoes
- 1 cup dark molasses
- 1 cup packed dark brown sugar
- 1 tablespoon dried mustard
- ¼ teaspoon ground cloves

- 2 tablespoons tomato paste
- 2 tablespoons Worcestershire sauce
- Flaked sea salt
- Freshly ground black pepper
- 1 yellow onion, diced
- 1 red bell pepper, stemmed, seeded, and diced
- 1 green bell pepper, stemmed, seeded, and diced

Directions:

1. Preheat the electric smoker to 250°F. Ensure the drip tray is clean and in place. Seal the door.
2. Place the wood chips in the smoking tray or firebox, get a good smoke rolling, and seal the door.
3. Place a large cast iron casserole, such as a Dutch oven, on a smoking rack to preheat, then pour in the olive oil and add the bacon. Smoke the bacon for 30 to 45 minutes, tossing occasionally, until completely cooked.
4. In a large bowl, stir together the beans, beef stock, tomatoes, molasses, sugar, mustard, cloves, and tomato paste until blended. Stir in the Worcestershire sauce and season the mixture with salt and pepper. Set aside.
5. Add the onion, red bell pepper, and green bell pepper to the casserole. Season with salt and pepper. Toss to coat. Smoke for 30 minutes.
6. Stir the bean mixture into the casserole. Smoke for 90 minutes. Remove the casserole from the smoker. Season with salt and pepper to taste.

Smoked Sweet Mushroom

Servings: 1
Cooking Time: 45 Minutes

Ingredients:
- 1 tablespoon onion powder
- 1 teaspoon sugar
- Salt, to taste
- Pepper to taste
- 4 cups mushroom
- 1 tablespoon canola oil

Directions:

1. Wash and clean the mushroom and pat dry with paper towel.
2. Preheat the smoker to 350 degrees F by adding apple wood chips.

3. Combine mushroom along with all the listed ingredients in a bowl.
4. Transfer the mushroom to rack and place inside the smoker for cooking.
5. Cook for 30 minutes and then turn the temperature to 450 degrees F and smoker for additional 15 minutes.
6. Serve.

Cast Iron Corn Bread

Servings: 8
Cooking Time: 1 Hour

Ingredients:
- ½ cup corn oil, plus ½ tablespoon
- 1 cup yellow cornmeal
- 1¼ cups all-purpose flour
- ½ cup granulated sugar
- 1 tablespoon baking powder
- 1 teaspoon baking soda
- ½ teaspoon flaked sea salt
- 1 cup buttermilk
- ¼ cup clover honey
- 3 tablespoons unsalted butter, melted
- 2 large eggs, lightly beaten
- 1 cup corn kernels

Directions:

1. Preheat the electric smoker to 275°F. Ensure the drip tray is clean and in place. Seal the door.
2. Place the wood chips in the smoking tray or firebox, get a good smoke rolling, and seal the door.
3. Brush a large cast iron skillet with ½ tablespoon of the corn oil. Set aside.
4. In a medium bowl, whisk together the cornmeal, flour, sugar, baking powder, baking soda, and salt.
5. In a large bowl, whisk together the buttermilk, remaining ½ cup of corn oil, honey, melted butter, and eggs until smooth.
6. Pour the dry ingredients into the wet ingredients and fold to combine. Do not overmix the batter. Pour the batter into the prepared skillet and smooth the top. Scatter the corn kernels over the top. Place the skillet on a smoking rack and smoke for 1 hour, or until a toothpick inserted into the thickest part of the corn bread comes out clean.

Smoked Vegetable Casserole

Servings: 6
Cooking Time: 10 Minutes

Ingredients:

- 1 zucchini, cut into ½-inch-thick slices
- 1 yellow summer squash, cut into ½-inch-thick slices
- 1 carrot, cut into ½-inch-thick slices
- 1 red onion, cut into eighths
- 1 green bell pepper, cut into eighths
- 1 red bell pepper, cut into eighths
- 1 yellow bell pepper, cut into eighths
- ¼ cup olive oil
- 2 tablespoons balsamic vinegar
- 1 tablespoon maple syrup
- 3 tablespoons minced garlic
- 2 teaspoons coarse salt
- 1 teaspoon freshly ground black pepper

Directions:

1. Preheat the smoker to 225°F.
2. Place the zucchini, squash, carrot, onion, and bell peppers in a large bowl. In a small bowl, whisk together the olive oil, vinegar, maple syrup, garlic, salt, and black pepper. Add the dressing to the vegetables. Mix them up, making sure all the vegetables are coated.
3. Place them in a glass baking dish. Smoke for 1 hour 30 minutes, or until tender and caramelized.
4. Serve immediately.

Grilled Pumpkin With Cinnamon Whiskey Glaze

Servings: 2
Cooking Time: 2-3 Hours

Ingredients:

- 1 large pie pumpkin
- Oil spray, for greasing
- Seasoning Ingredients:
- 2 tablespoons light brown sugar
- 2 teaspoons ground cinnamon
- ½ teaspoon grated nutmeg
- ½ teaspoon ground ginger,
- ½ teaspoon orange zest, dried
- ¼ teaspoon ground allspice
- For The Glaze Ingredients:
- 1 cup chicken stock
- ¼ cup light brown sugar
- 2 tablespoons cornstarch
- 2 tablespoons cold water
- 4 ounces cinnamon whiskey

Directions:

1. Take a small cooking pot and pour stock in it
2. Bring it to medium heat and cook for 10 minutes.
3. Once reduced to half add brown sugar and stir well until combined.
4. Add in the cornstarch and water together and cook for 2 minutes, while stirring the liquid.
5. Next, add cinnamon whiskey and stir to combine well.
6. Turn off the heat.
7. Wash and clean the pumpkin and cut into slices with the knife.
8. Take out the seeds and clean the inside of it.
9. Cut into cubes.
10. Spray the pumpkin slices with oil, then sprinkles the pumpkin with the seasoning ingredients.
11. Cover the pumpkin with glaze mixture and place in the smoker and let it cool for 2-3 hours at 225 degrees F.
12. Serve warm.

Hasselback Sweet Potatoes

Servings: 4 To 6
Cooking Time: 15 Minutes

Ingredients:

- 4 large sweet potatoes, scrubbed
- ¼ cup canola oil
- 2 tablespoons table salt
- ½ cup (1 stick) butter
- 4 serrano peppers, seeded and sliced
- 1 cup Glazed Spiced Pecans, coarsely chopped
- 1 tablespoon sea salt
- ¼ cup honey

Directions:

1. Preheat the smoker to 250°F with the pecan wood.

2. Rub the sweet potatoes all over with the oil and table salt.

3. Cut them thick-sliced Hasselback-style: Slice into the sweet potatoes, all the way across, making your cuts about ½ inch apart, and being careful not to cut all the way through the bottom of the sweet potato (see tip).

4. Place the sweet potatoes on a grill pan and put it into the smoker. Smoke for 1 hour, then remove from the heat.

5. Place a pat of butter between each slice.

6. Stuff serrano slices and pecans between the slices.

7. Sprinkle well with the sea salt and drizzle with the honey, getting it between the slices.

8. Smoke for 30 to 40 minutes more and remove from the smoker when the potatoes pass the squeeze test.

Smoked Cherry Tomatoes

Servings: 4
Cooking Time: 15 Minutes

Ingredients:
- 2 pounds cherry tomatoes, halved
- ¼ cup olive oil
- 1 tablespoon minced garlic
- 1 tablespoon coarse salt
- 2 teaspoons chipotle powder (optional)
- 2 teaspoons dried basil
- 1 teaspoon freshly ground black pepper
- ¼ cup balsamic reduction

Directions:
1. Preheat the smoker to 225°F.
2. Arrange the tomatoes in a large, shallow baking dish.
3. In a small bowl, mix together the olive oil, garlic, salt, chipotle powder (if using), basil, and black pepper. Brush the mixture over the tomatoes.
4. Smoke the tomatoes for 30 minutes.
5. Sprinkle the balsamic reduction over the tomatoes and smoke for another 30 minutes.
6. Let the tomatoes rest for 10 minutes before serving.

Smoked And Stuffed Zucchini

Servings: 4
Cooking Time: 15 Minutes

Ingredients:
- 4 medium zucchini
- 5 teaspoons olive oil
- 1 tablespoon salt
- 2 teaspoons freshly ground black pepper
- 2 teaspoons garlic powder
- 2 teaspoons paprika
- 1 small red onion, finely chopped
- ½ cup seasoned croutons
- ½ cup shredded mozzarella cheese
- 3 tablespoons grated Parmesan cheese

Directions:
1. Preheat the smoker to 225°F.
2. Wash the zucchini. Halve the zucchini lengthwise, then slice off a thin strip down the length of each half to allow the zucchini to lie flat.
3. With a teaspoon or melon baller, scoop out the pulp and seeds to make 8 zucchini boats, leaving about ⅛ inch of wall all around. Pat the outside of the zucchini dry with paper towels.
4. In a small bowl, mix together the oil, salt, pepper, garlic powder, and paprika. Brush the inside and outside of the zucchini boats with about 2 teaspoons of the seasoned oil.
5. In a skillet on the stovetop, heat the remaining seasoned oil over medium-high heat. Add the onion and sauté for about 3 minutes, or until softened. Remove from the heat and stir in the croutons.
6. Spoon the mixture into the zucchini boats.
7. Place the zucchini boats on a cooking rack or grill grate in the smoker. Smoke for 45 minutes.
8. Sprinkle the boats with the mozzarella and Parmesan. Return to the smoker for another 15 minutes.
9. Serve immediately.

Smoked Brussels Sprouts

Servings: 2
Cooking Time: 90 Minutes

Ingredients:
- 1.5 pounds of Brussels sprouts
- 6 tablespoons olive oil
- 2 tablespoons Dijon mustard
- 6 cloves garlic, minced
- 2 sprig thyme

- ½ teaspoon smoked paprika
- 2 teaspoons apple cider vinegar
- ½ teaspoon fresh-cracked pepper
- ¼ teaspoon kosher salt

Directions:

1. Preheat the electric smoker for two hours at 200 degrees F by adding a mild or any other wood chips.
2. Chop the Brussels sprouts in a large bowl.
3. Add in all the listed ingredients and toss well for fine coating.
4. Place the Brussels sprouts in a non-stick rack and place inside the smoker.
5. Cook for 90 minutes at 220 degrees F.
6. Enjoy.

Cast Iron Leek And White Beans

Servings: 8

Cooking Time: 2 Hours

Ingredients:

- 2 tablespoons extra-virgin olive oil
- 4 leeks, white parts only, quartered lengthwise and thinly sliced
- 8 fingerling potatoes, cut lengthwise into slices
- 1 garlic bulb, halved
- Flaked sea salt
- Freshly ground black pepper
- 1 cup white wine
- 3 parsley sprigs, leaves stripped and minced
- 4 cups cannellini beans (see tip)
- 1 cup chicken stock
- Grated zest of 1 lemon, plus juice of 1 lemon
- 1 cup finely grated Gruyère cheese

Directions:

1. Preheat the electric smoker to 275°F. Ensure the drip tray is clean and in place. Seal the door.
2. Place the wood chips in the smoking tray or firebox, get a good smoke rolling, and seal the door.
3. Place a large cast iron casserole, such as a Dutch oven, on a smoking rack to preheat, then pour in the olive oil.
4. Add the leeks and potatoes to the casserole. Place the garlic halves in the pot cut-side down. Season with salt and pepper. Smoke for 1 hour.
5. Stir in the white wine to deglaze the pan, scraping up any browned bits from the bottom.
6. Add the parsley, beans, chicken stock, lemon zest, and lemon juice. Season with salt and pepper. Smoke for about 1 hour more, or until your desired consistency is reached.
7. To serve, squeeze the garlic cloves from the head and add them back to the casserole. Taste and season with more salt and pepper, as needed, and top with the Gruyère cheese.

Smoked Onions With Cheese

Servings: 3

Cooking Time: 45 Minutes

Ingredients:

- 6 slices whole grain bread
- 6 tablespoons butter (more or less) at room temperature
- 6 slices good cheddar cheese
- 2 sweet onion, sliced thinly
- 6 thin slices prosciutto

Directions:

1. Preheat the smoker for 30 minutes at 350 degrees F.
2. Place onions inside the smoker and let it cook for 45 minutes.
3. Take out the onions and then slice thinly.
4. Place butter on each slice of bread and top three bread slices with one slice of cheese, generous amount of onion, one slice of prosciutto and one slice of cheddar cheese.
5. Place remaining slices on the top of the cheddar cheese.
6. Assemble all slices in the form of a sandwich.
7. Serve and enjoy.

Smoked Root Vegetables

Servings: 8 To 10
Cooking Time: 2 Hours

Ingredients:

- 2 tablespoons extra-virgin olive oil, plus more for garnish, as desired
- 8 red fingerling potatoes, scrubbed and halved lengthwise
- 8 white fingerling potatoes, scrubbed and halved lengthwise
- 8 heirloom carrots, trimmed and halved lengthwise
- 8 shallots, halved
- 4 parsnips, peeled, trimmed, and quartered lengthwise
- 4 red beets, peeled, trimmed, and quartered
- 4 golden beets, peeled, trimmed, and quartered
- 5 thyme sprigs, leaves stripped
- 5 rosemary sprigs, leaves stripped and chopped
- 1 garlic bulb, top cut off to expose the cloves
- Flaked sea salt
- Freshly ground black pepper

Directions:

1. Preheat the electric smoker to 275°F. Ensure the drip tray is clean and in place. Seal the door.
2. Place the wood chips in the smoking tray or firebox, get a good smoke rolling, and seal the door.
3. Place a large cast iron casserole, such as a Dutch oven, on a smoking rack to preheat, then pour in 2 tablespoons of the olive oil.
4. In a large bowl, combine the red potatoes, white potatoes, carrots, shallots, parsnips, red beets, golden beets, thyme, rosemary, and garlic. Drizzle with olive oil, if desired, toss to coat, and season with salt and pepper. Transfer the vegetables to the cast iron pan and smoke for about 1 hour, gently tossing occasionally, until the vegetables are tender and caramelized.

Jalapeño Honey-roasted Heirloom Carrots

Servings: 8
Cooking Time: 2 Hours

Ingredients:

- 1 tablespoon extra-virgin olive oil
- 1 tablespoon unsalted butter
- 24 rainbow heirloom carrots, scrubbed, trimmed, and quartered lengthwise
- 3 jalapeño peppers, trimmed, seeded, and cut into rings
- 3 rosemary sprigs, plus extra rosemary leaves for garnish
- Flaked sea salt
- Freshly ground black pepper
- Grated zest of 1 lemon
- 3 tablespoons wildflower honey

Directions:

1. Preheat the electric smoker to 250°F. Ensure the drip tray is clean and in place. Seal the door.
2. Place the wood chips in the smoking tray or firebox, get a good smoke rolling, and seal the door.
3. Place a large cast iron skillet on a smoking rack to preheat, then pour in the olive oil and add the butter to melt.
4. Add the carrots, jalapeños, and rosemary to the skillet. Season with salt and pepper and toss to coat. Spread the vegetables into an even layer and smoke for 1 hour, or until the vegetables are tender, caramelized, and golden brown, turning once during smoking. Remove the skillet from the smoker. Remove and discard the rosemary sprigs.
5. To serve, sprinkle with lemon zest, drizzle with honey, and garnish with fresh rosemary leaves.

Stuffed Jalapeños

Servings: 12
Cooking Time: 20 Minutes

Ingredients:

- 8 ounces sharp Cheddar cheese, shredded
- 8 ounces cream cheese, at room temperature
- 1 tablespoon red pepper flakes
- 12 jalapeño peppers, sliced lengthwise on one side (not halved), seeded and membranes removed
- 12 bacon slices
- 2 teaspoons freshly ground black pepper

Directions:

1. Preheat the smoker to 250°F with the maple wood.

2. In a large bowl, stir together the Cheddar, cream cheese, and red pepper flakes. Stuff some of the cheese mixture into each jalapeño.

3. Wrap each stuffed pepper with 1 bacon slice and secure it with toothpicks, or tuck the bacon ends in securely.

4. Sprinkle with the black pepper.

5. Place the stuffed jalapeños on a grill pan and put them inside the smoker. Smoke for 1 to 1½ hours until the bacon is cooked. You can speed the process by partially cooking the bacon before wrapping the peppers.

Smoked Stuffed Artichokes

Servings: 4
Cooking Time: 1 Hour

Ingredients:
- 4 large artichokes
- 4 teaspoons fresh lime juice, divided
- 4 slices smoked bacon
- 4 tablespoons (½ stick) unsalted butter
- 1 yellow onion, cut into medium dice
- 2 tablespoons minced garlic
- ¾ cup white wine
- 8 cups seasoned bread crumbs
- 1 ½ cups chopped fresh parsley
- 4 tablespoons grated Romano cheese

Directions:
1. Preheat the smoker to 275°F.

2. Wash the artichokes with lots of cold water. Cut just enough off the bottom of each artichoke so that it sits flat. Remove the tough outer leaves. Use kitchen scissors to cut any of the pointy ends off the rest of the leaves. Pull the leaves in the middle open. With a spoon that has a sharp edge (like a grapefruit spoon), dig out the fuzzy choke in the center by scraping it away. Sprinkle the 2 teaspoons lime juice over the artichokes.

3. In a vegetable steamer, steam the artichokes for 15 minutes. Set them aside.

4. In a skillet on the stovetop, fry the bacon over high heat for about 5 minutes, or until crisp. Remove the bacon and drain on paper towels. Reduce the heat to medium. Add the butter and onion to the bacon fat and sauté for 2 minutes. Add the garlic and cook for another

5 minutes, or until the onion is tender and translucent. Stir in the wine and remaining 2 teaspoons lime juice and simmer, stirring, for another 5 minutes.

5. Mix in the seasoned bread crumbs and parsley. Remove the pan from the heat and let the mixture rest for about 10 minutes.

6. Set the steamed artichokes on the cooking rack. Fill the middle of the artichokes and in between the leaves with the seasoned bread crumb mixture. Spread the leaves out as you work to be able to fit all the stuffing.

7. Place the artichokes on the grill rack in the smoker. Smoke for 1 hour 10 minutes.

8. Remove the artichokes and sprinkle each with 1 tablespoon Romano. Return them to the smoker for 20 minutes.

9. Serve hot.

Bacon Wrapped Mushrooms

Servings: 4
Cooking Time: 90 Minutes

Ingredients:
- 12 white mushrooms
- 12 bacon strips, slices thin, center-cut bacon
- 1 tablespoon olive oil
- 2 garlic cloves, chopped
- Salt and pepper to taste
- 1-2 sliced jalapeno pepper
- ½ cup of hot sauce (optional)

Directions:
1. Preheat the smoker to 225 degrees F by adding apple wood chips and wait until smoke starts to come out.

2. Brush each mushroom with olive oil and then place sliced jalapeño ring on a cap of a mushroom.

3. Insert garlic pieces into the cavity of mushroom.

4. Wrap each mushroom with one bacon strip.

5. Twist the end of the bacon strips and let it drape down the sides of the mushrooms.

6. Place these stuffed mushrooms filling side up, onto a baking rack and smoke for 90 minutes.

7. Sprinkle salt and pepper at the end and then serve with hot sauce.

Smoked Whole Onions

Servings: 4
Cooking Time: 15 Minutes

Ingredients:

- 4 large Vidalia onions
- 4 tablespoons (½ stick) unsalted butter
- 4 teaspoons coarse salt
- 2 teaspoons freshly ground black pepper
- 1 teaspoon garlic powder

Directions:

1. Preheat the smoker to 275°F.
2. Slice the bottom of the onions, just above the root, so that they can sit flat. Then slice off the top of the onions.
3. With a paring knife, cut out a circle at the top of the onion that's about 1 ½ inches deep. Be sure that you don't cut through the bottom of the onion.
4. Wrap the bottom half of each onion with aluminum foil. Be sure that the onions are flat and not tilted.
5. Place 1 tablespoon butter on the top of each onion, then sprinkle with the salt, pepper, and garlic powder.
6. Smoke the onions for 1 hour 30 minutes. or until the skins have turned a golden-brown color.
7. Let the onions rest for 5 minutes before serving.

Smoked Corn On The Cob

Servings: 4
Cooking Time: 1 Hour

Ingredients:

- 8 large ears corn, husked
- ½ cup olive oil
- 1 tablespoon garlic powder
- 1 tablespoon smoked salt
- 2 teaspoons freshly ground black pepper

Directions:

1. Remove any silk from the corn and soak the ears in cold water for 1 hour. Do not add salt to the water because it makes the kernels shrink.
2. Preheat the smoker to 250°F.
3. In a small bowl, mix together the olive oil, garlic powder, smoked salt, and pepper. Pull the corn out of the water, pat the ears dry with paper towels, and brush them with the seasoned olive oil.
4. Smoke the corn for 1 hour, or until the kernels are tender and slightly browned. Brush the corn with the olive oil mix every 20 minutes.
5. Serve hot.

Cauliflower Roast With Tomato Gravy

Servings: 4
Cooking Time: 1 To 2 Hours

Ingredients:

- 3 tablespoons extra-virgin olive oil, plus more for brushing and garnish
- 1 leek, white part only, quartered lengthwise, and thinly sliced
- Flaked sea salt
- Freshly ground black pepper
- 1 cup white wine
- 5 Roma tomatoes, blanched, peeled, and diced (see tip)
- 1 cup vegetable stock
- 1 head cauliflower, rinsed, trimmed, and cored
- 1 garlic bulb, halved
- Smoked paprika, for garnish
- Grated zest of 1 lemon
- 3 thyme sprigs, leaves stripped
- 3 flat-leaf parsley sprigs, leaves stripped and minced
- Finely grated Pecorino-Romano cheese (optional)
- Sliced almonds, toasted (optional)

Directions:

1. Preheat the electric smoker to 275°F. Ensure the drip tray is clean and in place. Seal the door.
2. Place the wood chips in the smoking tray or firebox, get a good smoke rolling, and seal the door.
3. Place a large cast iron skillet on a smoking rack to preheat, then pour in 3 tablespoons of the olive oil.
4. Add the leek to the skillet, toss to coat it in the oil, and season with salt and pepper. Smoke for 15 minutes.

5. Stir in the white wine to deglaze the skillet, scraping up any browned bits from the bottom.

6. Add the tomatoes and vegetable stock. Season with salt and pepper.

7. Brush the cauliflower and the garlic with enough olive oil to coat them. Nestle the cauliflower and the garlic halves on top of the tomatoes. Season everything in the skillet with salt and pepper. Smoke for 60 to 90 minutes, until a paring knife passes easily into the cauliflower.

8. Squeeze the garlic cloves from the head and add them to the sauce.

9. Top with a dusting of paprika to taste. Garnish with lemon zest, thyme, and parsley. Cut the cauliflower into ½-inch-thick steaks and serve topped with the tomato sauce and sprinkled with the Pecorino-Romano cheese and almonds, as desired.

Smoked Green Beans

Servings: 3

Cooking Time: 2 Hours

Ingredients:

- 2.5 pounds fresh green beans
- 4 cups chicken broth or stock
- 1 pound smoked turkey legs meat only
- 3 tablespoons apple cider vinegar
- Salt and pepper, to taste

Directions:

1. Add wood chips to the smoker and preheat the smoker for 40 minutes at 220 degrees F.

2. Wash and then trim the edges of the green beans and place it in a microwave-safe container.

3. Pour water over the beans and then microwave for 4 minutes.

4. Drain the water.

5. Pat dry the beans with the paper towel.

6. Transfer the beans to a pan and cover with aluminum.

7. Add stock and turkey to the same pan.

8. Set the temperature of the smoker to 250 degrees F. Now cooks the green beans for 2 hours

9. Once done, drain the excess liquid.

10. Remove the turkey leg as well, and sprinkle the beans with the seasoning of salt, pepper, and a drizzle of apple cider vinegar and pepper.

11. Serve with shredded turkey leg meat on top.

12. Enjoy.

BEEF RECIPES

Smoked Pot Roast

Servings: 6
Cooking Time: 15 Minutes

Ingredients:
- 1 (3- to 4-pound) beef chuck roast
- 2 tablespoons olive oil
- 2 teaspoons coarse salt
- 2 teaspoons freshly ground black pepper
- 1 teaspoon cayenne pepper
- 2 teaspoons granulated garlic
- 2 teaspoons onion powder
- 1 ½ pounds fingerling or small potatoes, halved
- 1 ½ pounds carrots, cut into 1 ½- to 2-inch pieces
- 1 pound pearl onions, peeled
- 2 rosemary sprigs
- 1 tablespoon chipotle powder
- 1 cup red wine
- 2 cups beef broth

Directions:
1. Preheat the smoker to 190°F.
2. Pat the chuck roast with paper towels to dry it. Brush the roast with the olive oil, then sprinkle the salt, pepper, cayenne, garlic, and onion powder over all sides of the meat.
3. Smoke the roast for 1 hour 30 minutes.
4. Put the potatoes, carrots, onions, rosemary, and chipotle powder in a Dutch oven or baking dish that you can cover with aluminum foil. Pour the wine and beef broth over the vegetables and spices.
5. Take the chuck roast out of the smoker and place it over the vegetables, then cover the dish.
6. Increase the smoker temperature to 275°F. Place the Dutch oven or covered baking dish in the smoker and cook for another 4 hours, or until the internal temperature of the meat reaches 165°F.
7. Serve warm.

Reverse-seared And Smoked Steak

Servings: 2
Cooking Time: 4 Hours 30 Minutes

Ingredients:
- 1 (2-pound) rib-eye steak (2 to 2 ½ inches thick)
- 3 teaspoons coarse salt, divided
- 2 tablespoons granulated garlic
- 1 tablespoon freshly ground black pepper
- 2 teaspoons olive oil

Directions:
1. Rub the steak with 1 teaspoon salt on both sides. Cover it tightly with plastic wrap and refrigerate for 4 hours.
2. Wipe the salt off the steak and let it come to room temperature. It should take about 30 minutes.
3. Preheat the smoker to 225°F and fill the water pan.
4. In a small bowl, mix together the garlic, pepper, and remaining 2 teaspoons salt. Brush the steak all over with the olive oil. Then, generously sprinkle the garlic mixture on both sides of the steak.
5. Smoke the steak for 1 hour 30 minutes, or until the internal temperature reaches 100°F Check it after the first hour.
6. If you have a pellet smoker with a searing feature that gets you above 600°F, crank it up. Otherwise, heat a cast-iron skillet over high heat on the stovetop.
7. Give the meat a good sear on each side, 2 to 4 minutes per side, until the internal temperature reaches 125°F for rare or 135°F for medium.
8. To keep the steak juicy, let it rest for 10 minutes before serving.

Smoked Philly-style Sandwiches

Servings: 4
Cooking Time: 30 Minutes

Ingredients:

- 1 ½ pounds prime rib or sirloin, shaved into very thin slices
- 6 tablespoons olive oil, plus more for drizzling
- 1 teaspoon coarse salt
- 1 teaspoon freshly ground black pepper
- 2 teaspoons garlic powder
- 1 teaspoon onion powder
- 1 pound onions, sliced
- 1 pound green bell peppers, cut into thin strips
- 1 tablespoon Beef Rub
- 8 ounces mushrooms, sliced
- 4 tablespoons cheddar cheese spread or Cheez Whiz
- 4 kaiser rolls, split and toasted
- 8 slices provolone cheese

Directions:

1. Season the beef slices with 2 tablespoons olive oil, the salt, pepper, garlic powder, and onion powder. Toss to combine.
2. Preheat the smoker to 275°F.
3. Place the meat on a perforated BBQ skillet and set it on a rack in the smoker.
4. Place the onions and bell peppers in a baking dish. Add the remaining 4 tablespoons olive oil and the beef rub. Mix it all up, then place it in the smoker under the beef.
5. Smoke the beef and veggies for 1 hour, or until the internal temperature of the beef reaches 135°F.
6. During the last 5 minutes of smoking, warm a skillet on the stovetop over medium heat and fry the mushrooms.
7. For each sandwich, spread 1 tablespoon of cheese spread onto the bottom half of a roll. Top with a slice of provolone and then the meat, onions, peppers, mushrooms, and a second slice of provolone. Close up the sandwich and serve warm.

Garlic Pepper Steaks

Servings: 4
Cooking Time: 5 Minutes

Ingredients:

- 2 tablespoons coarse kosher salt
- 4 teaspoons dried dill weed
- 4 teaspoons coarsely ground black pepper
- 4 teaspoons coarsely ground coriander seeds
- 2 teaspoons garlic powder
- 2 teaspoons paprika
- 1 to 2 teaspoons red pepper flakes
- 4 (6-ounce) rib-eye steaks
- 6 cloves garlic, finely minced
- ½ cup (1 stick) butter

Directions:

1. In a small bowl, combine the salt, dill weed, black pepper, coriander, garlic powder, paprika, and red pepper flakes. Sprinkle 1 to 2 teaspoons of this rub mixture on all sides of each steak. (Store any leftover seasoning in an airtight container for up to 6 months.)
2. Prepare the smoker's water pan according to the manufacturer's instructions and preheat the smoker to 250°F. While it heats, fill a medium bowl with water and add 3 or 4 handfuls of pecan wood chips to soak.
3. Heat a grill to high and sear the steaks for 1 minute on each side, then place them directly on a smoker rack. Add a small handful of the soaked pecan chips to the chip loading area.
4. In a small saucepan, gently warm the minced garlic and butter until melted. Alternatively, heat the garlic and butter in the microwave for 20 to 30 seconds in a microwave-safe bowl. Stir to combine. Every 30 minutes, baste the steaks with the garlic butter and add more wood chips. Smoke the steaks for 1¼ to 2 hours, or until they are done the way you like them. For a medium steak, cook to an internal temperature of 155°F.

Smoked Chuck Roast

Servings: 4 To 6
Cooking Time: 15 Minutes

Ingredients:

- 1 (4- to 5-pound) chuck roast
- ¼ cup olive oil
- ¼ cup firmly packed brown sugar
- 2 tablespoons Cajun seasoning

- 2 tablespoons paprika
- 2 tablespoons cayenne pepper

Directions:

1. Preheat the smoker to 225°F with the mesquite or oak wood.

2. Rub the chuck roast all over with the olive oil.

3. In a small bowl, mix together the brown sugar, Cajun seasoning, paprika, and cayenne. Coat the roast generously with the spice mix.

4. Place the roast on the smoker rack and smoke for 1 hour per pound. Remove from the heat when the internal temperature reaches 165°F. This temperature works well for meat that will be sliced.

5. If you desire a more traditional fall-apart texture (some even serve this pulled) continue to smoke to an internal temperature of 180°F to 190°F. Wrap with aluminum foil and let it rest for 30 minutes.

Hickory-smoked Tomahawk Rib Eyes

Servings: 4
Cooking Time: 2 Hours

Ingredients:

- 3 tablespoons flaked sea salt
- 3 tablespoons dark brown sugar
- 2 tablespoons sweet paprika
- 1 tablespoon garlic powder
- 1 tablespoon dried mustard
- 1 tablespoon freshly ground black pepper
- 1 tablespoon dried oregano
- 1 teaspoon ground coriander
- 1 teaspoon ground cumin
- 2 (2-inch thick) bone-in tomahawk rib eye steaks

Directions:

1. Preheat the electric smoker to 275°F. Ensure the drip tray is clean and in place. Seal the door.

2. Place the wood chips in the smoking tray or firebox, get a good smoke rolling, and seal the door.

3. In a large bowl, whisk together the salt, sugar, paprika, garlic powder, mustard, pepper, oregano, coriander, and cumin. Season the steaks on all sides with the dry rub. Cover the steaks with plastic wrap and refrigerate them for 24 hours.

4. Remove the steaks from the refrigerator 20 minutes before smoking.

5. Place the steaks on the smoking rack, leaving space between them. Insert a probe thermometer (if available) into the thickest part of the meat, not touching the bone. Set the target temperature for 125°F for rare, 135°F for medium-rare, 145°F for medium, 150°F for medium-well, and 160°F for well-done. Smoke for about 2 hours, or until the internal thermometer reads 5°F lower than your desired doneness.

6. Transfer the steaks to a cutting board, loosely tent them with aluminum foil, and let them rest for 15 minutes. The temperature of the beef will continue to rise while resting, achieving desired doneness.

7. Serve as desired.

Spicy Smoked Quesadillas

Servings: 8
Cooking Time: 2 Hours

Ingredients:

- 2 pounds chuck roast, trimmed and ground
- 2 tablespoons ground ancho chili powder
- 2 tablespoons ground cumin
- 1 tablespoon ground coriander
- 1 tablespoon paprika
- 1 tablespoon garlic powder
- ¼ teaspoon ground cayenne pepper
- 1 tablespoon extra-virgin olive oil
- 1 tablespoon unsalted butter
- 8 scallions, trimmed and finely sliced
- 2 yellow onions, diced
- 2 red bell peppers, cored and diced
- Flaked sea salt
- Freshly ground black pepper
- 1 (12-ounce) bottle pilsner beer
- 16 (12-inch) flour tortillas, divided
- Corn oil, for brushing
- 2 pounds Cheddar (or Monterey Jack) cheese, shredded
- Spicy Black Beans
- Sour cream (optional)

- Pico de gallo (optional)

Directions:

1. Remove the beef from the refrigerator 20 minutes before preparation.

2. In a small bowl, whisk together the chili powder, cumin, coriander, paprika, garlic powder, and cayenne. Set aside.

3. Preheat the electric smoker to 275°F. Ensure the drip tray is clean and in place. Seal the door.

4. Place the wood chips in the smoking tray or firebox, get a good smoke rolling, and seal the door.

5. Place a large cast iron skillet on a smoking rack to preheat, then pour in the olive oil and add the butter to melt.

6. In the skillet, combine the scallions, onions, and red bell peppers. Season with salt and pepper. Smoke for 20 minutes.

7. Add the ground beef to the skillet and season with salt, pepper, and the spice mixture. Smoke the beef for 20 minutes.

8. Stir in the beer to deglaze the skillet, scraping up any browned bits from the bottom. Smoke for 10 minutes until the liquid is reduced and almost dry. Remove the skillet from the smoker and let the liquid cool slightly.

9. Brush 8 flour tortillas with corn oil and arrange them on a work surface, oiled-side down. Build the quesadillas with the beef, cheese, and black beans. Top each quesadilla with 1 of the remaining 8 tortillas. Brush each top tortilla with corn oil and season with salt and pepper. Arrange the quesadillas on smoking racks, leaving spaces between them. Smoke them for 10 to 15 minutes, until the tortillas are crisp and the cheese is melted.

10. Remove the quesadillas from the smoker and let them rest for 1 minute before slicing and serving them. Serve with sour cream and pico de gallo on the side, if desired.

Cast Iron Osso Buco

Servings: 4
Cooking Time: 2 To 3 Hours

Ingredients:

- 2 tablespoons extra-virgin olive oil
- 2 tablespoons unsalted butter
- 4 (1½-inch-thick) bone-in beef shanks, tied with butcher's twine
- Flaked sea salt
- Freshly ground black pepper
- 2 cups diced carrots
- 2 cups diced celery hearts
- 2 cups diced yellow onions
- 4 garlic cloves, minced
- 4 thyme sprigs, leaves stripped and finely chopped, plus more for garnish
- 4 flat-leaf parsley sprigs, leaves stripped and finely chopped, plus more for garnish
- 3 fresh bay leaves
- 3 tablespoons tomato paste
- ½ cup all-purpose flour
- 3 cups sauvignon blanc
- 3 cups beef stock
- Grated zest of 2 lemons, for garnish
- 2 lemons, cut into slices, for serving

Directions:

1. Preheat the electric smoker to 250°F. Ensure the drip tray is clean and in place. Seal the door.

2. Place the wood chips in the smoking tray or firebox, get a good smoke rolling, and seal the door.

3. Place a large cast iron casserole on a smoking rack to preheat, then pour in the olive oil and add the butter to melt.

4. Season the beef shanks on all sides with salt and pepper. Arrange the shanks on smoking racks above the casserole, leaving space between each shank.

5. In the preheated casserole, combine the carrots, celery, onions, garlic, thyme, parsley, and bay leaves. Season with salt and pepper. Smoke for 1 hour.

6. To the casserole, add the tomato paste and flour, and stir to incorporate.

7. Stir in the sauvignon blanc to deglaze the pan, scraping up any browned bits from the bottom. Add the beef stock and transfer the beef shanks to the casserole. Smoke for 1 hour or until your desired texture is reached, spooning the cooking liquid over the shanks occasionally.

8. Garnish with fresh parsley and lemon zest. Season with salt and pepper. Serve with lemon slices.

Garlic-studded Prime Rib Roast

Servings: 4
Cooking Time: 3 To 4 Hours

Ingredients:

- 4 pounds bone-in (2 guests per bone) prime rib roast, trimmed and excess fat removed
- 1 garlic bulb, cloves separated, peeled, and halved
- 4 thyme sprigs, leaves stripped
- 2 tablespoons Italian seasoning
- 1 tablespoon ground paprika
- 1 tablespoon onion powder
- 1 tablespoon ground coriander
- 1 tablespoon coarsely ground black pepper
- 3 tablespoons extra-virgin olive oil, for drizzling
- Coarse sea salt
- Freshly ground black pepper

Directions:

1. Remove the roast from the refrigerator 1 hour before preparation.
2. Preheat the electric smoker to 275°F. Ensure the drip tray is clean and in place. Seal the door.
3. Place the wood chips in the smoking tray or firebox, get a good smoke rolling, and seal the door.
4. Using a boning knife, make incisions into the roast deep enough to press in half of a garlic clove below the surface of the meat. Space the incisions evenly so each slice of beef will have several cloves in it. Insert ½ garlic clove into each incision.
5. In a medium bowl, whisk together the thyme, Italian seasoning, paprika, onion powder, coriander, and pepper.
6. Drizzle the roast with the olive oil and massage the spice mixture all over the roast. Season with salt and pepper. Insert a probe thermometer (if available) into the thickest part of the meat, not touching the bone. Set the target temperature for 125°F for rare, 135°F for medium-rare, 145°F for medium, 150°F for medium-well, and 160°F for well-done. Place the roast, fat-side up (rib bones down), on a smoking rack. Smoke for 3 to 4 hours.
7. Remove the roast from the smoker when the thermometer reads 5°F lower than your desired doneness. The temperature of the beef will continue to rise while resting, achieving desired doneness.
8. Transfer the roast to a cutting board, loosely tent it with aluminum foil, and let it rest for 30 minutes before slicing and serving it.

Pepper-crusted Filet Of Beef

Servings: 6
Cooking Time: 2 Hours

Ingredients:

- 2 tablespoons extra-virgin olive oil, plus more for brushing
- 2 tablespoons unsalted butter
- 1 center-cut beef tenderloin
- Flaked sea salt
- 1 cup black peppercorns, partially crushed
- 3 shallots, finely diced
- 3 garlic cloves, crushed
- 3 rosemary sprigs, plus more for garnish
- Freshly ground black pepper
- 1 cup Cognac (or bourbon)
- 1 cup heavy (whipping) cream
- 1 tablespoon green peppercorns, whole

Directions:

1. Preheat the electric smoker to 275°F. Ensure the drip tray is clean and in place. Seal the door.
2. Place the wood chips in the smoking tray or firebox, get a good smoke rolling, and seal the door.
3. Place a large cast iron skillet on a smoking rack to preheat. Pour in 2 tablespoons of the olive oil and add the butter to melt.
4. Brush the beef with olive oil and season it on all sides with salt.
5. Spread the crushed black peppercorns on a piece of parchment paper. Roll the beef in the pepper, coating all sides.
6. In the preheated skillet, combine the shallots, garlic, and 3 rosemary sprigs. Toss to coat with the oil and butter, and season with salt and pepper.
7. Place the beef on the smoking rack above the skillet. Insert a probe thermometer (if available) into the thickest part of the meat. Set the target temperature for 125°F for rare, 135°F for medium-rare, 145°F for

medium, 150°F for medium-well, and 160°F for well-done. Smoke for 1 hour.

8. Stir in the Cognac to deglaze the skillet, scraping up any browned bits from the bottom. Add the heavy cream and green peppercorns.

9. Continue to smoke the meat until the internal thermometer reads 5°F lower than your desired doneness.

10. Transfer the beef to a cutting board and let it rest, uncovered, for 15 minutes before slicing. The temperature of the beef will continue to rise while resting, achieving desired doneness.

11. Serve with the pan sauce and garnish with rosemary.

Bulgogi

Servings: 4
Cooking Time: 5 Minutes

Ingredients:

* 1 pound flank steak
* ⅓ cup soy sauce or tamari
* 3 tablespoons sugar
* 6 garlic cloves, finely minced
* ⅛ teaspoon black pepper
* 1 teaspoon grated fresh ginger
* 1 tablespoon mirin or seasoned rice wine vinegar
* 2 tablespoons canola or vegetable oil
* cooked rice
* sliced green onions (optional)
* sesame seeds (optional)

Directions:

1. Place the steak in a 1-gallon zip-top plastic bag. Add the soy sauce, sugar, garlic, pepper, ginger, and mirin and mix well to combine. Seal the bag and place in the fridge for at least 6 hours, or overnight.

2. Prepare the smoker's water pan according to the manufacturer's instructions and preheat the smoker to 275°F. While it heats, fill a medium bowl with water and add 3 or 4 handfuls of hickory wood chips to soak.

3. Remove the steak from the marinade and place directly on one of the lower smoker racks. Add a small handful of the soaked hickory chips to the chip loading area, and keep adding more wood chips at least every 30 minutes. The steak is done when it reaches an internal

temperature of 150° to 155 °F, about 1 hour. Remove from the smoker and let rest under a foil tent for 10 minutes before thinly slicing the meat against the grain.

4. While the steaks rests, heat your grill to high. Set a large cast-iron skillet directly over the heat and add 2 tablespoons oil. Add the steak slices and heat for about 5 minutes, stirring occasionally, until they become slightly caramelized. Remove from the grill and serve the bulgogi over rice, topped with a sprinkling of sesame seeds and green onions, if desired.

Smoked Maple-bacon Cheeseburgers

Servings: 6
Cooking Time: 15 Minutes

Ingredients:

* 12 ground beef patties (80% lean, 4 ounces each)
* 1 tablespoon coarse salt
* 1 tablespoon coarsely ground black pepper
* 1 tablespoon granulated garlic
* 12 leaves lettuce
* 6 large burger buns, split and toasted
* 12 slices cheese of your choice
* 12 slices Smoked Candied Bacon
* 6 slices tomato
* 6 slices onion

Directions:

1. Preheat the smoker to 225°F.

2. Season the patties with the salt, pepper, and granulated garlic.

3. Smoke the burgers for 1 hour, or until their internal temperature reaches 145°F.

4. To build the burgers, place with a layer of lettuce on the bottom of each bun. Place a patty over the lettuce, then a slice of cheese on top, then 2 slices of candied bacon, crisscrossed. Add another patty, another slice of cheese, and a slice each of tomato and onion.

5. Serve the burgers on a big serving board.

Big Mcfatty

Servings: 6 To 8

Cooking Time: 25 Minutes

Ingredients:

- FOR BILL'S SPECIAL SAUCE
- ¼ cup mayonnaise
- ¼ cup Miracle Whip
- 3 tablespoons French dressing
- 1½ tablespoons dill-pickle relish
- 1½ teaspoons sweet pickle relish
- 1 teaspoon sugar
- 1 teaspoon dry minced onion
- 1 teaspoon vinegar
- 1 teaspoon ketchup
- Pinch salt
- FOR THE FATTY
- 1 pound bacon slices
- 2 pounds ground beef
- Salt
- Freshly ground black pepper
- ½ cup dill-pickle slices
- 4 slices American cheese
- 1 onion, sliced
- 2 tablespoons sesame seeds, divided

Directions:

1. TO MAKE BILL'S SPECIAL SAUCE
2. In a small microwave-safe bowl, stir together the mayonnaise, Miracle Whip, French dressing, dill and sweet relishes, sugar, onion, vinegar, ketchup, and salt. Microwave on high power for 30 seconds and stir. Refrigerate until needed.
3. TO MAKE THE FATTY
4. Preheat the smoker to 250°F with the hickory wood.
5. Line a rimmed baking sheet with parchment paper. On the sheet, place 6 bacon slices side by side vertically and weave another 6 pieces through them horizontally in an over-under pattern.
6. Layer the ground beef on top to cover the bacon.
7. Season with salt and pepper.
8. Layer the pickles, American cheese, and onion on the ground beef, leaving a 1-inch border all the way around. Using the parchment paper as an aid, roll the fatty into a roll (think sushi).
9. Spread half of the sauce on the fatty, sprinkle with 1 tablespoon of sesame seeds, and transfer to the smoker. Smoke for about 2 hours, or until the internal temperature reaches 160°F.
10. Top with the remaining sauce and 1 tablespoon of sesame seeds. Let the fatty rest for a few minutes.
11. Slice to serve (an electric carving knife works well).

Barbecue Meatloaf

Servings: 4 To 6

Cooking Time: 20 Minutes

Ingredients:

- 1½ pounds lean ground beef
- 1 cup Tangy Smoked Barbecue Sauce (page 17), divided
- ¾ cup quick-cooking rolled oats
- 1 large egg
- ¼ cup finely minced onion
- 2 teaspoons Basic Barbecue Rub (page 19)

Directions:

1. Prepare the smoker's water pan according to the manufacturer's instructions and preheat the smoker to 225°F. While it heats, fill a medium bowl with water and add 3 or 4 handfuls of cherry wood chips to soak.
2. In a large bowl, combine the ground beef, ¾ cup barbecue sauce, oats, egg, onion, and rub. Mix with your hands just until combined, then transfer onto a piece of parchment paper and form into a large log shaped like a bread pan. Spread the remaining ¼ cup barbecue sauce over the top of the meatloaf.
3. Place the meatloaf—on the parchment paper—directly on a smoker rack. Add a small handful of the soaked cherry chips to the chip loading area, and keep adding more chips at least every 30 minutes while the meatloaf cooks. The meatloaf is done when its internal temperature is 160°F, about 2 to 2½ hours.
4. Remove from the smoker to slice and serve immediately.

Spicy Korean Rib Eye Barbecue

Servings: 4

Cooking Time: 10 Minutes

Ingredients:

- ¼ cup soy sauce
- ¼ cup chopped scallion, white and green parts
- 2 tablespoons minced garlic
- 2 tablespoons gochujang Korean chili paste
- 1 tablespoon honey
- 2 teaspoons ground ginger
- 2 teaspoons onion powder
- 2 (8- to 12-ounce) boneless rib eye steaks
- Smoked Coleslaw
- 12 flour tortillas

Directions:

1. Preheat the smoker to 200°F with the peach or pear wood.

2. In a small bowl, whisk the soy sauce, scallion, garlic, gochujang, honey, ginger, and onion powder to make a paste. Spread the paste on both sides of the steaks.

3. Place the steaks in the smoker and smoke for about 15 minutes per pound. Remove from the heat when the internal temperature reaches 115°F to 120°F, and quickly sear on both sides on a hot grill or in a skillet. Final temperature is a matter of taste, with 145°F suggested by the USDA for medium-rare.

4. Cut the steaks into strips and serve with the coleslaw all wrapped in the flour tortillas.

Smoked Shutters Deluxe Hamburger

Servings: 4

Cooking Time: 1 Hour

Ingredients:

- 2 pounds chuck roast, trimmed and medium ground
- 2 tablespoons extra-virgin olive oil
- 2 tablespoons unsalted butter
- 2 yellow onions, cut into ½-inch rings
- 2 thyme sprigs, leaves stripped and finely chopped
- Flaked sea salt
- Freshly ground black pepper
- 8 smoked bacon slices
- 1 pound aged Cheddar cheese, shredded
- 4 country-style rolls
- 4 Roma tomatoes, seeded and finely diced
- Pickled beets
- Dill pickles, thinly sliced lengthwise

Directions:

1. Preheat the electric smoker to 250°F. Ensure the drip tray is clean and in place. Seal the door.

2. Place the wood chips in the smoking tray or firebox, get a good smoke rolling, and seal the door.

3. Remove the meat from the refrigerator 20 minutes before smoking it.

4. Place a large cast iron skillet on a smoking rack to preheat, then pour in the olive oil and add the butter to melt.

5. In the skillet, combine the onions and thyme. Toss to coat with the oil and butter, and season with salt and pepper. Smoke for about 10 minutes or until onions slightly brown. Remove the skillet from the smoker and set aside.

6. Divide the chuck into 4 equal portions and press each piece flat, to ½-inch thickness. Season with salt and pepper. Place the hamburgers and bacon slices on smoking racks, leaving space between each burger. Insert a probe thermometer into the thickest part of the meat. Set the target temperature for 125°F for rare, 135°F for medium-rare, 145°F for medium, 150°F for medium-well, and 160°F for well-done. Smoke for about 1 hour, or until the internal thermometer reads 5°F lower than your desired doneness.

7. Top each burger with shredded Cheddar cheese. Smoke for about 10 minutes, until the cheese melts.

8. Remove the hamburgers from the smoker. Loosely tent them with aluminum foil and let them rest for 5 minutes. The temperature of the beef will continue to rise while resting, achieving desired doneness.

9. Serve the hamburgers on country-style rolls, topped with the smoked bacon, onions, tomatoes, beets, and pickles, as desired.

Smoked Burnt Ends Of Brisket

Servings: 6
Cooking Time: 20 Minutes

Ingredients:
- ½ cup Beef Rub
- 2 tablespoons molasses
- 4 tablespoons light brown sugar, divided
- 1 teaspoon freshly ground black pepper
- 1 (6- to 8-pound) fatty point of beef brisket
- ½ cup olive oil
- 1 cup Bacon-Flavored BBQ Sauce

Directions:
1. Preheat the smoker to 250°F.
2. In a small bowl, mix together the beef rub, molasses, 2 tablespoons brown sugar, and the pepper. Brush the brisket with the olive oil, then rub the paste into the meat.
3. Smoke the brisket for 6 hours, or until the internal temperature reaches 195°F.
4. Take the brisket out of the smoker and let it rest for 15 minutes.
5. Cut the brisket into 1 ½-inch chunks and place them in a baking dish. Add the BBQ sauce and remaining 2 tablespoons brown sugar. Mix it all up to coat the brisket.
6. Place the baking dish in the smoker and smoke for 2 more hours, stirring every 30 minutes.
7. Serve hot.

Smoked Beef Brisket

Servings: 6 To 8
Cooking Time: 15 Minutes

Ingredients:
- 1 (10- to 12-pound) whole beef brisket, fat trimmed to a ¼-inch thickness
- 1 cup Beef Rub

Directions:
1. Preheat the smoker to 225°F.
2. Generously season the brisket all over with the beef rub.
3. Place the brisket fat-side down in the smoker. Insert a thermometer into the thickest part of the meat.
4. Smoke the brisket for 3 to 5 hours, or until it reaches an internal temperature of 160°F.
5. Remove it from the smoker and double-wrap it in butcher paper (preferred) or aluminum foil. Return the brisket to the smoker and cook for as much as another 8 or so hours (see Smoking tip), or until it reaches an internal temperature of 204°F.
6. Remove the brisket, wrap it in a towel, and let it rest for at least 30 minutes before serving.

Smoked Brisket Grilled Cheese

Servings: 4
Cooking Time: 15 Minutes

Ingredients:
- 8 slices thick-sliced French bread
- Pineapple–Brown Sugar Sauce
- 4 tablespoons soft, spreadable herbed goat cheese (chèvre)
- 2 ounces Gruyère cheese, thinly shaved
- 4 thick slices Unbelievably Moist Brisket
- 4 slices smoked Cheddar cheese
- 4 or 8 tomato slices
- 1 avocado, peeled, pitted, and sliced
- 4 tablespoons (½ stick) butter, melted
- Dill pickle slices, for serving

Directions:
1. Preheat the smoker to 275°F with the cherrywood.
2. Slather one side of each bread slice with the pineapple sauce and place on the smoker's grill rack sauce-side down. Lightly smoke the bread for about 5 minutes, then flip it.
3. Spread the sauced side of four bread slices with the goat cheese and top the remaining four "bottom buns" with the Gruyère. Smoke for 5 to 10 minutes more.
4. When the cheese begins to melt, top the Gruyère-side bread with the brisket. Top the brisket with the Cheddar.
5. Place 1 or 2 tomato slices and avocado slices on top of the Cheddar. Place the remaining bread slices on top, brush with the melted butter, and smoke for about 5 more minutes.
6. Serve with dill pickle slices.

Fireball Whiskey Meatballs

Servings: 24
Cooking Time: 40 Minutes

Ingredients:
- FOR THE FIREBALL BARBECUE SAUCE
- 2 cups ketchup
- ½ cup Fireball Cinnamon Whisky
- ¼ cup molasses
- ¼ cup firmly packed brown sugar
- 2 tablespoons olive oil
- 2 tablespoons apple cider vinegar
- 2 tablespoons Dijon mustard
- 2 tablespoons Worcestershire sauce
- 1 tablespoon garlic powder
- 1 tablespoon onion powder
- Salt
- Freshly ground black pepper
- FOR THE MEATBALLS
- 1 pound lean ground beef
- 1 pound ground pork
- 1 egg, beaten
- ½ cup finely chopped onion
- ½ cup panko bread crumbs
- ¼ cup shredded mozzarella cheese
- ¼ cup grated Parmesan cheese
- 2 tablespoons tomato paste
- 2 tablespoons Fireball Cinnamon Whisky
- 1 tablespoon Italian seasoning
- 1 tablespoon minced garlic
- 1 teaspoon salt
- 1 teaspoon freshly ground black pepper
- 2 teaspoons red pepper flakes
- 12 bacon slices, cooked and crumbled
- ½ cup chopped fresh parsley leaves

Directions:
1. TO MAKE THE FIREBALL BARBECUE SAUCE
2. In a medium saucepan over medium heat, combine the ketchup, whiskey, molasses, brown sugar, olive oil, vinegar, mustard, Worcestershire sauce, garlic powder, and onion powder. Season with salt and pepper. Bring to a boil and simmer for 20 to 30 minutes. Remove from the heat and set aside.

3. TO MAKE THE MEATBALLS
4. Preheat the smoker to 225°F with the oak wood.
5. In a large bowl, combine the ground beef and pork with the egg, onion, bread crumbs, mozzarella, Parmesan, tomato paste, whiskey, Italian seasoning, garlic, salt, pepper, red pepper flakes, and bacon. Using your hands, mix until well incorporated and roll into 24 balls.
6. Place a Frogmat nonstick grill mat directly on the grate. Arrange the meatballs on the mat leaving space between them for good air and smoke flow. Smoke for 1 to 1½ hours. During the last 15 minutes of cooking, brush the meatballs with some of the barbecue sauce.
7. When an instant-read thermometer registers 160°F, remove the meatballs from the smoker.
8. Sprinkle with the parsley and serve hot with the remaining fireball barbecue sauce.

Classic Texas Brisket

Servings: 4
Cooking Time: 15 Minutes

Ingredients:
- 4 pounds beef brisket, fat trimmed
- 2 tablespoons coarse kosher salt
- 2 tablespoons garlic powder
- 2 tablespoons onion powder
- 2 tablespoons celery powder
- 1 tablespoon ground cumin
- 1½ cups Tangy Smoked Barbecue Sauce (page 17), divided

Directions:
1. Prepare the smoker's water pan according to the manufacturer's instructions and preheat the smoker to 225°F. While it heats, fill a medium bowl with water and add 5 or 6 handfuls of pecan wood chips to soak.
2. Remove the brisket from its packing, dry with paper towels, and set aside. In a small bowl, combine the seasonings (salt through cumin). Rub this mixture over the brisket to cover all surfaces heavily.
3. Place the brisket in the smoker, fatty side up, and add a small handful of the soaked pecan chips to the chip loading area. Keep adding more chips every 30 minutes. At about the 4-hour mark, remove the meat from the

smoker and place it on a piece of foil. Pour half the barbecue sauce over the top and then wrap it tightly in foil before returning it to the smoker. There's no need to keep adding wood chips at this point unless you are also smoking something else. Smoke for a total of 6 to 8 hours, or until the meat is tender and has reached an internal temperature of 165°F.

4. Remove the brisket from the smoker and let it rest in the foil for 30 minutes before serving. Cut in thick slices or chop with reserved sauce that's been gently warmed.

Mopped Burnt Ends

Servings: 8
Cooking Time: 6 To 7 Hours

Ingredients:

- FOR THE MOP SAUCE
- 1 cup apple cider vinegar
- ½ cup packed dark brown sugar
- ½ cup dark molasses
- ½ cup bourbon
- 3 tablespoons finely chopped canned chipotle peppers in adobo sauce
- 3 tablespoons Worcestershire sauce
- 3 tablespoons tomato purée
- 3 tablespoons garlic powder
- 3 tablespoons onion powder
- 1 tablespoon fine sea salt
- Juice of 1 lime
- FOR THE BEEF BRISKET
- 2 cups packed dark brown sugar
- 3 tablespoons ground paprika
- 3 tablespoons ancho chili powder
- 3 tablespoons ground chipotle pepper
- 3 tablespoons coarsely ground black pepper
- 3 tablespoons garlic powder
- 3 tablespoons onion powder
- 3 tablespoons fine sea salt
- 4 pounds beef brisket point cut, trimmed and excess fat removed

Directions:

1. TO MAKE THE MOP SAUCE

2. In a large bowl, whisk together the vinegar, sugar, molasses, bourbon, peppers, Worcestershire sauce, tomato purée, garlic powder, onion powder, salt, and lime juice. Set aside.

3. TO MAKE THE BEEF BRISKET

4. In a large bowl, combine the sugar, paprika, chili powder, chipotle pepper, black pepper, garlic powder, onion powder, and salt. Whisk to blend.

5. Season the brisket with the dry rub mixture and wrap it tightly in plastic wrap.

6. Refrigerate the brisket for 24 hours. Remove it from the refrigerator 20 minutes before smoking and remove the plastic wrap.

7. Preheat the electric smoker to 225°F. Ensure the drip tray is clean and in place. Seal the door.

8. Place the wood chips in the smoking tray or firebox, get a good smoke rolling. Seal the door.

9. Place a large cast iron skillet on a smoking rack to preheat.

10. Place the brisket on a smoking rack. Insert a probe thermometer (if available) into the thickest part of the meat, not touching the bone. Set the target temperature for 190°F. Smoke for 5 to 6 hours, or until tender.

11. Transfer the brisket to a cutting board, loosely tent it with aluminum foil, and let cool. The temperature of the beef will continue to rise while resting, achieving desired doneness.

12. Slice the brisket into 1-inch cubes and place them in the preheated cast iron skillet.

13. Toss the cubes with enough mop sauce to completely coat the brisket (reserving the rest for the finish). Return the skillet to the smoker, tossing the meat occasionally.

14. Continue to smoke the brisket until the burnt ends are heavily glazed, for 20 to 30 minutes, and finish with the reserved mop sauce.

Hickory-smoked Beef Tri-tip

Servings: 6 To 8
Cooking Time: 2 To 3 Hours

Ingredients:

- ½ cup packed light brown sugar
- ½ cup coarse sea salt

- 1 tablespoon peppercorns, whole
- 1 teaspoon allspice berries, whole
- ½ teaspoon cloves, whole
- 3 fresh bay leaves
- 2 cups ice water
- 1 (4- to 5-pound) tri-tip beef roast, trimmed
- Extra-virgin olive oil, for brushing
- Flaked sea salt
- Freshly ground black pepper

Directions:

1. In a medium saucepan over medium heat, combine the sugar, salt, peppercorns, allspice, cloves, and bay leaves. Whisk to combine. Cook until steam begins to form, then remove from the heat. Stir in the ice water to cool the brine.

2. In a large food-grade plastic bag, combine the beef and the cooled brine. Remove as much air as possible from the bag and seal it. Refrigerate for 24 hours, turning 2 or 3 times.

3. Remove the tri-tip from the refrigerator 20 minutes before smoking. Drain the meat, rinse it, and pat it dry with a paper towel. Discard the brine.

4. Preheat the electric smoker to 225°F. Ensure the drip tray is clean and in place. Seal the door.

5. Place the wood chips in the smoking tray or firebox, get a good smoke rolling, and seal the door.

6. Brush the tri-tip with olive oil, season on all sides with salt and pepper, and place the meat on a smoking tray. Insert a probe thermometer (if available) into the thickest part of the meat. Set the target temperature for 125°F for rare, 135°F for medium-rare, 145°F for medium, 150°F for medium-well, and 160°F for well-done. Smoke for 2 to 3 hours, or until the internal thermometer reads 5°F lower than your desired doneness.

7. Transfer the beef to a cutting board, loosely tent it with aluminum foil, and let it rest for 20 minutes. The temperature of the beef will continue to rise while resting, achieving desired doneness.

8. Serve as desired.

Simple Brisket

Servings: 10 To 12

Cooking Time: 10 Minutes

Ingredients:

- 4 pounds beef brisket, fat trimmed
- 2 tablespoons coarse kosher salt
- 2 tablespoons garlic powder
- 1 tablespoon black pepper
- 1 cup Tangy Smoked Barbecue Sauce (page 17)
- ½ cup Worcestershire sauce
- ½ cup water

Directions:

1. Prepare the smoker's water pan according to the manufacturer's instructions and preheat the smoker to 225°F. While it heats, fill a medium bowl with water and add 3 or 4 handfuls of wood chips to soak.

2. Remove the brisket from its wrapping, dry with paper towels, and set aside. In a small bowl, combine the salt, garlic powder, and pepper. Rub the mixture over the brisket, making sure to cover everything heavily.

3. In a medium bowl, combine the barbecue sauce, Worcestershire, and water; mix well. Pour half into a small container with a lid and refrigerate until after the meat is cooked. The remainder will be used to baste the meat.

4. Place the brisket in the smoker, fatty side up, and add a small handful of the soaked wood chips to the chip loading area. Add more chips at least every 30 minutes, and also baste the meat with the sauce mixture every 30 minutes. Smoke for 4 to 6 hours, or until the internal temperature of the meat is 165°F.

5. Remove the brisket from the smoker, wrap tightly in foil, and let rest for 30 minutes. Meanwhile, gently warm the reserved sauce mixture in a small saucepan on the stovetop. Cut the meat into thick slices and serve along with the sauce, or chop up the meat with the sauce.

Smoked Meat Loaf

Servings: 4

Cooking Time: 20 Minutes

Ingredients:

- 1 tablespoon olive oil
- 2 cups diced red onions
- 4 garlic cloves, thinly sliced
- 2 slices bread

- 2 large eggs, lightly beaten
- ¾ cup beef stock
- 1 tablespoon Worcestershire sauce
- 2 pounds ground beef (80% lean)
- 1 teaspoon granulated garlic
- 1 teaspoon dried parsley
- 1 teaspoon dried thyme
- 1 teaspoon coarse salt
- 3 teaspoons freshly ground black pepper, divided
- ½ cup ketchup
- ½ cup packed light brown sugar

Directions:

1. Preheat the smoker to 250°F and fill the water pan.

2. In a skillet on the stovetop, heat the olive oil over medium-high heat. Add the onions and cook for about 5 minutes, or until they start to turn translucent. Add the sliced garlic during the last minute. Let cool slightly.

3. Put the bread in a food processor and pulse to make coarse bread crumbs. Place the crumbs in a large bowl. Add the beaten eggs, beef stock, Worcestershire sauce, and fried onions and garlic. Toss the mixture very lightly, just enough to coat the bread crumbs. Add the ground beef, granulated garlic, parsley, thyme, salt, and 1 teaspoon pepper. Mix it all up lightly, leaving it coarse.

4. Dump the mixture onto a strip of wax paper long enough to fit the loaf with some extra at each end for "handles." Form the mixture into a loaf shape, then put it (with the wax paper) into a loaf pan.

5. In a small bowl, whisk together the ketchup, brown sugar, and remaining 2 teaspoons pepper. Pour half of the glaze over the meat loaf.

6. Smoke the meat loaf for 3 hours, or until the internal temperature reaches 165°F.

7. Remove the meat loaf and pour the rest of the glaze over it. Let it rest for 10 minutes before serving.

Bacon-wrapped Meatloaf

Servings: 8
Cooking Time: 2 Hours

Ingredients:

- 1 tablespoon extra-virgin olive oil
- 1 tablespoon unsalted butter
- 1 yellow onion, finely diced
- 4 garlic cloves, minced
- 1 tablespoon fresh thyme leaves, stripped and finely chopped
- Flaked sea salt
- Freshly ground black pepper
- 1 pound bacon slices
- 3 pounds chuck, medium ground
- 2 large eggs, lightly beaten
- 1 cup fresh bread crumbs
- 1 cup tomato sauce

Directions:

1. Preheat the electric smoker to 225°F. Ensure the drip tray is clean and in place. Seal the door.

2. Place the wood chips in the smoking tray or firebox, get a good smoke rolling, and seal the door.

3. Place a large cast iron skillet on a smoking rack to preheat, then pour in the olive oil and add the butter to melt.

4. In the skillet, combine the onion, garlic, and thyme. Toss to coat with the oil and butter, and season with salt and pepper. Smoke for 10 to 15 minutes, until slightly browned. Remove the skillet from the smoker and transfer the ingredients to a medium stainless steel bowl. Let the ingredients cool to below 39°F.

5. Place a 24-inch-long sheet of plastic wrap on a work surface. Lay out the bacon slices on the plastic so they're touching but not overlapping.

6. Add the beef, eggs, bread crumbs, and tomato sauce to the onion mixture. Season with salt and pepper and mix to combine. Turn the mixture out onto the bacon slices. Form the mixture into a uniform meatloaf across the center of the bacon.

7. Use the plastic wrap to pull up each side of the bacon tightly and fully wrap the meatloaf in the bacon. Overlap the bacon seams, tightly wrap the plastic, and twist the ends of the plastic wrap snug. Let rest for 5 minutes.

8. Remove the plastic wrap, season the loaf with pepper, and lay the meatloaf on a smoking rack, overlapped-side down. Insert a probe thermometer (if available) into the thickest part of the meat. Set the target temperature for 165°F. Smoke for about 2 hours, or until the internal temperature reaches 165°F.

9. Remove the meatloaf from the smoker. Loosely tent it with aluminum foil and let it rest for 20 minutes before slicing and serving.

Korean-style Short Ribs

Servings: 4
Cooking Time: 5 Hours

Ingredients:
- 6 cups cold water
- 1 tablespoon coarse salt
- 2 pounds cross-cut or flanken-style short ribs
- 7 tablespoons soy sauce
- ¼ cup rice wine
- ¼ cup packed light brown sugar
- 3 tablespoons minced garlic
- 1 teaspoon grated fresh ginger
- 1 teaspoon freshly ground black pepper
- ½ teaspoon cayenne or red pepper flakes (optional)
- ½ cup apple juice
- 2 tablespoons apple jelly

Directions:
1. In a large bowl, combine the water and salt and stir to dissolve. Add the short ribs and let soak for 30 minutes. Remove the ribs and pat dry with paper towels.
2. In a small bowl, mix together the soy sauce, rice wine, brown sugar, garlic, ginger, black pepper, and cayenne (if using) to make the marinade.
3. Place the ribs in a large zip-top bag and pour the marinade over them. Squeeze the air out of the bag, seal it, and refrigerate the ribs for 4 hours.
4. Take the ribs out of the bag and dry them with paper towels. Let them come to room temperature, about 30 minutes.
5. Preheat the smoker to 225°F.
6. Smoke the ribs for 2 hours.
7. Meanwhile, in a bowl, mix the apple juice and jelly.
8. Brush the ribs with the apple mixture and smoke for another 1 hour 30 minutes, or until the internal temperature reaches 195°F. Baste the ribs with the apple mixture every hour.
9. Serve warm.

Cast-iron Chili

Servings: 4 To 6
Cooking Time: 15 Minutes

Ingredients:
- 1½ pounds lean ground beef
- 2 (15-ounce) cans tricolored beans (or kidney or pinto beans), drained and rinsed
- 1 (15-ounce) can tomato sauce
- 2 cups water
- 3 tablespoons chili powder
- 3 tablespoons dried onion flakes
- 1½ tablespoons ground cumin
- 4 teaspoons coarse kosher salt
- 2 teaspoons dried minced garlic
- 1 teaspoon red pepper flakes
- ½ teaspoon cayenne pepper
- ½ teaspoon sugar
- chopped white onions, grated cheese, and sour cream, as toppings

Directions:
1. Prepare the smoker's water pan according to the manufacturer's instructions and preheat the electric smoker to 275°F. While it heats, fill a medium bowl with water and add 3 or 4 handfuls of hickory wood chips to soak.
2. Meanwhile, cook the ground beef in a large cast-iron pot on the stovetop over high heat. Stir and break the meat apart until it is crumbly and no longer pink. Drain off any fat liquid and add the beans, tomato sauce, water, and seasonings (chili powder through sugar). Stir well to combine and bring to a simmer.
3. Place the pot on the top rack of the smoker. Add a small handful of the soaked hickory chips to the chip loading area. Stir the chili and add more chips at least every 30 minutes. The chili is already fully cooked, but let it smoke for about 2 hours to let the flavors fully develop.
4. To serve, ladle the chili into bowls and top with chopped onions, cheese, and dollops of sour cream.

Juicy Beef Short Ribs

Servings: 4 Or 5
Cooking Time: 10 To 15 Minutes

Ingredients:
- 8 to 10 English-cut beef short ribs
- ¼ cup olive oil
- ½ cup apple cider vinegar

- ½ cup apple juice
- Java Rub

Directions:

1. Preheat the smoker to 225°F with the mesquite or oak wood.

2. Trim some of the fat off the ribs and rub the ribs with the olive oil.

3. In a kitchen spray bottle, mix the vinegar and apple juice together.

4. Coat the ribs with the rub and head outside. Place the ribs in the smoker and smoke for 1 hour. Spray them with the vinegar-and-apple-juice mixture. Smoke for about 2 hours more, spraying the ribs every 1 5 to 20 minutes until done. Total cook time should be 3 to 4 hours with a target temperature of 175°F to 205°F. The ribs will appear beautifully browned and, if cooked to the higher temperature, will be falling off the bone.

5. Serve with Smoked Bacon-Wrapped Onion Rings, if desired.

Hickory-smoked Meatballs

Servings: 8
Cooking Time: 2 Hours

Ingredients:

- 2 tablespoons extra-virgin olive oil
- 4 shallots, cut into ¼-inch rings
- 2 pounds chuck roast beef, medium ground
- 1 pound pork shoulder, medium ground
- 8 ounces bacon, cut into thin slices
- 2 tablespoons fresh oregano leaves, finely chopped
- 2 large eggs, lightly beaten
- 1 cup fresh bread crumbs
- Flaked sea salt
- Freshly ground black pepper
- 4 cups tomato sauce
- 4 cups beef stock
- 2 cups red wine
- 4 ounces finely grated Parmesan cheese, for garnish
- 1 loaf country bread, sliced or torn into 8 pieces

Directions:

1. Preheat the electric smoker to 225°F. Ensure the drip tray is clean and in place. Seal the door.

2. Place the wood chips in the smoking tray or firebox, get a good smoke rolling, and seal the door.

3. Place a large cast iron casserole on a smoking rack to preheat, then pour in the olive oil and add the shallots.

4. In a large bowl, combine the ground beef, ground pork, bacon, oregano, eggs, and bread crumbs. Using clean hands, mix the ingredients together thoroughly. Divide the meat mixture into 24 meatballs. Season with salt and pepper. Arrange the meatballs on smoking racks above the casserole, leaving space between each meatball.

5. In the preheated casserole, whisk together the tomato sauce, beef stock, and red wine. Season with salt and pepper. Insert a probe thermometer (if available) into the thickest meatball. Set the target temperature for 160°F. Smoke the meatballs for 1 hour.

6. Transfer the meatballs into the casserole. Smoke for 30 to 60 minutes to finish, or until the internal temperature reaches 160°F.

7. Top with the Parmesan cheese and serve the meatballs and sauce with the bread.

Smoked Beef Chili

Servings: 6
Cooking Time: 30 Minutes

Ingredients:

- 2 pounds ground chuck
- 2 teaspoons chili powder
- 2 teaspoons paprika
- 2 teaspoons coarse salt
- 1 teaspoon ancho powder or red pepper flakes
- 1 teaspoon chipotle powder
- 1 teaspoon ground cumin
- 1 teaspoon garlic powder
- 1 teaspoon onion powder
- 1 teaspoon dried oregano
- 1 teaspoon freshly ground black pepper
- 1 large red onion, diced
- 1 red bell pepper, chopped
- 1 green bell pepper, chopped
- 2 tablespoons minced garlic
- 2 tablespoons olive oil
- 1 (28-ounce) can crushed tomatoes
- ½ cup tomato paste
- 1 (16-ounce) can pinto beans, drained and rinsed
- 1 (16-ounce) can kidney beans, drained and rinsed

* 2 cups beef broth

Directions:

1. Preheat the smoker to 250°F.
2. In a large bowl, combine the ground chuck, chili powder, paprika, salt, ancho powder, chipotle powder, cumin, garlic powder, onion powder, oregano, and black pepper. Mix thoroughly.
3. In the bottom of a large baking dish, spread the onions, bell peppers, and minced garlic. Drizzle the olive oil over them.
4. Place the ground beef in a perforated BBQ skillet and set it in the smoker. Place the baking dish with the vegetables under the skillet. Smoke for 1 hour, breaking up the burger as it cooks.
5. Stir the crushed tomatoes and tomato paste into the vegetables in the baking dish. Then add the pinto beans, kidney beans, smoked ground beef, and beef broth. Stir to combine.
6. Smoke for 1 more hour, stirring every 20 minutes.
7. Serve warm.

Mesquite-smoked Barbacoa

Servings: 4

Cooking Time: 7 Hours

Ingredients:

* 1 (3-pound) bone-in beef chuck roast
* ¼ cup Beef Rub
* 1 tablespoon light brown sugar
* 2 tablespoons minced garlic
* 2 teaspoons chopped jalapeño
* 1 teaspoon ancho powder or red pepper flakes
* 1 teaspoon chipotle powder
* 1 teaspoon coarsely ground black pepper
* 1 teaspoon ground cumin
* 1 teaspoon ground cinnamon
* 1 cup bitter orange juice (also called Seville orange juice)
* 1 teaspoon chopped fresh oregano
* 1 tablespoon chopped fresh cilantro
* 1 teaspoon olive oil
* 1 teaspoon salt
* 1 teaspoon cayenne pepper
* 2 teaspoons granulated garlic
* ½ cup Bacon-Flavored BBQ Sauce

* 1 tablespoon fresh lime juice

Directions:

1. With a sharp knife, trim the fat off the side of the roast. Don't leave more than ¼ inch.
2. In a large bowl or container with a cover, combine the beef rub, brown sugar, minced garlic, jalapeño, ancho powder, chipotle powder, black pepper, cumin, and cinnamon. Mix in the orange juice, oregano, and cilantro.
3. Place the meat in the container and coat it completely. Refrigerate for 7 hours.
4. Preheat the smoker to 225°F.
5. Remove the meat from the marinade and pat it dry with paper towels.
6. Brush the olive oil over the roast and then sprinkle the salt, cayenne, and granulated garlic on all sides.
7. Smoke the chuck roast for 3 to 5 hours, or until the internal temperature reaches 145°F.
8. Remove the roast, cover in aluminum foil, return to the smoker and smoke for 1 more hour.
9. Remove it again, take off the foil, and smoke it for 30 more minutes.
10. While the roast is smoking, mix the BBQ sauce with the lime juice. Baste the roast, then cook for 30 more minutes, still unwrapped.
11. Serve warm.

Bourbon-marinated Beef Roast

Servings: 3 Or 4

Cooking Time: 15 Minutes

Ingredients:

* ½ cup firmly packed light-brown sugar
* ½ cup soy sauce
* ½ cup olive oil
* ¼ cup bourbon
* Juice of 1 lemon
* 1 tablespoon freshly ground black pepper
* 1 (3- to 4-pound) beef roast

Directions:

1. In a medium bowl, whisk together the brown sugar, soy sauce, olive oil, bourbon, lemon juice, and pepper to make the marinade.

2. In a large bowl, combine the meat and marinade. Cover loosely with plastic wrap and refrigerate overnight.

3. Preheat the smoker to 225°F with the apple, hickory, or oak wood.

4. Remove the meat from the bowl and discard the marinade. Place the roast on the smoker rack and smoke for 1 hour per pound. Remove from the heat when the internal temperature reaches 145°F.

Smoked Roast Beef Hash

Servings: 4
Cooking Time: 2 Hours

Ingredients:

- 2 pounds eye of round roast, trimmed
- 2 tablespoons extra-virgin olive oil
- 2 tablespoons unsalted butter
- Paprika, for seasoning
- Flaked sea salt
- Freshly ground black pepper
- 8 new red potatoes, blanched and diced
- 1 yellow onion, diced
- 1 red bell pepper, cored and diced
- 4 garlic cloves, minced
- 4 thyme sprigs, leaves stripped, plus more for garnish
- 2 ears corn, kernels cut off
- 4 flat-leaf parsley sprigs, leaves stripped and finely chopped
- 8 large eggs

Directions:

1. Remove the roast from the refrigerator 20 minutes before preparation.

2. Preheat the electric smoker to 250°F. Ensure the drip tray is clean and in place. Seal the door.

3. Place the wood chips in the smoking tray or firebox, get a good smoke rolling, and seal the door,

4. Place a large cast iron skillet on a smoking rack to preheat, then pour in the olive oil and add the butter to melt.

5. Season the roast all over with paprika, salt, and pepper. Place the roast on a smoking rack. Insert a probe thermometer (if available) into the thickest part of the meat, not touching the bone. Set the target temperature for 125°F for rare, 135°F for medium-rare, 145°F for medium, 150°F for medium-well, and 160°F for well-done. Smoke the meat for 30 minutes.

6. In the skillet, combine the potatoes, onion, red bell pepper, garlic, and thyme. Season with salt and pepper. Cook for about 90 minutes more, or until the internal thermometer reads 5°F lower than desired doneness. Remove the skillet and the roast from the smoker. The temperature of the beef will continue to rise while resting, achieving desired doneness.

7. Transfer the roast to a cutting board, loosely tent it with aluminum foil, and let it rest for 20 minutes. Thinly slice the beef and add it to the skillet, along with the corn and parsley. Toss to incorporate. Place the skillet back on a smoking rack and smoke for 10 minutes.

8. Crack the eggs into the hash, leaving space between them for individual portions. Season with salt and pepper. Return the skillet to the smoker to cook the eggs to your desired doneness. Serve garnished with thyme.

Prime Rib

Servings: 6 To 8
Cooking Time: 10 Minutes

Ingredients:

- ¼ cup whole peppercorns
- ¼ cup coarse kosher salt
- ¼ cup minced garlic (about 20 cloves)
- 1 tablespoon olive oil
- 7 to 8-pound boneless beef prime rib roast

Directions:

1. Grind or smash the peppercorns until coarsely ground, using a coffee grinder, a heavy-duty blender, or even a rolling pin. This will add a nice crust to the outside of your prime rib. In a small bowl, combine the ground peppercorns, salt, and garlic.

2. Rub the olive oil on the roast and then rub the pepper mixture all over the meat. It will be very thick (you'll use all of it) and should cover the entire roast. Place the pepper-coated roast on a plate and cover with plastic wrap and refrigerate for 1 to 2 hours.

3. Prepare the smoker's water pan according to the manufacturer's instructions and preheat the electric smoker to 250°F. While it heats, fill a medium bowl with water and add 3 or 4 handfuls of cherry wood chips to soak.

4. When the smoker is ready, place the prime rib directly on a smoker rack and add a small handful of the soaked cherry wood chips to the chip loading area. Keep adding chips at least every 30 minutes. Use a meat thermometer to monitor the temperature of the roast, and remove it from the smoker when it is about 15°F under the recommended temperature for the degree of doneness you want. Prime rib takes anywhere from 1½ to 2½ hours, depending on whether you like yours rare, medium-rare, or medium.

5. When the meat is close to being ready to take out of the smoker, heat your outdoor grill as hot as it will allow. Transfer the roast to the hot grill and let the outside crust crisp for 3 to 4 minutes per side. After the quick grill, let the meat rest for 15 to 20 minutes under a loose foil tent to finish cooking and allow the juices to be absorbed back into the meat.

6. Cut and serve in ½-inch thick slices with horseradish sauce, if desired.

Pecan-smoked Beef Short Ribs

Servings: 4

Cooking Time: 3 To 4 Hours

Ingredients:

- 1 tablespoon extra-virgin olive oil
- 1 tablespoon unsalted butter
- 1 (12-bone) bone-in beef short ribs, membrane removed (see tip)
- Flaked sea salt
- Freshly ground black pepper
- 24 pearl onions, blanched, trimmed, and peeled
- 1 cup diced carrots
- 1 cup diced celery hearts
- 1 cup diced yellow onions
- 2 cups ruby port
- 3 fresh bay leaves
- 4 cups beef stock

Directions:

1. Preheat the electric smoker to 225°F. Ensure the drip tray is clean and in place. Seal the door.

2. Place the wood chips in the smoking tray or firebox, get a good smoke rolling, and seal the door.

3. Place a large cast iron casserole on a smoking rack to preheat, then pour in the olive oil and add the butter to melt.

4. Remove the ribs from the refrigerator 20 minutes before smoking. Season the meat on all sides with salt and pepper.

5. Add the pearl onions, carrots, celery, and yellow onions to the casserole, toss to coat them with the oil and butter, and season with salt and pepper. Smoke for 20 to 30 minutes, until lightly browned in color.

6. Stir the port into the casserole to deglaze the pan, scraping up any browned bits from the bottom. Add the bay leaves and beef stock. Place the ribs into the casserole. Smoke the ribs for 2 to 3 hours, basting the ribs with cooking liquid every 30 minutes. The ribs are finished when the meat shrinks from the bones and is tender, and the ribs pull apart with ease.

7. Remove the casserole from the smoker and loosely tent it with aluminum foil. Let the ribs rest for 20 minutes.

8. Remove the ribs from the casserole and cover them with aluminum foil. Strain the cooking liquid through a fine-mesh sieve set over a bowl. Reserve the pearl onions; discard the vegetables. Return the ribs, onions, and strained liquid to the casserole. Return the casserole to the smoker, spooning cooking liquid over the ribs until the sauce reaches your desired consistency.

9. Gently slice the ribs into portions and serve with the sauce and pearl onions.

Smoked Brisket And Cheese Pizza

Servings: 2 Or 3

Cooking Time: 15 To 20 Minutes

Ingredients:

- 1 tablespoon butter
- 1 tablespoon all-purpose flour
- ½ cup cold milk
- 2 garlic cloves, minced
- ¼ teaspoon salt
- ⅛ teaspoon freshly ground black pepper
- ⅛ teaspoon ground nutmeg
- ¼ cup grated Parmesan cheese

- 1 (12-inch) Boboli pizza crust (or use a smaller size for individual pizzas)
- 1 cup leftover chopped smoked brisket
- ½ onion, sliced
- ½ bell pepper (any color), sliced
- ½ cup (torn thin strips) provolone cheese
- ½ cup (torn thin strips) white American cheese

Directions:

1. Preheat the smoker to 275°F with the hickory or mesquite wood.

2. In a saucepan over medium heat, make a roux by melting the butter, adding the flour, and whisking continuously for about 1 minute.

3. Slowly pour in the cold milk while continuing to whisk.

4. Add the garlic, salt, pepper, and nutmeg, and continue stirring until thickened.

5. Remove from the heat and stir in the Parmesan cheese until it has melted and is fully incorporated. Remove from the heat and let the sauce cool.

6. Spread the cooled sauce over the crust. Layer on the brisket, onion, and bell pepper. Sprinkle the provolone and American cheeses on top.

7. Place the pizza directly on the smoker rack or on a Frogmat grill mat and smoke for 1 to 1½ hours until the veggies are tender and the cheeses are bubbly.

Herb-crusted Beef Tenderloin

Servings: 4 To 6

Cooking Time: 2 Hours

Ingredients:

- 4 shallots, finely diced
- 6 thyme sprigs, leaves stripped and finely chopped
- 6 rosemary sprigs, leaves stripped and finely chopped
- 6 parsley sprigs, leaves stripped and finely chopped
- ¼ cup whole-grain mustard
- 3 tablespoons extra-virgin olive oil
- 2 tablespoons ground fennel seeds
- 2 tablespoons ground cumin seeds
- 2 tablespoons ground coriander seeds
- Flaked sea salt
- Freshly ground black pepper

- 1 center-cut beef tenderloin, silver skin removed

Directions:

1. Preheat the electric smoker to 275°F. Ensure the drip tray is clean and in place. Seal the door.

2. Place the wood chips in the smoking tray or firebox, get a good smoke rolling, and seal the door.

3. In a large bowl, whisk together the shallots, thyme, rosemary, parsley, mustard, and olive oil.

4. Add the fennel, cumin, and coriander and season with salt and pepper. Fold the ingredients together to form a paste.

5. Season the tenderloin on all sides with salt and pepper, then spread the herb paste across the top. Wrap the tenderloin with plastic wrap and refrigerate it for 4 hours. Remove the meat from the refrigerator 20 minutes before smoking.

6. Place the tenderloin on the smoking rack, herb crust up. Insert a probe thermometer (if available) into the thickest part of the meat. Set the target temperature for 125°F for rare, 135°F for medium-rare, 145°F for medium, 150°F for medium-well, and 160°F for well-done. Smoke for about 2 hours, or until the internal thermometer reads 5°F lower than your desired doneness.

7. Transfer the tenderloin to a cutting board, loosely tent it with aluminum foil, and let it rest for 20 minutes. The temperature of the beef will continue to rise while resting, achieving desired doneness.

Smoked Beef Brisket Chili

Servings: 6 To 8

Cooking Time: 20 Minutes

Ingredients:

- 1 tablespoon olive oil
- 1 small onion, chopped
- 2 garlic cloves, minced
- ½ cup chili powder (Feeling adventurous? See the tip for homemade chili powder.)
- 1 large fresh poblano pepper, fire-roasted and seeded
- 1 (28-ounce) can crushed tomatoes
- 1 (15-ounce) can kidney beans, rinsed and drained
- 1 (12-ounce) bottle robust beer

* 2 beef bouillon cubes
* 1 tablespoon salt
* 2 teaspoons smoked paprika
* 2 teaspoons ground cumin
* 1½ teaspoons cayenne pepper
* 2 pounds leftover Unbelievably Moist Brisket, chopped

Directions:

1. In a soup pot over medium-high heat, heat the olive oil and sauté the onion and garlic for about 3 minutes until translucent.

2. Add the chili powder, poblano, tomatoes, kidney beans, beer, bouillon cubes, salt, paprika, cumin, and cayenne. Stir to combine and bring to a boil. Reduce the heat to low and simmer for 1 to 2 hours.

3. Stir in the brisket and heat through before serving.

T-bone Kebabs

Servings: 8
Cooking Time: 20 Minutes

Ingredients:

* 1 pound beef tenderloin, cut into 1-inch cubes
* 2 pounds strip steak, cut into 1-inch cubes
* 1 large onion, cut into 1-inch cubes
* 1 bell pepper (any color), cut into 1-inch cubes
* 1 zucchini, cut into 1-inch cubes
* 1 pint (about 10 ounces) cherry tomatoes
* ¼ cup olive oil
* ½ cup steak seasoning

Directions:

1. In a large bowl, combine the tenderloin, strip steak, onion, bell pepper, zucchini, and tomatoes with the olive oil and steak seasoning. Gently stir until coated. Cover and refrigerate for 4 to 8 hours.

2. When ready to smoke, preheat the smoker to 225°F with the oak wood.

3. Make the kebabs by alternating different veggies and meat on your skewers, beginning and ending with meat. Transfer the skewers to a grill rack and smoke for 45 minutes to 1 hour. Remove from the smoker when the internal temperature of the steak is at least 135°F (rare) or 140°F (medium-rare).

Smoked Pulled Beef Sandwiches

Servings: 6
Cooking Time: 12 Hours

Ingredients:

* 2 (3-pound) boneless chuck roasts, at least 2 inches thick
* ¾ cup Beef Rub
* 1 tablespoon light brown sugar
* 1 teaspoon cayenne pepper
* 3 tablespoons olive oil
* ½ cup apple juice
* 1 cup Bacon-Flavored BBQ Sauce, divided
* 6 brioche buns, split and toasted
* 6 lettuce leaves

Directions:

1. Pat the roasts dry with paper towels.

2. In a small bowl, mix together the beef rub, brown sugar, and cayenne. Brush the roasts all over with the olive oil and rub on all sides with the seasoning mixture. Refrigerate the roasts, uncovered, for 8 to 12 hours.

3. Take the chuck roasts out of the fridge and bring to room temperature, about 45 minutes.

4. Preheat the smoker to 225°F.

5. Smoke the roasts for about 3 hours, or until the internal temperature reaches 180°F. Fill a spray bottle with the apple juice.

6. Take the roasts out, spray them with the apple juice, and wrap them in butcher paper or foil. Return them to the smoker and cook for another 1 hour 30 minutes.

7. Take the roasts out of the smoker and unwrap them. Baste them with ½ cup BBQ sauce and return them to the smoker. Smoke for another 1 hour 30 minutes, or until the internal temperature reaches 210°F. The meat should be very tender, so that it has little resistance to a knife.

8. Remove the roasts, let them rest for 15 minutes, and then shred them.

9. On each bottom brioche bun, place a leaf of lettuce. Spoon some pulled beef onto the sandwiches, top with the remaining ½ cup BBQ sauce, and serve.

Bacon-wrapped Beef Tenderloin

Servings: 8
Cooking Time: 15 Minutes

Ingredients:

- 1 (5- to 6-pound) beef tenderloin
- 2 tablespoons olive oil
- ½ cup Beef Rub
- 12 to 14 slices bacon
- ½ cup Bacon-Flavored BBQ Sauce

Directions:

1. Preheat the smoker to 250°F.
2. Pat the tenderloin dry with paper towels. Then brush the meat with the olive oil and sprinkle the beef rub over all sides, rubbing it into the meat.
3. Cut a piece of wax paper that's the length of the tenderloin. Place the bacon slices on the wax paper so that they are slightly overlapping along the edges. Then set the tenderloin across the bacon strips at one end. Slowly and carefully, begin to roll the tenderloin. You can use toothpicks to help fasten the bacon to the beef, if needed.
4. Smoke the tenderloin for 1 hour.
5. Remove the tenderloin and brush it with the BBQ sauce. Continue to smoke for 30 minutes, or until the internal temperature reaches 135°F.
6. Let the tenderloin rest for 10 minutes before serving.

Smoked Steak Fajitas

Servings: 6
Cooking Time: 4 Hours

Ingredients:

- ¾ cup Basic Beef Marinade (here)
- 6 tablespoons tequila
- ¼ cup Beef Rub
- 1 teaspoon cayenne pepper (optional)
- 1 tablespoon granulated garlic
- 2 pounds skirt steak
- 2 large yellow or red onions, cut into rings
- 3 red or green bell peppers, cut into ½-inch rings
- 2 tablespoons olive oil

Directions:

1. In a small bowl, mix together the beef marinade, tequila, beef rub, cayenne (if using), and garlic.
2. Place the steak in a nonaluminum dish, large enough so that the meat lies flat. Cover both sides with the marinade. Cover the dish and refrigerate the steak for 4 hours, turning it every hour.
3. Preheat the smoker to 225°F.
4. Transfer the steak to a large ovenproof glass dish and pour the marinade over it.
5. Smoke the steak for 1 hour and 30 minutes. Place the onions and peppers on a grill mat or wire grill screen and drizzle the olive oil over them. Smoke them, along with the steak, for another 1 hour and 30 minutes. When the steak reaches an internal temperature of 100°F, it is ready for a quick sear.
6. If you're using a pellet smoker, increase the temperature to 550°F and cook the steak for 10 to 12 minutes, or until the internal temperature reaches 130°F for medium-rare. If not, heat a cast-iron skillet on the stovetop over high heat. Sear the steak for 2 to 3 minutes per side, brushing it with the extra smoked marinade, bringing the steak to 135°F for medium.
7. Let the steak rest for 10 minutes, then slice it across the grain, with the knife at a 45-degree angle to the cutting board, into thin strips. Place it on the serving platter with the onions and peppers.

Smoked Philly Cheesesteak

Servings: 4
Cooking Time: 2 Hours

Ingredients:

- 2 pounds top round beef roast, trimmed
- 4 tablespoons extra-virgin olive oil, divided
- Flaked sea salt
- Freshly ground black pepper
- 12 baby portobello mushrooms, trimmed and thinly sliced
- 2 yellow onions, very thinly sliced
- 1 green bell pepper, cored, seeded, and thinly sliced
- 1 red bell pepper, cored, seeded, and thinly sliced
- 4 garlic cloves, minced
- 4 Amoroso-style rolls (see tip)
- 8 slices provolone cheese

Directions:

1. Remove the beef from the refrigerator 20 minutes before preparation.

2. Preheat the electric smoker to 275°F. Ensure the drip tray is clean and in place. Seal the door.

3. Place the wood chips in the smoking tray or firebox, get a good smoke rolling, and seal the door.

4. Place a large cast iron skillet on a smoking rack to preheat, then pour in 2 tablespoons of olive oil.

5. Season the roast on all sides with salt and pepper. Place the roast on a smoking rack. Insert the probe thermometer (if available) into the thickest part of the meat. Set the target temperature for 125°F for rare, 135°F for medium-rare, 145°F for medium, 150°F for medium-well, and 160°F for well-done. Smoke for about 2 hours, or until the internal thermometer reads 5°F lower than your desired doneness.

6. While the beef cooks, add the mushrooms to the skillet, toss to coat with the olive oil and season with salt and pepper. Smoke for 20 minutes. Remove from the skillet and set aside.

7. In the same skillet, combine the remaining 2 tablespoons of olive oil with the onions, green and red bell peppers, and garlic. Season with salt and pepper. Smoke for 20 minutes.

8. Transfer the beef to a cutting board, loosely tent it with aluminum foil, and let it rest for 20 minutes. The temperature of the beef will continue to rise while resting, achieving desired doneness.

9. Thinly slice the beef across the grain.

10. Add the mushrooms to the onion and pepper mixture. Cover the vegetables with foil.

11. Layer each roll with thinly sliced beef and the vegetables. Top each sandwich with 2 slices of provolone cheese.

12. Arrange the sandwiches on smoking racks, leaving space between each one. Smoke the sandwiches for 10 minutes, until the rolls are slightly toasted and the cheese is melted.

13. Tightly wrap each sandwich in parchment or foil and eat by peeling back the wrapping as you go.

Mesquite-smoked Hanger Steak

Servings: 4

Cooking Time: 1 Hour

Ingredients:
- 2 shallots, finely diced
- 1 tablespoon finely grated peeled fresh ginger
- 1 tablespoon finely diced jalapeño pepper
- 2 tablespoons soy sauce
- 2 tablespoons fish sauce
- 2 tablespoons dark brown sugar
- 2 tablespoons toasted sesame oil
- 2 tablespoons canola oil
- 2 (1- to 1½-pound) hanger steaks
- Flaked sea salt
- Freshly ground black pepper

Directions:

1. Preheat the electric smoker to 275°F. Ensure the drip tray is clean and in place. Seal the door.

2. Place the wood chips in the smoking tray or firebox, get a good smoke rolling, and seal the door.

3. In a large bowl, stir together the shallots, ginger, jalapeño, soy sauce, fish sauce, sugar, sesame oil, and canola oil. Transfer to a large food-grade plastic bag and add the steaks. Remove as much air as possible from the bag and seal it. Refrigerate for 24 hours, turning the bag 2 or 3 times.

4. Remove the steaks from the refrigerator 20 minutes before smoking. Remove the steaks from the marinade, reserving the marinade in the refrigerator. Season the steaks on both sides with salt and pepper and place them on a smoking rack, leaving space between the steaks. Insert a probe thermometer (if available) into the thickest part of the meat. Set the target temperature for 125°F for rare, 135°F for medium-rare, 145°F for medium, 150°F for medium-well, and 160°F for well-done. Smoke the steaks for 30 minutes.

5. Baste the steaks with the reserved marinade. Smoke the meat for about 30 minutes more, or until the internal thermometer reads 5°F lower than your desired doneness.

6. Transfer the steaks to a cutting board, loosely tent them with aluminum foil, and let them rest for 15 minutes. The temperature of the beef will continue to rise while resting, achieving desired doneness.

7. Serve as desired.

Texas-style Smoked Beef Short Ribs

Servings: 4

Cooking Time: 8 Hours

Ingredients:

- 1 tablespoon coarse salt
- 8 pounds chuck or plate ribs, trimmed of fat and membrane
- ¾ cup plus 2 tablespoons Beef Rub
- 2 tablespoons light brown sugar
- 2 teaspoons chipotle powder
- 2 tablespoons olive oil
- 1 tablespoon molasses
- 1 cup apple juice

Directions:

1. Sprinkle the salt over the ribs. Wrap them in plastic wrap and refrigerate overnight.

2. Preheat the smoker to 225°F.

3. Pat the ribs dry with paper towels, removing any excess salt.

4. In a small bowl, mix together the beef rub, brown sugar, chipotle powder, olive oil, and molasses. Rub that paste onto the ribs.

5. Place the ribs in the smoker meat-side up. Smoke for 3 hours. Fill a spray bottle with the apple juice.

6. Spray them with the apple juice and smoke for another 2 hours, spritzing again with the juice every hour, or until the internal temperature reaches 205°F. Be prepared to cook them for another couple of hours if the internal temperature stalls.

7. Let them rest for 10 minutes before serving.

Beef Churrasco With Chimichurri

Servings: 4

Cooking Time: 1 Hour

Ingredients:

- 1 bunch fresh flat-leaf parsley, leaves stripped and chopped
- 1 garlic bulb, cloves separated, peeled, and crushed
- 1 cup extra-virgin olive oil
- Grated zest of 1 lemon, plus 1 lemon, halved, for serving
- Grated zest of 1 lime, plus juice of 1 lime
- Flaked sea salt
- Freshly ground black pepper
- 4 (2-inch-thick) beef striploins, trimmed and excess fat removed

Directions:

1. In a large bowl, whisk together the parsley, garlic, olive oil, lemon zest, and lime zest. Add the lime juice and season with salt and pepper. Refrigerate until needed.

2. Preheat the electric smoker to 275°F. Ensure the drip tray is clean and in place. Seal the door.

3. Place the wood chips in the smoking tray or firebox, get a good smoke rolling, and seal the door.

4. If refrigerated, allow the steaks to rest at room temperature for 20 minutes before smoking. Season the striploin on both sides with salt and pepper. Rub half the chimichurri sauce over the steaks. Insert a probe thermometer (if available) into the thickest part of the meat. Set the target temperature for 125°F for rare, 135°F for medium-rare, 145°F for medium, 150°F for medium-well, and 160°F for well-done. Smoke the meat for about 1 hour. Remove the steaks from the smoker when the thermometer reads 5°F lower than your desired doneness.

5. Transfer the steaks to a cutting board, loosely tent them with aluminum foil, and let them rest for 10 minutes. The temperature of the beef will continue to rise while resting, achieving desired doneness.

6. Taste and season with salt and pepper, as needed. Thinly slice the steak across the grain and serve with the remaining half of the chimichurri sauce and a squeeze of fresh lemon juice.

Homemade Pastrami

Servings: 10 To 12

Cooking Time: 30 Minutes

Ingredients:

- FOR THE PICKLING SEASONING:
- 6 bay leaves, roughly crumbled
- 2 tablespoons mustard seed

- 2 tablespoons whole allspice
- 2 tablespoons whole coriander
- 2 tablespoons whole black peppercorns
- 1 tablespoon whole cloves
- 1 tablespoon red pepper flakes
- 1 cinnamon stick, broken in several pieces
- TO PREPARE THE MEAT:
- 5 tablespoons Pickling Seasoning
- 1 cup plus 1 tablespoon light brown sugar, divided
- 1 cup coarse kosher salt
- 6 cloves garlic, smashed
- 1 onion, quartered
- 3 teaspoons pink curing salt (page 88)
- 1 gallon water
- 4 pounds beef brisket, fat trimmed
- 2 tablespoons black pepper
- 2 tablespoons paprika
- ¼ cup ground coriander
- 1 tablespoon garlic powder

Directions:

1. Combine all the ingredients for the homemade pickling seasoning and store in an airtight container for up to 6 months.

2. In a 3 to 4-gallon container with a lid, combine the pickling seasoning, 1 cup brown sugar, kosher salt, garlic, onion, and pink salt with 1 gallon water. Stir well to combine and to dissolve the salt and sugar. Add the brisket and place a heavy bowl upside down on top of the meat to keep it submerged in the brine. Place the lid on the container and refrigerate for 5 to 7 days.

3. Prepare the smoker's water pan according to the manufacturer's instructions and preheat the smoker to 225°F. While it heats, fill a medium bowl with water and add 4 or 5 handfuls of hickory wood chips to soak.

4. Remove the brisket from the brine and rinse well under cool water for a couple minutes. The meat will feel denser and have a different texture and color than before it went into the brine. Dry with paper towels and set aside. In a small bowl, combine the black pepper, paprika, ground coriander, 1 tablespoon brown sugar, and garlic powder. Rub the mixture over the brisket to cover the entire surface with the seasonings.

5. Place the brisket in the smoker, fatty side up, and add a small handful of the soaked hickory chips to the chip loading area. Keep adding more chips at least every 30 minutes (or every 15 minutes, for a more intense smoke flavor). Smoke for 4 to 6 hours, or until the meat reaches an internal temperature of 165°F.

6. Remove from the smoker, wrap tightly in foil, and let sit for 2 hours. The meat will become even more tender as it sits. Thinly slice and store in an airtight container in the refrigerator for up to a week.

Texas-style Beef Brisket

Servings: 8
Cooking Time: 8 Hours

Ingredients:

- 3 tablespoons dark brown sugar
- 2 tablespoons chili powder
- 2 tablespoons smoked paprika
- 2 tablespoons fine sea salt
- 1 tablespoon ground cumin
- 1 tablespoon dried mustard
- 1 teaspoon ground cayenne pepper
- 7 pounds beef brisket (flat cut), trimmed and excess fat removed
- Flaked sea salt
- Freshly ground black pepper

Directions:

1. In a large bowl, whisk together the sugar, chili powder, paprika, salt, cumin, mustard, and cayenne. Season the brisket on all sides with this dry rub and wrap it tightly in plastic wrap. Refrigerate it for 24 hours.

2. Remove the brisket from the refrigerator 20 minutes before smoking. Remove the plastic wrap. Season the meat all over with salt and pepper.

3. Preheat the electric smoker to 200°F. Ensure the drip tray is clean and in place. Seal the door.

4. Place the wood chips in the smoking tray or firebox, get a good smoke rolling, and seal the door.

5. Place the brisket on the smoking rack and smoke it for 5 hours.

6. Remove the brisket from the smoker and wrap it in aluminum foil. Place the wrapped brisket on a baking sheet and return it to the smoker. Insert a probe thermometer (if available) into the thickest part of the meat. Set the target temperature for 190°F. Cook the

brisket for about 3 hours more, or until the target internal temperature is reached.

7.   Transfer the brisket to a cutting board. Remove the foil and loosely tent the meat with it. Let the meat rest for 30 minutes before slicing and serving it.

Smoked Tri-tip

Servings: 4
Cooking Time: 15 Minutes

Ingredients:

- 1 (2- to 3-pound) tri-tip
- 1 tablespoon olive oil
- 1 tablespoon coarse salt
- 1 tablespoon freshly ground black pepper
- 2 tablespoons granulated garlic
- 1 cup Bacon-Flavored BBQ Sauce, divided
- 2 tablespoons unsalted butter
- 1 rosemary sprig

Directions:

1.   Preheat the smoker to 225°F.

2.   Brush the meat with the olive oil and generously sprinkle with the salt, pepper, and garlic.

3.   Smoke the meat for 1 hour 30 minutes.

4.   Remove the trip-tip, brush it with ½ cup BBQ sauce, then smoke for another 30 minutes, or until the internal temperature reaches 110°F. Remove the meat from the smoker.

5.   In a cast-iron skillet on the stovetop, melt the butter over high heat until it's sizzling. Add the sprig of rosemary. Sear the meat on both sides for 3 to 4 minutes per side. The internal temperature should reach 125°F for rare and 135°F for medium.

6.   Let the tri-tip rest for 15 minutes before slicing. The grain of tri-tip meat changes, so to slice, start at the smallest tip and cut against the grain.

7.   Serve the tri-tip with the remaining ½ cup BBQ sauce.

Smoked Beef Jerky

Servings: 4
Cooking Time: 2 Hours

Ingredients:

- 1 pound London broil (such as top round)
- ½ cup apple cider vinegar
- ¼ cup beef broth
- ¼ cup Beef Rub
- 2 tablespoons blackstrap molasses
- 1 tablespoon light brown sugar

Directions:

1.   Trim the fat from the meat, then cut it into strips that are about ¼ inch thick. It's easier to cut when the meat is very cold.

2.   In a small bowl, mix together the vinegar, broth, beef rub, molasses, and brown sugar. Place the strips of beef in a glass dish (do not use an aluminum pan). Pour the marinade over the beef strips, making sure they are coated. Refrigerate for 2 hours.

3.   Preheat the smoker to 225°F.

4.   Pat the beef strips dry with paper towels.

5.   Place the beef strips in the smoker, making sure there is space between the strips. Smoke for 2 hours 30 minutes, or until the meat is firm and the internal temperatures reaches 150°F.

6.   Take the strips out of the smoker and let them rest for 10 minutes before enjoying.

Beef Stew With Dark Stout Beer

Servings: 8
Cooking Time: 3 To 4 Hours

Ingredients:

- 2 tablespoons extra-virgin olive oil
- 2 tablespoons unsalted butter
- 3 pounds stewing beef, excess fat removed, diced
- 3 tablespoons all-purpose flour
- Flaked sea salt
- Freshly ground black pepper
- 3 tablespoons tomato paste
- 2 cups diced carrots
- 2 cups diced celery hearts
- 2 cups diced yellow onions
- 2 cups leeks, white parts only, quartered lengthwise and thinly sliced
- 3 garlic cloves, minced
- 1 (12-ounce) bottle dark stout beer

- 1 tablespoon fresh thyme leaves, stripped and finely chopped
- 1 tablespoon fresh rosemary leaves
- 3 fresh bay leaves
- 1 tablespoon fresh flat-leaf parsley leaves, finely chopped

Directions:

1. Preheat the electric smoker to 250°F. Ensure the drip tray is clean and in place. Seal the door.
2. Place the wood chips in the smoking tray or firebox, get a good smoke rolling, and seal the door.
3. Place a large cast iron Dutch oven on a smoking rack to preheat, then pour in the olive oil and add the butter to melt.
4. In a large bowl, toss together the beef and flour to coat. Season with salt and pepper. Transfer the beef to the preheated Dutch oven. Smoke the beef for 20 minutes.
5. To the preheated skillet, add the tomato paste, carrots, celery, onions, leeks, and garlic. Stir to coat the ingredients with the oil and butter. Smoke for 20 minutes more.
6. Stir in the beer to deglaze the pan, scraping up any browned bits from the bottom.
7. Add the thyme, rosemary, and bay leaves and enough water to just cover ingredients. Smoke for 2 to 3 hours more, until the liquid has thickened and the meat is tender.
8. Remove and discard the bay leaves. Taste and season with salt and pepper, as needed. Top with the fresh parsley before serving.

Smoked Porterhouse With Roasted Garlic

Servings: 4
Cooking Time: 2 Hours

Ingredients:

- 4 (2-inch-thick) porterhouse steaks
- ¼ cup extra-virgin olive oil, plus more for brushing
- Flaked sea salt
- Freshly ground black pepper
- 8 rosemary sprigs
- 4 garlic bulbs, tops cut off to expose the cloves
- 4 tablespoons unsalted butter

Directions:

1. Preheat the electric smoker to 275°F. Ensure the drip tray is clean and in place. Seal the door.
2. Place the wood chips in the smoking tray or firebox, get a good smoke rolling, and seal the door.
3. Remove the steaks from the refrigerator 20 minutes before smoking them.
4. Brush each steak with olive oil and season them on both sides with salt and pepper. Place 2 rosemary sprigs on each steak.
5. Place the garlic bulbs on a piece of aluminum foil and pour ¼ cup of olive oil over the exposed cloves. Season with salt and pepper.
6. Place the steaks and garlic on the smoking racks, leaving space between them. Insert a probe thermometer (if available) into the thickest part of the meat, not touching the bone. Set the target temperature for 125°F for rare, 135°F for medium-rare, 145°F for medium, 150°F for medium-well, and 160°F for well-done. Smoke for about 2 hours, or until the internal thermometer reads 5°F lower than your desired doneness.
7. Transfer the steaks to a cutting board, loosely tent them with aluminum foil, and let them rest for 15 minutes. The temperature of the beef will continue to rise while resting, achieving desired doneness.
8. Top each steak with 1 tablespoon of butter and serve with a roasted garlic bulb on the side.

Sunday Shank Roast

Servings: 4
Cooking Time: 3 To 4 Hours

Ingredients:

- 1 (5-pound) bone-in beef shank roast
- Flaked sea salt
- Freshly ground black pepper
- 2 tablespoons extra-virgin olive oil
- 12 shiitake mushrooms, brushed clean, stemmed, and quartered
- 12 garlic cloves, halved lengthwise
- 8 shallots, halved lengthwise

- 4 thyme sprigs
- 3 cups Riesling (or Gewürztraminer)
- 3 fresh bay leaves
- 4 cups beef (or vegetable) stock

Directions:

1. Remove the roast from the refrigerator 20 minutes before smoking. Season it on all sides with salt and pepper.

2. Preheat the electric smoker to 225°F. Ensure the drip tray is clean and in place. Seal the door.

3. Place the wood chips in the smoking tray or firebox, get a good smoke rolling, and seal the door.

4. Place a large cast iron skillet on a smoking rack to preheat, and pour in the olive oil.

5. In the skillet, combine the mushrooms, garlic, shallots, and thyme. Toss to coat with the oil and season with salt and pepper. Smoke for 10 to 15 minutes, until slightly browned.

6. Stir in the Riesling to deglaze the pan, scraping up any browned bits from the bottom. Add the bay leaves and beef stock and return the skillet to the smoker.

7. Place the roast on a smoking rack directly above the skillet, so the skillet will catch any drippings. Insert a probe thermometer (if available) into the thickest part of the meat, without touching the bone. Set the target temperature for 125°F for rare, 135°F for medium-rare, 145°F for medium, 150°F for medium-well, and 160°F for well-done. Smoke for about 1 hour. Transfer the roast to the skillet, basting it with the cooking liquid. Continue to smoke until the internal thermometer reads 5°F lower than your desired doneness.

8. Remove the skillet from the smoker and loosely tent the meat with aluminum foil. Let it rest for 20 minutes. The temperature of the beef will continue to rise while resting, achieving desired doneness.

9. Slice the roast into portions and season with salt and pepper.

10. Remove and discard the thyme and bay leaves. Serve with the mushrooms, garlic, and shallots, topped with au jus.

Stuffed And Smoked Burgers

Servings: 6
Cooking Time: 45 Minutes

Ingredients:

- 1 hot dog
- 1 teaspoon olive oil
- 4 ounces sliced mushrooms
- 3 tablespoons crumbled blue cheese
- ¼ cup crumbled cooked bacon
- 1 (8-ounce) jar caramelized red onion chutney
- 3 tablespoons shredded pepper Jack cheese
- Cooking spray
- 2¼ pounds ground beef (80% lean)
- 2 tablespoons coarse salt
- 2 tablespoons freshly ground black pepper
- ¼ cup granulated garlic
- 6 large burger buns, split and toasted
- Burger condiments and toppings of choice

Directions:

1. Preheat the smoker to 275°F.

2. Slice the hot dog lengthwise. In a frying pan over medium heat, warm 1 teaspoon olive oil and sear the hot dog on both sides. Then, remove it from the heat and cut it into ½-inch pieces.

3. Place the hot dog pieces, sliced mushrooms, blue cheese, bacon, onion chutney, and pepper Jack all in their own separate bowls to make a "stuffing bar."

4. Mist the burger press with cooking spray. To make each burger, take 4 ounces ground beef and place it in the press, pressing it onto the bottom and sides. Fill the burger with 3 tablespoons of the toppings of your choice. Then form the top of the burger with another 2 ounces meat. Seal the top layer and sides of the meat together, pressing with your fingers. Flip the burger out of the mold and onto a tray lined with wax paper. Repeat to make a total of 6 burgers.

5. Sprinkle the burgers with the salt, pepper, and granulated garlic.

6. Smoke the burgers for 1 hour, or until the internal temperature reaches 165°F.

7. Let the burgers rest for 10 minutes. Serve the burgers on the buns topped with your favorite condiments and toppings.

Unbelievably Moist Brisket

Servings: 8 To 12
Cooking Time: 30 To 40 Minutes

Ingredients:

- 1 cup kosher salt
- 1 cup coarsely ground black pepper

- 1 (8- to 12-pound) brisket, trimmed of hardened fat thicker than ½ inch
- 2 cups prepared yellow mustard

Directions:

1. Preheat the smoker to 225°F with the oak wood for indirect heat.
2. In a medium bowl, mix together the salt and pepper.
3. Slather the brisket with the mustard to act as an adherent.
4. Coat the entire surface of the meat with the salt-and-pepper blend. It's a lot of salt and pepper but a roast this size uses it nicely.
5. Arrange the meat in the center for your smoker, fat-side up. If the whole brisket won't fit, use a sharp knife to trim off the point by following the flat's fat cap, to make a second roast. Smoke for 4 to 5 hours (typically) until the internal temperature reaches about 165°F.
6. Following Texas tradition, wrap the meat tightly with pink butcher's paper to seal in the juices. Continue to cook to an internal temperature of around 205°F, typically 4 to 5 hours more. Smoke is no longer a big factor. Look for a dark mahogany bark and a spring to the touch.
7. Remove the meat from the smoker, uncover it, and let it rest off the heat for up to 1 hour before slicing.
8. Separate the point and reserve for burnt ends, if desired (see tip). Slice the flat against the grain in pencil-thin slices.
9. Serve with Smoked Cauliflower Steaks, if desired.

Smoked Prime Rib

Servings: 8 To 10
Cooking Time: 25 Minutes

Ingredients:

- 1 (4-bone, about 8-pound) prime rib roast (see tip)
- 2 onions, thickly sliced
- Smoky Teriyaki Marinade
- Salt
- Freshly ground black pepper

Directions:

1. In a container large enough to hold the meat and marinade, combine the roast and onion slices. Pour the marinade over. Cover tightly and refrigerate to marinate for 2 hours.

2. Turn the meat over, replace the lid, and refrigerate for 2 hours more.
3. Preheat the smoker to 225°F with the oak wood.
4. Remove the roast and onions from the container and discard the marinade.
5. Skewer the onion slices to make "onion lollipops."
6. Season the prime rib on both sides with salt and pepper. Place the meat and onions on the smoker rack.
7. Smoke the meat for 4 to 6 hours and the onions until done (about 2 hours).
8. Remove the prime rib from the smoker when the internal temperature reaches at least 135°F. Let it rest for 15 minutes. Serve with the onion lollipops.

Smoked Tri-tip Roast

Servings: 3 To 4
Cooking Time: 10 Minutes

Ingredients:

- ¾ cup soy sauce
- ½ cup rice wine vinegar
- ½ cup water
- ¼ cup sesame oil
- 3 tablespoons firmly packed dark-brown sugar
- 2 scallions, white and green parts, minced
- 1 tablespoon sesame seeds
- 1 teaspoon garlic powder
- 1 teaspoon red pepper flakes
- 1 teaspoon freshly ground black pepper
- 1 (2-pound) tri-tip roast

Directions:

1. In a medium bowl, stir together the soy sauce, vinegar, water, sesame oil, brown sugar, scallions, sesame seeds, garlic powder, red pepper flakes, and pepper until well blended.
2. Place the roast in a shallow container and pour the marinade over the beef. Cover and refrigerate for a minimum of 4 hours, turning the meat as necessary to coat.
3. Preheat the smoker to 225°F with the red-oak wood.
4. Remove the meat and discard the marinade. Place the roast in the smoker for 2 to 3 hours. The internal temperature needs to be 135°F to 145°F depending on how well done you prefer your meat.

SAUCES, RUBS & MORE RECIPES

Basic Marinade With Variations

Servings: 8
Cooking Time: 5 Minutes

Ingredients:

- 6 cups dry red wine (about one 750 ml bottle)
- ½ cup olive oil
- 1 medium to large onion, diced
- ¼ cup minced garlic
- ¼ cup chopped fresh parsley
- 1 teaspoon smoked salt
- 1 teaspoon coarsely ground black pepper
- Variations (see list below)

Directions:

1. In a large bowl, whisk together the wine, oil, onion, garlic, parsley, smoked salt, pepper, and any additional ingredients outlined in the Variations.

Spicy Peanut Sauce

Servings: 3
Cooking Time: 30 Minutes

Ingredients:

- 1 large head garlic
- 4 tablespoons sesame oil, divided
- ⅔ cup raw peanuts
- 2 tablespoons unsalted butter, melted
- 1 teaspoon coarse salt
- 3 scallions, diced
- 1 tablespoon grated peeled fresh ginger
- 1 cup water
- ¼ cup soy sauce
- ¼ cup distilled white vinegar
- 3 tablespoons light brown sugar
- ½ teaspoon red pepper flakes

Directions:

1. Preheat the smoker to 250°F.
2. Cut the top off the garlic head, set it cut-side up, and drizzle it with 2 tablespoons sesame oil.
3. Set the garlic in the smoker on a piece of aluminum foil and smoke for 40 minutes, until softened and browned. Squeeze the cloves out of their skins and measure out 1 to 2 tablespoons (save any remainder for another use).
4. Meanwhile, in a bowl, toss the peanuts and melted butter together. Sprinkle with the salt and toss again. Place the peanuts in a perforated BBQ skillet or a shallow baking dish and smoke them for 45 minutes, stirring every 15 minutes. Don't let them burn!
5. Take the peanuts out the smoker and let cool for about 20 minutes.
6. Transfer the peanuts to a food processor and process for 4 to 5 minutes, until the peanuts turn into a creamy peanut butter. There should be just a little more than ½ cup.
7. In a skillet on the stovetop, heat the remaining 2 tablespoons sesame oil over medium heat until it's hot but not smoking. Add the smoked garlic, scallions, and ginger and cook, stirring constantly, for 90 seconds.
8. Stir in the water, peanut butter, soy sauce, vinegar, brown sugar, and red pepper flakes. Bring to a simmer, stirring constantly until it's smooth. Let it cool to room temperature before serving.

Carolina Mustard Sauce

Servings: 1
Cooking Time: 10 Minutes

Ingredients:

- ¾ cup prepared yellow mustard
- ¼ cup maple syrup
- ¼ cup apple cider vinegar
- 2 tablespoons firmly packed brown sugar
- 2 tablespoons ketchup
- 1 tablespoon Worcestershire sauce
- 2 teaspoons hot sauce
- 1 teaspoon pumpkin-pie spice
- 1 teaspoon salt
- 1 teaspoon freshly ground black pepper

Directions:

1. In a medium bowl, whisk the mustard, maple syrup, vinegar, brown sugar, ketchup, Worcestershire sauce, hot sauce, pumpkin-pie spice, salt, and pepper. Refrigerate in an airtight container for up to 2 weeks.

Beef Rub

Servings: 2½
Cooking Time: 10 Minutes

Ingredients:
- ½ cup coarse smoked salt
- ½ cup smoked paprika
- ½ cup packed light brown sugar
- ½ cup minced fresh or granulated garlic
- 6 tablespoons dried minced or granulated onion
- 1 tablespoon dried oregano
- 1 tablespoon freshly ground black pepper
- 1 teaspoon ground cumin

Directions:
1. In a medium bowl, mix the salt, paprika, brown sugar, garlic, onion, oregano, pepper, and cumin together. If you use fresh garlic, use the rub within 4 days. With granulated garlic, store in a sealed container for up to 1 month.

Pork Rub

Servings: 2½
Cooking Time: 10 Minutes

Ingredients:
- ½ cup coarse salt
- ½ cup smoked paprika
- ½ cup packed light brown sugar
- ½ cup minced fresh or granulated garlic
- 6 tablespoons dried minced or granulated onion
- 2 tablespoons chopped fresh thyme or 2 teaspoons dried thyme
- 1 tablespoon freshly ground black pepper
- ½ teaspoon ground nutmeg

Directions:
1. In a medium bowl, mix the salt, paprika, brown sugar, garlic, onion, thyme, pepper, and nutmeg together. If you use fresh garlic, use the rub within 4 days. With granulated garlic, store in a sealed container for up to 1 month.

Maple Turkey Brine

Servings: 12 To18
Cooking Time: 15 Minutes

Ingredients:
- 4 quarts water
- 1½ teaspoons coarse sea salt
- 12 peppercorns
- 12 cloves, whole
- 6 allspice berries, whole
- 6 star anise, whole
- 6 fresh bay leaves
- 1 cup pure maple syrup
- 1 cup diced carrots
- 1 cup diced celery hearts
- 1 cup diced yellow onions
- 2 rosemary sprigs
- 2 sage sprigs
- 2 thyme sprigs

Directions:
1. In a large stockpot over medium heat, combine the water, salt, peppercorns, cloves, allspice, star anise, and bay leaves. Bring to a simmer. Stir in the maple syrup and then remove the pan from the heat. Let the brine cool, and then refrigerate the pot of brine until it is completely cool.
2. Add the carrots, celery, onions, rosemary, sage, and thyme to the brine.
3. In a large pot (or other food-grade container large enough to hold the turkey and brine), combine the turkey and brine. Place a weight, such as a heavy plate, on the turkey to keep it fully submerged. Refrigerate the marinating turkey for at least 4 hours, or ideally overnight, before cooking according to the recipe instructions.

Korean-style Bbq Sauce

Servings: 4
Cooking Time: 20 Minutes

Ingredients:
- 1 large head garlic
- 3 tablespoons sesame oil, divided
- 1 ¼ cups soy sauce
- 1 tablespoon rice vinegar
- 1 ½ cups packed light brown sugar
- 3 tablespoons gochujang or similar red chili paste
- 1 tablespoon grated fresh ginger

- 1 teaspoon coarsely ground black pepper
- ½ cup plus 2 tablespoons water
- 2 tablespoons cornstarch

Directions:

1. Preheat the smoker to 250°F.
2. Cut the top off the garlic head, set it cut-side up, and drizzle it with 2 tablespoons sesame oil.
3. Set the garlic in the smoker on a piece of aluminum foil and smoke for 40 minutes, or until it is soft and brown.
4. When the garlic has cooled enough to handle, squeeze the cloves out of their skins and measure out 2 tablespoons (save any remaining smoked garlic for another use).
5. In a saucepan, combine the smoked garlic, soy sauce, vinegar, remaining 1 tablespoon sesame oil, brown sugar, gochujang, ginger, and black pepper. Mix to blend.
6. Set the saucepan over medium-high heat and bring to a boil.
7. Meanwhile, in a small bowl, stir the water into the cornstarch until it's smooth.
8. As soon as the garlic mixture starts to boil, add the cornstarch slurry, whisking thoroughly. Simmer the sauce for 2 minutes to thicken.
9. Let the sauce cool slightly. Use immediately or store for up to 10 days.

Fish Rub

Servings: 2½
Cooking Time: 10 Minutes

Ingredients:

- ½ cup coarse smoked salt
- ½ cup smoked paprika
- ½ cup packed light brown sugar
- ½ cup minced fresh or granulated garlic
- 6 tablespoons dried minced or granulated onion
- 1 tablespoon freshly ground black pepper
- 1 teaspoon grated lemon zest
- 1 teaspoon chopped fresh or dried dill

Directions:

1. In a medium bowl, mix the salt, paprika, brown sugar, garlic, onion, pepper, lemon zest, and dill together. If you use fresh garlic, use the rub within 4

days. With granulated garlic, store in a sealed container for up to 1 month.

Chimichurri Sauce

Servings: 1½
Cooking Time: 30 Minutes

Ingredients:

- 1 large head garlic
- ½ cup extra-virgin olive oil, plus 3 tablespoons
- 2 tablespoons red wine vinegar
- ½ cup finely chopped parsley
- ¾ teaspoon minced fresh oregano
- 1 teaspoon coarse salt
- ½ teaspoon freshly ground black pepper

Directions:

1. Preheat the smoker to 250°F.
2. Cut the top off the garlic head, set it cut-side up, and drizzle it with 3 tablespoons olive oil.
3. Set the garlic in the smoker on a piece of aluminum foil and smoke for 40 minutes, or until it is soft and brown.
4. When the garlic has cooled enough to handle, squeeze the cloves out of their skins and measure out 2 tablespoons (save any remaining smoked garlic for another use).
5. In a bowl, stir together the remaining ½ cup olive oil, the vinegar, parsley, oregano, salt, pepper, and smoked garlic. Let the chimichurri rest for at least 30 minutes before using. You can store chimichurri in the refrigerator for up to 1 week.

Ruby Port Cranberry Sauce

Servings: 12
Cooking Time: 1 Hour

Ingredients:

- 1 cup ruby port
- 1 pound fresh or frozen cranberries
- ½ cup packed dark brown sugar
- Grated zest of 1 orange, plus juice of 1 orange
- 5 star anise, whole
- 5 cloves, whole
- 1 cinnamon stick, whole

- Flaked sea salt

Directions:
1. If you would like to reduce the alcohol content slightly, preheat a saucepan over medium heat, then pour in the port and let it cook for 1 minute.
2. Add the cranberries, sugar, orange zest, orange juice, star anise, cloves, cinnamon stick, and a pinch of salt. (If you skipped step 1, stir in the port now.) Bring the mixture to a boil. Reduce the heat to maintain a simmer and cook for about 1 hour, or until your desired consistency is reached. Remember, the sauce will thicken considerably when it cools.
3. Remove and discard the whole spices.

Asian-inspired Marinade

Servings: 3 To 4
Cooking Time: 15 Minutes

Ingredients:
- 1 cup fresh cilantro leaves, finely chopped
- 3 garlic cloves, minced
- 2 limes, thinly sliced
- 1 jalapeño pepper, trimmed, seeded, and diced
- ¼ cup packed dark brown sugar
- 3 tablespoons canola oil
- 3 tablespoons soy sauce
- 3 tablespoons fish sauce
- 1 tablespoon toasted sesame oil
- 1 teaspoon ground coriander
- 1 teaspoon freshly ground black pepper

Directions:
1. In a large stockpot over medium heat, combine the cilantro, garlic, limes, jalapeño, sugar, canola oil, soy sauce, fish sauce, sesame oil, coriander, and black pepper. Bring to a simmer and cook for 5 minutes.
2. Whisk to combine the ingredients, remove the marinade from the heat, and cool it completely in the refrigerator before using.
3. To use, in a large food-safe plastic bag, combine the meat and marinade. Remove as much air as possible from the bag and seal it. Refrigerate to marinate your meat for 24 hours for best results. Massage the marinade into the meat and turn the bag occasionally.

4. Remove the meat from the marinade and cook it according to the recipe's instructions.

Bbq Rub

Servings: 2
Cooking Time: 60-120 Minutes

Ingredients:
- ½ cup brown sugar
- ½ cup paprika
- 1 tablespoon ground black pepper
- ½ tablespoon salt
- 3 tablespoons chili powder
- 4 tablespoons garlic powder
- 4 tablespoons onion powder
- 1 teaspoon cayenne pepper

Directions:
1. Combine all the spice in a bowl.
2. Preheat the electric smoke to 220 degrees F.
3. Use a cold smoker attachment and fire up the apple wood chips until the temperature reaches 100 degrees F.
4. Next, take an aluminum pie pan and place the spices from the bowl into it.
5. Place the pan inside the smoker and let it smoke for 1 to 2 hours.
6. Store it in the tight jar for future use.

Bleu Cheese Cowboy Butter

Servings: 1
Cooking Time: 5 Minutes

Ingredients:
- 1 cup unsalted butter, softened
- 4 ounce bleu cheese crumbles, room temperature
- 1 teaspoon cayenne pepper
- 1 teaspoon garlic powder
- ¼ cup chopped scallions, white and green parts
- 1 tablespoon brown sugar, firmly packed

Directions:
1. Cream the butter and bleu cheese with a mixer.
2. Add the cayenne pepper, garlic powder, scallions, and brown sugar, and blend well.
3. Using wax paper, roll the mixture into a cylindrical log and wrap well.
4. Refrigerate for a minimum of 4 hours.
5. When ready to serve, unwrap and cut into 1-inch slices.

Queens Of Cuisine Seafood Seasoning

Servings: 4
Cooking Time: 120 Minutes

Ingredients:

- 2 teaspoons paprika
- 4 teaspoons cinnamon
- 3 teaspoons ground ginger
- 2 teaspoons ground cumin
- 2 teaspoons ground coriander
- 2 teaspoons dried lemon peel
- 4 teaspoons onion powder
- 2 teaspoons lemon pepper
- 2 teaspoons dried parsley
- 2 teaspoons dried cilantro
- 2 teaspoons garlic powder

Directions:

1. Combine all the spice in a bowl.
2. Preheat the electric smoke to 220 degrees F.
3. Use a cold smoker attachment and fire up with the cherry wood chips until the temperature reaches 100 degrees F.
4. Next, take an aluminum pie pan and place bowl spices into it.
5. Place the pan inside the smoker and let it smoke for 2 hours.
6. After 2 hours, the spices are smoked to perfection.
7. Store in the tight jar for future use.

Jerky Seasoning

Servings: 1
Cooking Time: 2 Hours

Ingredients:

- 6 tablespoons dried minced onion
- 4 teaspoons dried thyme
- 2 teaspoons ground allspice powder
- 1 teaspoon ground black pepper
- 2 teaspoons ground cinnamon
- 2 teaspoons cayenne pepper
- 1 teaspoon salt

Directions:

1. Combine all the spice in a bowl.
2. Preheat the smoke to 220 degrees F.
3. Use a cold smoker attachment and fire up the apple flavored wood chips until the temperature reached 100 degrees F.
4. Next, take an aluminum pie pan and place bowl spices into it.
5. Place the pan inside the smoker and let it smoke for 2 hours.
6. Store spices in a tight jar for future use.

Bill's Best Barbecue Rub

Servings: ¾
Cooking Time: 10 Minutes

Ingredients:

- ¼ cup paprika
- ¼ cup Sugar In The Raw, or other turbinado sugar
- 3 tablespoons Cajun seasoning
- 1 tablespoon firmly packed brown sugar
- 1½ teaspoons chili powder
- 1½ teaspoons cayenne pepper
- 1½ teaspoons ground cumin

Directions:

1. In a small bowl, stir together the paprika, sugar, Cajun seasoning, brown sugar, chili powder, cayenne, and cumin. Refrigerate in an airtight container for up to 2 weeks.

Magical Rub Mix

Servings: 3
Cooking Time: 120 Minutes

Ingredients:

- ½ cup paprika
- ½ teaspoon brown sugar
- 2 tablespoons salt
- 4 tablespoons white pepper
- 4 tablespoons mustard

Directions:

1. Combine all the spice in a bowl.
2. Preheat the smoke to 220 degrees F.
3. Use a cold smoker attachment and fire up the apple wood chips until the temperature reaches 100 degrees F.

4. Next, take an aluminum pie pan and place bowl spices into it.
5. Place the pan inside the smoker and let it smoke for 2 hours.
6. After an hour, the spices are smoked to perfection.
7. Store it in the tight jar for future use.

Zesty Guacamole

Servings: 4 To 6
Cooking Time: 10 To 15 Minutes

Ingredients:

*   3 avocados, halved, pitted, and diced
*   1 Roma tomato, cored, quartered, and finely chopped
*   ½ cup finely diced red onion
*   1 jalapeño pepper, trimmed, seeded, and finely chopped (optional)
*   3 tablespoons fresh cilantro leaves, finely chopped
*   Grated zest of 1 lime, plus juice of 1 lime
*   Flaked sea salt
*   Freshly ground black pepper

Directions:

1. In a medium bowl, stir together and mash the avocados, tomato, onion, jalapeño (if using), cilantro, lime zest, and lime juice until your desired consistency is reached—leave chunky or mix until smooth.
2. Taste and season with salt and pepper.

Watermelon Salsa

Servings: 8
Cooking Time: 10 To 15 Minutes

Ingredients:

*   ½ seedless watermelon, peeled and diced
*   ½ cucumber, peeled, seeded, and diced
*   ½ cup red onion, diced
*   1 jalapeño pepper, trimmed, seeded, and finely chopped (optional)
*   3 tablespoons fresh cilantro leaves, finely chopped
*   Grated zest of 1 lime, plus juice of 1 lime
*   Flaked sea salt
*   Freshly ground black pepper

Directions:

1. In a large bowl, gently fold together the watermelon, cucumber, onion, jalapeño (if using), cilantro, lime zest, and lime juice.
2. Taste and season with salt and pepper. Cover and refrigerate until well-chilled. Serve cold.

Seafood Seasoning

Servings: 1⅓
Cooking Time: 10 Minutes

Ingredients:

*   ½ cup minced fresh or granulated garlic
*   ¼ cup smoked paprika
*   3 tablespoons dried minced or granulated onion
*   3 tablespoons coarse smoked salt
*   1 tablespoon celery salt
*   1 tablespoon freshly ground black pepper
*   1 teaspoon chopped fresh or dried dill
*   1 teaspoon grated lemon zest
*   ½ teaspoon ground ginger
*   ½ teaspoon mustard powder

Directions:

1. In a medium bowl, mix the garlic, paprika, onion, smoked salt, celery salt, pepper, dill, lemon zest, ginger, and mustard powder together. If you use fresh garlic, use the rub within 4 days. With granulated garlic, store in a sealed container for up to 1 month.

Blue Cheese Dip

Servings: 4 To 6
Cooking Time: 10 To 15 Minutes

Ingredients:

*   1 cup sour cream, lightly whipped
*   ½ cup buttermilk
*   ½ cup mayonnaise, lightly whipped
*   Grated zest of 1 lemon, plus juice of 1 lemon
*   Flaked sea salt
*   Freshly ground black pepper
*   8 ounces blue cheese, crumbled into fine pieces

Directions:

1. In a medium bowl, whisk together the sour cream, buttermilk, mayonnaise, lemon zest, and lemon juice. Taste and season with salt and pepper.
2. Fold in the blue cheese. Taste again and add more salt and pepper, as needed. Cover and refrigerate until serving.

Cajun Spice Rub

Servings: 4

Cooking Time: 60 Minutes

Ingredients:

- ½ tablespoon salt
- 4 teaspoons ground cayenne pepper
- 3 teaspoons ground white pepper
- 4 teaspoons ground black pepper
- 4 teaspoons paprika
- 4 teaspoons onion powder
- 3 teaspoons garlic powder

Directions:

1. Combine all the spice in a bowl.
2. Preheat the smoke to 220 degrees F.
3. Use a cold smoker attachment and fire up the apple wood chips until the temperature reaches 100 degrees F.
4. Next, take an aluminum pie pan and place bowl spices into it.
5. Place the pan inside the smoker and let it smoke for one hour.
6. After an hour, the spices are smoked to perfection.
7. Store spices in a tight jar for future use.

Classic Rub Recipes

Servings: 1

Cooking Time: 2 Hours

Ingredients:

- 4 tablespoons brown sugar
- 1 tablespoon paprika
- 2 tablespoons salt
- 1 tablespoon ground black pepper
- 2 teaspoons garlic powder

Directions:

1. Combine all the spice in a bowl.
2. Preheat the smoker to 220 degrees F.
3. Use a cold smoker attachment and fire up the mildly flavored wood chips until the temperature reaches 100 degrees F.
4. Next, take an aluminum pie pan and place bowl spices into it.
5. Place the pan inside the smoker and let it smoke for 2 hours.
6. After 2 hours, the spices are smoked to perfection.
7. Store it in a tight jar for future use.

Surefire Beef Rub

Servings: 6 To 7

Cooking Time: 15 Minutes

Ingredients:

- 10 allspice berries, whole
- 5 star anise, whole
- 3 tablespoons fennel seeds, whole
- 3 tablespoons coriander seeds, whole
- 1 tablespoon peppercorns
- 3 tablespoons paprika
- 1 tablespoon fine sea salt
- 1 teaspoon ground cayenne pepper
- 1 tablespoon dark brown sugar

Directions:

1. In a large sauté pan or skillet over medium heat, combine the allspice, star anise, fennel, coriander, and peppercorns. Cook, tossing the spices frequently to toast them evenly, until light brown and fragrant, about 5 minutes. Be careful not to burn the spices. Transfer them to a mortar or clean spice grinder and let them cool slightly.
2. Grind or pulse the cooled spices to a fine consistency. Transfer the powder to a medium bowl and let it cool completely.
3. Stir in the paprika, salt, cayenne, and sugar, stirring until evenly combined. Use immediately, or if the ingredients are fresh, store in an airtight container or resealable plastic bag for up to 12 months.

Pineapple–brown Sugar Sauce

Servings: 2

Cooking Time: 10 Minutes

Ingredients:

- 1 (20-ounce) can pineapple chunks, with juice
- 1 cup firmly packed brown sugar
- 2 tablespoons prepared mustard
- 2 tablespoons tomato paste
- 1 tablespoon ground cloves
- 1 teaspoon ground nutmeg

- 1 teaspoon ground cinnamon
- 1 teaspoon ancho chile powder (or chipotle)

Directions:

1.   In a large bowl, combine the pineapple chunks and juice, brown sugar, mustard, tomato paste, cloves, nutmeg, cinnamon, and chile powder. Stir well to mix. Refrigerate in an airtight container for up to 2 weeks.

Three Pepper Rub

Servings: 4
Cooking Time: 2 Hours

Ingredients:

- 4 tablespoons black pepper
- 4 tablespoons white pepper
- 1 tablespoon red pepper
- 2 tablespoons onion powder
- 2 teaspoons garlic powder
- 1 tablespoon dried thyme
- 2 tablespoons paprika
- 4 tablespoons dried oregano

Directions:

1.   Combine all the spice in a bowl.
2.   Preheat the smoke to 220 degrees F.
3.   Use a cold smoker attachment and fire up the hickory wood chips until the temperature reaches 100 degrees F.
4.   Next, take an aluminum pie pan and place bowl spices into it.
5.   Place the pan inside the smoker and let it smoke for 2 hours.
6.   After 3 hours, the spices are smoked to perfection.
7.   Store it in the tight jar for future use.

Hot Pepper Vinegar Barbecue Sauce

Servings: 3
Cooking Time: 30 Minutes

Ingredients:

- 2 cups ketchup
- 1 cup firmly packed light-brown sugar
- 1 cup hot-pepper vinegar sauce
- 2 tablespoons white vinegar

- 2 tablespoons salt
- 1 tablespoon chili powder
- 2 teaspoons freshly ground black pepper
- 1 teaspoon garlic powder
- 1 teaspoon cayenne pepper
- ½ teaspoon ground allspice

Directions:

1.   In a saucepan over medium heat, stir together the ketchup, brown sugar, hot-pepper vinegar sauce, white vinegar, salt, chili powder, pepper, garlic powder, cayenne, and allspice. Bring to a boil, reduce the heat to low, and simmer, covered, for 25 minutes, stirring occasionally. Refrigerate in an airtight container for up to 2 weeks.

Java Rub

Servings: 1
Cooking Time: 10 Minutes

Ingredients:

- ¼ cup finely ground roasted coffee beans
- ¼ cup paprika
- ¼ cup garlic powder
- 2 tablespoons chili powder
- 1 tablespoon firmly packed light-brown sugar
- 1 tablespoon ground allspice
- 1 tablespoon ground coriander
- 1 tablespoon freshly ground black pepper
- 2 teaspoons dry mustard
- 1½ teaspoons celery seed

Directions:

1.   In a blender or food processor, combine the coffee beans, paprika, garlic powder, chili powder, brown sugar, allspice, coriander, pepper, mustard, and celery seed. Pulse until fine. Store in an airtight container for up to 3 months, after which it starts to lose its flavor.

Bacon-flavored Bbq Sauce

Servings: 2¼
Cooking Time: 15 Minutes

Ingredients:

- 3 slices bacon
- 1 ½ cups ketchup

- ¼ cup pineapple juice
- 2 tablespoons light corn syrup
- 1 teaspoon Worcestershire sauce
- 2 teaspoons chili powder
- 1 teaspoon ground cumin
- ¼ teaspoon salt
- ¼ teaspoon freshly ground black pepper
- 1 tablespoon olive oil
- 6 tablespoons chopped yellow onion
- 2 teaspoons minced garlic

Directions:

1. Preheat the smoker to 275°F.

2. Lay the bacon slices on a wire rack or grill screen (or directly on the smoker rack, perpendicular to the grate). Smoke for 30 minutes, or until crisp. When cool enough to handle, cut them into ½-inch pieces.

3. In a bowl, combine the ketchup, pineapple juice, corn syrup, Worcestershire sauce, chili powder, cumin, salt, and pepper.

4. In a large saucepan on the stovetop, heat the oil over medium-high heat. Add the onion and garlic and cook for about 5 minutes, or until the onion is tender.

5. Add the ketchup mixture to the saucepan and bring to a boil. Reduce the heat to low. Cook, stirring occasionally, for about 8 minutes to thicken it slightly. Stir in the bacon pieces.

6. Pour the sauce into the bowl and let cool to room temperature before using.

Simple Smoked Salt Recipe

Servings: 2
Cooking Time: 60 Minutes

Ingredients:

- ½ cup kosher salt

Directions:

1. Preheat the eclectic smoke to 220 degrees F.

2. Use a cold smoker attachment and fired up the apple wood chips until the temperature reaches 100 degrees F.

3. Next, take an aluminum pie pan and place about ½ cup of kosher salt into it.

4. Place in the smoker to start the smoking process.

5. After an hour the salt is smoked to its perfection.

6. Store it in a tight jar for future use.

Jerk Spice Rub

Servings: 4 To 5
Cooking Time: 10 To 15 Minutes

Ingredients:

- 2 tablespoons dark brown sugar
- 2 tablespoons ground allspice
- 1 tablespoon garlic powder
- 1 tablespoon onion powder
- 1 tablespoon ground cinnamon
- 1 tablespoon fine sea salt
- 1 teaspoon ground cayenne pepper
- 1 teaspoon ground cloves
- 1 teaspoon ground nutmeg
- 1 teaspoon freshly ground black pepper

Directions:

1. In a large bowl, whisk together the sugar, allspice, garlic powder, onion powder, cinnamon, salt, cayenne, cloves, nutmeg, and black pepper. If the ingredients are fresh, the rub can be kept in an airtight container for up to 12 months.

Smoky Teriyaki Marinade

Servings: 1½
Cooking Time: 10 Minutes

Ingredients:

- ½ cup low-sodium soy sauce
- ½ cup teriyaki sauce
- ¼ cup firmly packed brown sugar
- ¼ cup granulated sugar
- 1 small onion, finely chopped
- ¼ cup rice wine vinegar
- ¼ cup canola oil
- 3 tablespoons hoisin sauce
- 2 teaspoons ground ginger
- 1 tablespoon minced garlic
- 1 teaspoon liquid smoke

Directions:

1. In a small bowl, stir together the soy sauce, teriyaki sauce, brown sugar, and granulated sugar until dissolved and well blended.

2. Add the onion, vinegar, oil, hoisin sauce, ginger, garlic, and liquid smoke. Stir to combine.

3. Pour it over your steak as a marinade, or bring to a boil and serve as a sauce for steak or chicken. Refrigerate any leftovers in an airtight container for up to 2 weeks (but this is so good you won't have any left!).

Spicy Hickory-smoked Barbecue Sauce

Servings: 3
Cooking Time: 30 Minutes

Ingredients:
- 1 small onion, finely chopped
- 2 garlic cloves, finely minced
- 2 cups ketchup
- 1 cup water
- ½ cup molasses
- ½ cup apple cider vinegar
- 5 tablespoons granulated sugar
- 5 tablespoons firmly packed brown sugar
- 1 tablespoon Worcestershire sauce
- 1 tablespoon freshly squeezed lemon juice
- 2 teaspoons hickory liquid smoke
- 1½ teaspoons freshly ground black pepper
- 1½ teaspoons dry mustard

Directions:
1. Preheat the smoker to 225°F with the hickory wood.
2. In a saucepan over medium heat, stir together the onion, garlic, ketchup, water, molasses, vinegar, granulated sugar, brown sugar, Worcestershire sauce, lemon juice, liquid smoke, pepper, and mustard. Bring to a boil. Transfer the sauce to a small metal or aluminum-foil pan and place it in the smoker for 30 minutes to absorb the smoke's flavor.
3. If you prefer a smooth sauce, strain out the chunks before serving. Refrigerate in an airtight container for up to 2 weeks.

Chicken Spice Rub

Servings: 2
Cooking Time: 1-2 Hours

Ingredients:

- 1 teaspoon sea salt
- 4 teaspoons dried basil
- 4 teaspoons crushed dried rosemary
- 2 teaspoons garlic powder
- 4 teaspoons dry mustard powder
- 1 teaspoon paprika
- ¼ teaspoon ground black pepper
- ¼ teaspoon ground dried thyme
- ½ teaspoon celery seed
- 1 teaspoon dried parsley
- ½ teaspoon ground cumin
- ½ teaspoon cayenne pepper

Directions:
1. Combine all the spice in a large bowl.
2. Preheat the electric smoke to 220 degrees F.
3. Use a cold smoker attachment and fired up the apple wood chips until the temperature reaches 100 degrees F.
4. Take an aluminum pie pan and place bowl spices into it.
5. Place inside the smoker and close the door.
6. After 1-2 hours the spices are smoked to perfection.
7. Store it in a tight jar for future use.

Alabama White Sauce

Servings: 1
Cooking Time: 10 Minutes

Ingredients:
- 1 cup mayonnaise
- ¼ cup apple cider vinegar
- 1 tablespoon hot chili powder
- 1 teaspoon Worcestershire sauce
- ½ teaspoon celery seed
- ½ teaspoon red pepper flakes
- ¼ teaspoon cayenne pepper
- Salt
- Freshly ground black pepper

Directions:
1. In a medium bowl, whisk the mayonnaise, vinegar, chili powder, Worcestershire sauce, celery seed, red pepper flakes, and cayenne until well blended. Season with salt and pepper and whisk again to combine.
2. Refrigerate in an airtight container for up to 2 weeks.

Smoked Garlic Tomato Sauce

Servings: 8
Cooking Time: 2 To 3 Hours

Ingredients:

- 3 tablespoons extra-virgin olive oil, plus more for drizzling
- 1 tablespoon unsalted butter
- 1 garlic bulb, top cut off to expose the cloves
- Flaked sea salt
- Freshly ground black pepper
- 2 cups cremini mushrooms, or white mushrooms, trimmed and cut into slices
- 1 cup diced carrots
- 1 cup diced celery
- 1 cup diced yellow onions
- 1 cup leeks, white parts only, quartered lengthwise and thinly sliced
- 3 tablespoons tomato paste
- 2 cups Cabernet Sauvignon, Merlot, or Pinot Noir
- 12 cups fresh or canned diced Roma tomatoes
- 3 tablespoons fresh thyme leaves, stripped and finely chopped
- 3 tablespoons fresh oregano leaves, minced
- 3 fresh bay leaves
- 2 cups chicken (or vegetable) stock
- Finely grated Parmesan cheese (optional)
- 3 tablespoons fresh flat-leaf parsley leaves, minced

Directions:

1. Preheat the electric smoker to 275°F. Ensure the drip tray is clean and in place. Seal the door.
2. Place the wood chips in the smoking tray or firebox, get a good smoke rolling, and seal the door.
3. Place a large cast iron Dutch oven on a smoking rack to preheat it. Pour in 3 tablespoons of the olive oil and add the butter to melt.
4. Place the garlic on a sheet of aluminum foil. Drizzle the garlic bulb with olive oil and season it with salt and pepper. Wrap the foil to enclose the garlic. Smoke the garlic for 1 hour, or until golden brown and tender. Remove the garlic from the foil and set it aside.
5. In the Dutch oven, combine the mushrooms, carrots, celery, onions, and leeks. Season with salt and pepper. Smoke the vegetables, uncovered, for 30 to 45 minutes, until golden brown. Move the vegetables to one side of the pan.
6. Add the tomato paste to the other side of the pan and smoke for 10 to 12 minutes, until browned and fragrant. Stir in the red wine to deglaze the pan, scraping up any browned bits stuck to the bottom. Smoke for 10 to 12 minutes more, or until the wine is reduced and the pan is dry.
7. Stir in the tomatoes, thyme, oregano, bay leaves, and chicken stock. Smoke for 2 hours, or until your desired consistency is reached.
8. Squeeze the garlic cloves from the head and add to the sauce along with the Parmesan cheese, if desired. Stir to combine. Remove and discard the bay leaves. Leave the sauce chunky, or purée it using an immersion blender for a smooth sauce, if desired.
9. Taste and season with more salt and pepper, as needed. Top with the parsley.

Zest Herbal Rub

Servings: 3
Cooking Time: 60 -120 Minutes

Ingredients:

- ½ cup cane sugar
- ⅓ cup chili powder
- 2 tablespoons granulated onion
- 2 tablespoons granulated garlic
- 1 tablespoon dried chilies
- 1 tablespoon dill weed
- 3 tablespoons lemon powder
- 2 tablespoons cumin, ground
- 2 tablespoons celery seeds
- 2 tablespoons basil
- ½ tablespoon dried rosemary
- ½ tablespoon mustard powder

Directions:

1. Combine all the spice in a bowl.
2. Preheat the eclectic smoke to 220 degrees F.
3. Use a cold smoker attachment and fire up the apple wood chips until the temperature reaches 100 degrees F.
4. Next, take an aluminum pie pan and place bowl spices into it.

5. Place the pan inside the smoker and let it smoke for 1 or 2 hours.

6. After an hour, the spices are smoked to perfection.

7. Store it in the tight jar for future use.

Plum Sauce

Servings: 1
Cooking Time: 30 Minutes

Ingredients:

- 12 ounces plum jam
- 2 tablespoons apple cider vinegar
- 1 tablespoon firmly packed brown sugar
- 1 tablespoon dry minced onion
- 1 teaspoon red pepper flakes
- 1 garlic clove, minced
- ½ teaspoon ground ginger
- Salt
- Freshly ground black pepper

Directions:

1. In a medium saucepan over high heat, whisk together the jam, vinegar, brown sugar, onion, red pepper flakes, garlic, and ginger. Season with salt and pepper and bring to a boil.

2. Reduce the heat to low and simmer for about 20 minutes.

3. Refrigerate in an airtight container for up to 2 weeks.

Pork Marinade

Servings: 10 To 12
Cooking Time: 15 Minutes

Ingredients:

- 2 quarts apple cider
- 12 garlic cloves, peeled and halved
- 3 shallots, trimmed and very thinly sliced
- 2 lemons, very thinly sliced
- 1 jalapeño pepper, sliced
- 3 thyme sprigs, rinsed
- 3 rosemary sprigs, rinsed
- 3 star anise, whole
- 1 tablespoon fennel seeds, whole
- 1 tablespoon coriander seeds, whole
- 1 tablespoon allspice berries, whole

Directions:

1. In a large stockpot over medium heat, combine the cider, garlic, shallots, lemons, pepper, thyme, rosemary, anise, fennel, coriander, and allspice. Bring the marinade to a simmer and cook for 5 minutes.

2. Whisk to combine the ingredients, remove the marinade from the heat, and cool it completely in the refrigerator before using.

3. To use, in a large food-safe plastic bag, combine the pork and marinade. Remove as much air as possible from the bag and seal it. Refrigerate the marinating pork for 24 hours for best results. Massage the marinade into the pork and turn the bag occasionally.

4. Remove the pork from the marinade and cook it according to the recipe's instructions.

Poultry Rub

Servings: 2½
Cooking Time: 10 Minutes

Ingredients:

- ½ cup coarse salt
- ½ cup smoked paprika
- ½ cup packed light brown sugar
- ½ cup minced fresh or granulated garlic
- 6 tablespoons dried minced or granulated onion
- 1 tablespoon grated lemon zest
- 1 tablespoon freshly ground black pepper
- 1 teaspoon ground cumin
- 1 teaspoon dried rosemary or oregano

Directions:

1. In a medium bowl, mix the salt, paprika, brown sugar, garlic, onion, lemon zest, pepper, cumin, and oregano together. If you use fresh garlic, use the rub within 4 days. With granulated garlic, store in a sealed container for up to 1 month.

OTHER FAVORITE RECIPES

Hot-smoked Gouda Bacon Dip

Servings: 4 To 6
Cooking Time: 10 Minutes

Ingredients:

- 1 pound Gouda cheese, cut into 4-by-2-inch blocks, at room temperature
- 4 tablespoons butter
- 2 tablespoons all-purpose flour
- 1 cup whole milk
- 8 bacon slices, cooked and crumbled
- Crackers or pita points, for serving

Directions:

1. Prepare the smoker for cold-smoking (under 90°F) with the hickory or mesquite wood, and maintain the temperature.
2. Place the cheese blocks on the top rack and smoke for about 2 hours.
3. Remove the cheese from the smoker and wrap the smoked cheese blocks in parchment paper, wax paper, or vacuum pack them with a food sealer. Refrigerate for 1 to 7 days to mellow the flavor.
4. When ready to serve the dip, shred the smoked Gouda blocks (you should get about 1½ cups).
5. In a large saucepan over medium heat, melt the butter.
6. Whisk in the flour and continue whisking for 1 minute to make the roux.
7. Slowly add the milk and continue to whisk for about 5 minutes, or until thickened.
8. Stir in the smoked Gouda and bacon. Remove from the heat when the cheese melts.
9. Preheat the smoker to 225°F with the hickory or mesquite wood.
10. Transfer the dip into a small metal or aluminum-foil pan and place it in the smoker for 1 hour before serving to get that added smoke flavor and keep it hot.
11. Serve warm with crackers or pita points.

Smoked Brie With Brown Sugar And Pecans

Servings: 8 To 10
Cooking Time: 5 Minutes

Ingredients:

- 1 (16-ounce) Brie wheel, rind intact
- ½ cup firmly packed brown sugar
- 1 teaspoon ground cinnamon
- ½ cup chopped Glazed Spiced Pecans, divided
- Crackers or pear and Granny Smith apple wedges, for serving

Directions:

1. Preheat the smoker to 200°F with the apple or cherrywood.
2. Place the whole Brie wheel on a piece of aluminum foil. Bring the foil up the sides but leave the top of the Brie uncovered. Place the foil-wrapped Brie in a metal or foil pie pan. Carefully cut off the rind from the top of the Brie only, leaving a ¼-inch border intact.
3. Cover the top of the cheese with the brown sugar and sprinkle with the cinnamon and ¼ cup of pecans.
4. Place the pan on the top rack of the smoker and smoke for 20 to 30 minutes. Remove when the cheese is melty, and top with the remaining ¼ cup of pecans.
5. Serve warm with crackers or pear and apple wedges.

Smoked Stuffed Pumpkin Squash

Servings: 8
Cooking Time: 30 Minutes

Ingredients:

- 4 pumpkin squash, or acorn squash, halved horizontally, pulp and seeds discarded
- 3 tablespoons olive oil
- Salt
- Freshly ground black pepper
- 8 ounces dry seasoned stuffing mix
- ½ cup hot water

- ½ cup (1 stick) butter, melted
- 1 egg, beaten
- ½ cup chopped celery
- ½ cup chopped onion
- 2 teaspoons chili powder
- Spicy mustard, for drizzling

Directions:

1. Preheat the smoker to 225°F with the maple wood.
2. Lightly drizzle the cut squash halves with the olive oil and sprinkle with salt and pepper.
3. In a medium bowl, stir together the stuffing mix, water, butter, egg, celery, onion, and chili powder. Stuff the mixture into the squash halves and place the squash directly on the rack inside the smoker. Smoke the stuffed squash for 1 to 1½ hours.
4. Drizzle with spicy mustard and serve warm.

Smokehouse Almonds

Servings: 2
Cooking Time: 10 Minutes

Ingredients:

- Nonstick cooking spray
- 3 tablespoons butter, melted
- 2½ teaspoons garlic powder
- 2 teaspoons salt
- 1 teaspoon freshly ground black pepper
- 1 teaspoon onion powder
- 1 teaspoon dried thyme
- 2 cups (16 ounces) raw almonds

Directions:

1. Preheat the smoker to 225°F with the hickory or mesquite wood.
2. Line a rimmed baking sheet with parchment paper (or aluminum foil), and grease the parchment with nonstick cooking spray.
3. In a medium bowl, stir together the butter, garlic powder, salt, pepper, onion powder, and thyme.
4. Add the almonds and stir until they are well coated. Arrange the nuts in a single layer on the prepared baking sheet. Place the sheet in the smoker and smoke for about 1 hour, turning once.

5. Remove from the smoker and let the nuts cool. Dry overnight and store in an airtight container away from heat, light, and moisture.

Glazed Spiced Pecans

Servings: 2
Cooking Time: 10 Minutes

Ingredients:

- Nonstick cooking spray
- ¼ cup firmly packed brown sugar
- 1 tablespoon butter, melted
- 1 tablespoon light corn syrup
- 1 teaspoon ground cinnamon
- 2 teaspoons salt
- 2 cups (16 ounces) pecan halves

Directions:

1. Preheat the smoker to 225°F with the apple, peach, or pear wood.
2. Line a rimmed baking sheet with parchment paper (or aluminum foil), and grease the parchment with nonstick cooking spray.
3. In a medium bowl, stir together the brown sugar, butter, corn syrup, cinnamon, and salt.
4. Add the nuts and stir until they are well coated. Arrange the nuts in a single layer on the prepared baking sheet. Place the sheet in the smoker and smoke for about 1 hour, turning once. Look for a glazed finish and roasted aroma.
5. When done, remove the nuts from the smoker and let them cool. Dry them overnight to enhance the flavor.
6. Store in an airtight container.

Smoked Cheesecake

Servings: 14 To 16
Cooking Time: 15 Minutes

Ingredients:

- FOR THE CRUST
- 2 cups crushed gingersnap cookies (or Oreo or graham cracker crumbs)
- 6 tablespoons butter, melted, plus more for the pan
- 3 tablespoons firmly packed brown sugar
- FOR THE FILLING

- 4 (8-ounce) packages cream cheese, at room temperature
- 4 eggs, beaten
- 1 cup sugar
- 1 teaspoon vanilla extract
- FOR THE TOPPINGS (OPTIONAL)
- Fresh berries
- Whipped cream
- Chocolate syrup
- Caramel sauce

Directions:

1. TO MAKE THE CRUST

2. In a food processor, pulse the cookie crumbs, butter, and brown sugar until combined.

3. Butter a springform pan and press the crumb mixture into the bottom and ½ inch up the sides.

4. TO MAKE THE FILLING

5. Preheat the smoker to 275°F with the apple, cherry, or peach wood.

6. In a large bowl, beat together the cream cheese, eggs, sugar, and vanilla until well blended. Pour the filling into the crust and place the pan inside the smoker. Fill a pan (any size that will fit on the rack next to the cheesecake) with 1 inch of water and place it in the smoker with the cheesecake. Smoke for 1½ to 2 hours until the cheesecake is firm.

7. Remove the cheesecake from the smoker, let it cool and then refrigerate it for 4 hours to set before serving with your toppings of choice.

Smoked Mac And Cheese

Servings: 8
Cooking Time: 25 Minutes

Ingredients:

- 4 tablespoons butter
- 3 tablespoons all-purpose flour
- 3 cups whole milk
- 2 cups shredded sharp Cheddar cheese, divided
- 2 cups shredded Monterey Jack cheese
- 1 cup grated Parmesan cheese, or Asiago or Roman
- 8 ounces cream cheese, cubed
- 2 teaspoons salt
- 1 teaspoon freshly ground black pepper

- 1 pound elbow macaroni, cooked according to package directions, drained
- Nonstick cooking spray

Directions:

1. Preheat the smoker to 225°F with the hickory or mesquite wood.

2. In a large saucepan over medium heat, melt the butter.

3. Whisk in the flour, continuing to whisk for about 1 minute until the flour is well incorporated.

4. Slowly whisk in the milk and bring to a boil. Reduce the heat to low and cook for 5 minutes until thickened. Remove from the heat.

5. Add 1½ cups of Cheddar, the Monterey Jack, Parmesan, and cream cheese. Stir the sauce until the cheeses melt.

6. Stir in the salt, pepper, and cooked macaroni.

7. Spray a half-size steam-table aluminum-foil roasting pan with nonstick cooking spray. Transfer the mac and cheese to the prepared pan and top with the remaining ½ cup of Cheddar cheese.

8. Place the pan in the smoker and smoke for about 1 hour until the cheese is bubbly.

Smoked Seasoned Duck

Servings: 4
Cooking Time: 25 Minutes

Ingredients:

- 1 (5-pound) whole duck
- ¾ cup soy sauce
- ¾ cup honey
- ¾ cup red table wine
- 2 tablespoons freshly ground black pepper
- 1½ tablespoons garlic powder

Directions:

1. Preheat the smoker to 225°F with the cherry or peach wood.

2. Pierce the skin of the duck with a fork (or tip of a pin) all over the surface of the duck, especially over the fatty areas to aid in rendering the fat out. Use caution NOT to pierce too deeply and hit the meat. This will help crisp the skin (tricky with lower temperatures).

3.   In a small bowl, stir together the soy sauce, honey, wine, pepper, and garlic powder. Season the duck inside the cavity and outside on the skin with the mixture. Reserve some liquid for basting later. Put the duck on the grates, breast-side down. Smoke for 2 hours.

4.   After the first 2 hours, baste the top of the duck twice, about every hour. The entire smoking time will take 3½ to 4 hours depending on the temperature of your smoker. Cook the duck until the internal breast temperature reaches 165°F.

5.   For crisp skin you'll need to enlist the help of high heat for the final 15 minutes. Move the duck to your grill, or even your oven, preheated to 500°F. Many electric smokers cannot achieve high temperatures.

Stuffed Cornish Game Hens

Servings: 2
Cooking Time: 30 Minutes

Ingredients:
- 2 Cornish game hens
- Salt
- Freshly ground black pepper
- 4 tablespoons butter, divided
- 1 cup quick-cooking seasoned brown rice
- 1 small onion, coarsely chopped
- ½ cup freshly squeezed orange juice
- ½ cup apricot jelly

Directions:
1.   Preheat the smoker to 275°F with the apple or olive wood.
2.   Season both birds with salt and pepper, including inside the cavities.
3.   In a small saucepan over low heat, melt 2 tablespoons of butter and stir in the rice and onion. Stuff the hens with the rice mixture and secure the legs with kitchen twine.
4.   Rinse out the saucepan and put it back over low heat. Melt the remaining 2 tablespoons of butter and stir in the orange juice and apricot jelly until smooth. Baste the hens with some of the jelly glaze.
5.   Place the birds in the smoker and smoke for 2 to 3 hours until the internal temperature reaches 170°F.
6.   Brush with the remaining jelly to serve.

Spicy Smoky Snack Mix

Servings: 12
Cooking Time: 10 Minutes

Ingredients:
- Nonstick cooking spray
- ½ cup (1 stick) butter, melted
- 2 tablespoons Worcestershire sauce
- 1 teaspoon onion powder
- 1 teaspoon garlic powder
- 2 cups oyster crackers
- 2 cups mini pretzels
- 2 cups (16 ounces) honey-roasted peanuts
- 2 cups garlic bagel chips, broken
- 2 cups sesame sticks
- 2 cups Cheez-It crackers

Directions:
1.   Preheat the smoker to 225°F with the hickory or mesquite wood.
2.   Line two rimmed baking sheets with parchment paper (or aluminum foil), and grease the parchment with nonstick cooking spray.
3.   In a small bowl, stir together the butter, Worcestershire sauce, onion powder, and garlic powder.
4.   In a large bowl, combine the oyster crackers, pretzels, peanuts, bagel chips, sesame sticks, and cheese crackers.
5.   Pour the butter mixture over the snack mix and stir until all is well coated. Spread the snack mix in a single layer on the prepared baking sheets and place them inside the smoker. Smoke for 2 to 2½ hours until dry.
6.   Store in an airtight container.

Smoked Venison Steaks

Servings: 8
Cooking Time: 10 Minutes

Ingredients:
- 1 cup canola oil
- 2 tablespoons dried oregano
- 1 tablespoon garlic powder
- 1 tablespoon dry minced onion
- 1 tablespoon sugar
- 1 tablespoon Lawry's seasoned salt

* 1 tablespoon dried basil
* 1 tablespoon dried parsley
* 1 teaspoon freshly ground black pepper
* ¼ teaspoon dried thyme
* ¼ teaspoon celery seed
* 8 venison steaks

Directions:

1. In a small bowl, whisk together the oil, oregano, garlic powder, onion, sugar, seasoned salt, basil, parsley, pepper, thyme, and celery seed. Place the steaks in a large shallow container and pour the marinade over the steaks. Cover and refrigerate for 4 to 8 hours.

2. Preheat the smoker to 225°F with the hickory wood.

3. Remove the steaks from the marinade and place them directly on the grill grate. Smoke for about 1 hour per pound (based on the weight of the individual steaks) until the internal temperature reaches 160°F.

Baba Ghanouj

Servings: 6 To 8
Cooking Time: 25 To 30 Minutes

Ingredients:

* 1 eggplant, halved lengthwise
* 1 tablespoon olive oil
* 2½ teaspoons salt, divided
* 2½ tablespoons tahini
* Juice of 1 lemon
* 1 garlic clove, minced
* 2 tablespoons chopped fresh parsley leaves
* Pita chips, for serving

Directions:

1. Preheat the smoker to 200°F with the maple wood.

2. Rub the eggplant halves with the olive oil and sprinkle with 2 teaspoons of salt. Place the halves on the smoker rack and smoke for 1 to 1½ hours.

3. Remove the eggplant from the smoker. Peel off and discard the skin.

4. Put the eggplant flesh into a food processor and add the tahini, lemon juice, garlic, and remaining ½ teaspoon of salt. Pulse until well blended. Transfer the mixture to a storage container.

5. Stir in the parsley and refrigerate until serving with pita chips.

Cajun Alligator Appetizer

Servings: 8 To 12
Cooking Time: 20 Minutes

Ingredients:

* FOR THE ALLIGATOR
* ½ gallon water
* ½ cup Worcestershire sauce
* ½ cup olive oil
* ½ cup white wine vinegar
* ¼ cup salt
* ¼ cup sugar
* 1 teaspoon red pepper flakes
* 2 pounds alligator meat
* 2 tablespoons Cajun seasoning
* FOR THE BUFFALO SAUCE
* ½ cup (1 stick) butter, melted
* ½ cup hot sauce
* 1 teaspoon garlic powder
* TO MAKE THE ALLIGATOR

Directions:

1. In a large bowl, stir together the water, Worcestershire sauce, olive oil, vinegar, salt, sugar, and red pepper flakes, stirring to dissolve the salt and sugar.

2. Place the alligator steaks into the brine, cover the bowl, and refrigerate overnight.

3. Preheat the smoker to 225°F with the mesquite wood.

4. Remove the meat from the marinade and pat it dry. Discard the marinade.

5. Spread the Cajun seasoning all over the alligator and place the pieces directly on the grill grate. Smoke for about 2 hours until the internal temperature reaches 165°F.

6. Remove the alligator from the smoker, cut it into chunks, and serve with the buffalo sauce for dipping.

7. TO MAKE THE BUFFALO SAUCE

8. While the meat smokes, in a small bowl, stir together the butter, hot sauce, and garlic powder. Set aside until serving.

Spicy Piggy Mac

Servings: 8 To 12
Cooking Time: 20 Minutes

Ingredients:

- 16 ounces elbow macaroni, cooked according to package directions
- 2 cups heavy whipping cream
- 8 ounces cream cheese, softened
- 1 teaspoon salt
- 1 teaspoon pepper
- 2 tablespoons Bisquick mix
- ½ cup panko bread crumbs
- 8 slices bacon, cooked and crumbled
- ½ cup coarsely chopped red onion
- 1 jalapeño pepper, seeded and finely chopped
- 2 cups Simple Smoked Pork Shoulder
- 1 cup Spicy Hickory-Smoked Barbecue Sauce
- 4 cups shredded sharp Cheddar cheese, divided

Directions:

1. Preheat smoker to 275°F and add hickory or mesquite woodchips.
2. Place the hot, cooked pasta in a shallow metal, nonstick baking pan.
3. Add in the whipping cream, cream cheese, salt, pepper, Bisquick mix, breadcrumbs, bacon, red onion, jalapeño, smoked pork shoulders, spicy sauce, and 2 cups of Cheddar, and stir until fully incorporated.
4. Top with the remaining Cheddar.
5. Place the pan in the preheated smoker and smoke for about 1 hour, until it's bubbly and the cheese is melted.

Barbecue Almonds And Cashews

Servings: 2
Cooking Time: 10 Minutes

Ingredients:

- Nonstick cooking spray
- 1 large egg white
- 1 tablespoon water
- 1 cup (8 ounces) raw almonds
- 1 cup (8 ounces) raw cashews
- ½ cup Bill's Best Barbecue Rub

Directions:

1. Preheat the smoker to 225°F with the hickory or pecan wood.
2. Line a rimmed baking sheet with parchment paper (or aluminum foil), and grease the parchment with nonstick cooking spray.
3. In a medium bowl, whisk the egg white and water.
4. Stir in the almonds and cashews until they are well coated. Arrange the nuts in a single layer on the prepared baking sheet.
5. Sprinkle with the rub.
6. Place the sheet in the smoker and smoke for about 1 hour, turning once.
7. Remove from the smoker and let the nuts cool. Dry overnight to enhance the smoke flavor.
8. Break up any clusters and store the nuts in an airtight container.

Smoked Peach Parfait

Servings: 8
Cooking Time: 20 Minutes

Ingredients:

- 4 barely ripe peaches, halved and pitted
- 1 tablespoon firmly packed brown sugar
- 1 pint vanilla ice cream
- 3 tablespoons honey

Directions:

1. Preheat the smoker to 200°F with the maple wood.
2. Sprinkle the cut peach halves with the brown sugar. Place them in the smoker, cut-side up. Also use a Frogmat to ease cleanup of sticky drippings. Smoke for 35 to 45 minutes.
3. Transfer the peach halves to dessert plates and top each with a scoop of vanilla ice cream.
4. Drizzle with the honey before serving.

Smoked Bologna

Servings: 18
Cooking Time: 20 Minutes

Ingredients:

- 2 tablespoons chili powder
- 2 tablespoons firmly packed brown sugar

- 1 teaspoon ground coriander
- 1 teaspoon ground nutmeg
- 1 teaspoon garlic powder
- 1 (5-pound) all-beef bologna chub
- ¼ cup prepared yellow mustard
- Salt
- Freshly ground black pepper

Directions:

1. Preheat the smoker to 250°F with the cherrywood.
2. In a small bowl, mix the chili powder, brown sugar, coriander, nutmeg, and garlic powder. Set aside.
3. Cut the bologna into ½-inch slices and make a few small cuts around the edges of the slices so they lie flat during the cooking process.
4. Coat both sides of each slice with the mustard and season with salt, pepper, and the spice mix. Place the slices on the smoker rack and smoke for 1 hour.

Big Fat Greek Fatty

Servings: 4
Cooking Time: 20 Minutes

Ingredients:

- FOR THE FATTY
- 1 pound ground lamb
- 1 pound ground beef
- 1 cup panko bread crumbs
- 6 garlic cloves, minced
- 2 eggs
- 2 tablespoons sesame seeds
- 2 tablespoons dried oregano
- 1 tablespoon Worcestershire sauce
- 1½ teaspoons salt
- 1 teaspoon freshly ground black pepper
- 1 cup halved cherry tomatoes, well drained, plus more for serving
- 1 medium red onion, thinly sliced
- 1 cucumber, seeded, dried and cut into julienne strips
- 1 tablespoon chopped fresh parsley leaves
- Pita points, for serving
- FOR THE TZATZIKI SAUCE
- 1 cucumber, seeded, dried and coarsely chopped
- Juice of 1 lemon
- 3 garlic cloves, minced
- 2 tablespoons chopped fresh dill

- 1 cup plain yogurt
- ½ teaspoon salt
- ¼ teaspoon freshly ground black pepper

Directions:

1. TO MAKE THE FATTY
2. Preheat the smoker to 225°F with the oak wood.
3. In a large bowl, mix the lamb, beef, bread crumbs, garlic, eggs, sesame seeds, oregano, Worcestershire sauce, salt, and pepper until well blended. On a rimmed baking sheet, roll or press the mixture out flat (about 8 to 10 inches square).
4. Starting on the left side and using half of each ingredient, create a row of cherry tomatoes, a row of red onion, and a row of cucumber. Repeat, leaving a clear space at the end.
5. From the left side, roll the fatty up tightly and place it in the smoker, seam-side down. Smoke for about 2 hours until the meat is cooked to an internal temperature of 145°F.
6. Sprinkle with the parsley. Slice and serve with pita-bread points, halved cherry tomatoes, and tzatziki sauce.
7. TO MAKE THE TZATZIKI SAUCE
8. While the fatty is smoking, in a medium bowl, stir together the cucumber, lemon juice, garlic, and dill until well blended.
9. Stir in the yogurt, salt, and pepper. Refrigerate until ready to serve.

Armadillo "eggs"

Servings: 6
Cooking Time: 35 To 40 Minutes

Ingredients:

- 8 ounces cream cheese, at room temperature
- 1 cup shredded Cheddar cheese
- 6 jalapeño peppers, cored and seeded
- 1 pound seasoned ground sausage

Directions:

1. Preheat the smoker to 225°F with the applewood.
2. In a medium bowl, stir together the cream cheese and Cheddar. Stuff the peppers with the cheese mixture.
3. Divide the sausage into six portions and wrap each jalapeño with one portion, covering the pepper completely. Place the "eggs" directly on the smoker grate. Smoke for about 2 hours until the sausage reaches an internal temperature of 165°F. Serve immediately.

Smoked Chorizo-stuffed Peppers

Servings: 8
Cooking Time: 10 Minutes

Ingredients:

- 3 cups shredded Cheddar cheese, divided
- 2 pounds ground chorizo sausage, casings removed (or ground hot sausage)
- 4 poblano peppers, halved lengthwise and seeded
- 8 bacon slices, uncooked

Directions:

1. Preheat the smoker to 225°F with the applewood.
2. In a large bowl, combine 2 cups of Cheddar with the sausage. Divide the mixture into eight portions and press one portion into each pepper half.
3. Sprinkle with the remaining 1 cup of Cheddar.
4. Wrap each pepper half with 1 bacon slice, tucking in the edges to secure. Place the peppers in the smoker and smoke for 2 hours, or until the sausage reaches an internal temperature of 165°F. Serve immediately.

Pineapple Pigtail

Servings: 6 To 8
Cooking Time: 45 Minutes

Ingredients:

- 2 tablespoons cayenne pepper
- 2 tablespoons ground cinnamon
- 1 tablespoon firmly packed brown sugar
- 1 whole pineapple
- 1 pound bacon slices
- ½ cup maple syrup

Directions:

1. Preheat the smoker to 250°F with the maple wood.
2. In a small bowl, stir together the cayenne, cinnamon, and brown sugar. Set aside.
3. Cut both ends off the pineapple and use a pineapple corer/slicer/peeler tool to core, slice, and peel the pineapple in one quick and easy step (see tip).
4. Tightly wrap the bacon slices around the pineapple spiral, completely covering the pineapple and overlapping the bacon to secure it, without severing the rings from each other. It should be one continuous bacon-wrapped corkscrew.

5. Baste the bacon with the maple syrup and sprinkle with the spice mixture. Place the pineapple on a Frogmats grill mat and put it in the smoker. Smoke for 1 to 1½ hours until the bacon is fully cooked.
6. Slice into rings to serve.

Cold-smoked Cheeses

Servings: 1
Cooking Time: 5 Minutes

Ingredients:

- 1 pound Cheddar, Gouda, mozzarella, provolone, Swiss, or Pepper Jack cheese, cut into 4-by-2-inch blocks, at room temperature to avoid condensation and sweating in the smoker

Directions:

1. Prepare the smoker for cold-smoking (under 90°F) with the applewood.
2. Blot the cheese completely dry with paper towels and place it in the coolest area of the smoker grate—typically away from the smoke source, near the wide-open ceiling vent. Allow steady smoke for 2 hours until the cheese displays a tint of smoke coloring.
3. Remove the cheese from the smoker and let it come to room temperature. Blot dry if necessary, wrap in parchment paper or wax paper, and refrigerate for 1 to 7 days for the smoke flavors to mellow.

Breakfast Fatty

Servings: 4 To 6
Cooking Time: 35 Minutes

Ingredients:

- FOR THE RUB
- ¼ cup firmly packed light-brown sugar
- 2 tablespoons paprika
- 1¼ teaspoons kosher salt
- 1 teaspoon cayenne pepper
- ½ teaspoon garlic powder
- ½ teaspoon onion powder
- ¼ teaspoon freshly ground black pepper
- FOR THE FATTY
- 5 large eggs, lightly beaten
- 1 small onion, chopped

- 1 small bell pepper (any color), chopped
- Salt
- Freshly ground black pepper
- 1 pound bacon slices, well chilled
- 1 pound ground hot sausage, well chilled
- 1 cup shredded Cheddar cheese

Directions:

1. TO MAKE THE RUB
2. In a small bowl, stir together the brown sugar, paprika, salt, cayenne, garlic powder, onion powder, and pepper. Set aside.
3. TO MAKE THE FATTY
4. Preheat the smoker to 275°F with the apple or hickory wood.
5. In a large skillet over medium-low heat, lightly scramble the eggs, incorporating the onion and bell pepper. Season with salt and pepper.
6. On a sheet of parchment paper (or plastic wrap), place 6 bacon slices side by side vertically and weave another 6 pieces through them horizontally in an over-under pattern.
7. Layer the sausage on top of the bacon, spreading it out to the edges.
8. Pour the scrambled-egg mixture evenly over the top of the sausage and top with the Cheddar.
9. Sprinkle a bit of the rub on top of the cheese, but reserve most for the outside of the fatty.
10. Roll the fatty up tightly and secure the ends with bacon. Spread the remaining rub all over the outside of the fatty. Place it into the smoker and smoke for 1½ to 2 hours until the internal temperature reaches 165°F. Look for a reddish crust and an impressive smoke ring.
11. Let the fatty rest for about 10 minutes before slicing and serving.

Porchetta Italian Pork Belly Roast

Servings: 4 To 6
Cooking Time: 30 Minutes

Ingredients:

- FOR THE RUB
- ¼ cup firmly packed brown sugar
- ¼ cup Cajun seasoning
- ¼ cup fennel seed
- ¼ cup dried oregano
- 2 tablespoons salt
- 2 tablespoons garlic powder
- 2 tablespoons dry minced onion
- 2 teaspoons freshly ground black pepper
- FOR THE BRINE
- 1 gallon water
- ½ cup firmly packed brown sugar
- ¼ cup salt
- ¼ cup Cajun seasoning
- 1 whole pork tenderloin
- 1 pork belly

Directions:

1. TO MAKE THE RUB
2. In a small bowl, stir together the brown sugar, Cajun seasoning, fennel seed, oregano, salt, garlic powder, onion, and pepper. Set aside.
3. TO MAKE THE BRINE
4. In a container large enough to hold the brine, tenderloin, and pork belly, stir together the water, brown sugar, salt, and Cajun seasoning, stirring to dissolve the sugar and salt. Submerge the tenderloin and the pork belly in the brine. Cover and refrigerate for a minimum of 6 hours.
5. Preheat the smoker to 225°F with the hickory wood.
6. Drain the meat and pat it dry with paper towels. Discard the liquid.
7. Season both pieces of meat well on all sides with the rub.
8. Wrap the pork belly around the pork tenderloin. With a sharp knife, score the outside with 2-inch slits. Secure the meat with kitchen twine. Add any remaining rub to the outside of the roast and place it on the smoker rack. Smoke the porchetta for 4 to 6 hours (depending on the weight) until the internal temperature reaches about 150°F.
9. Remove the porchetta from the heat and tent it with aluminum foil. Let it rest for 15 to 20 minutes before serving. The internal temperature needs to reach 160°F. This porchetta is great served alone or sliced for a sandwich.

Smoked Tomato-mozzarella Dip

Servings: 8 To 10
Cooking Time: 5 Minutes

Ingredients:

- 8 ounces smoked mozzarella cheese, shredded
- 8 ounces Colby cheese, shredded
- ½ cup grated Parmesan cheese
- 1 cup sour cream
- 1 cup sun-dried tomatoes
- 1½ teaspoons salt
- 1 teaspoon freshly ground black pepper
- 1 teaspoon dried basil
- 1 teaspoon dried oregano
- 1 teaspoon red pepper flakes
- 1 garlic clove, finely minced
- ½ teaspoon onion powder
- Crackers or toasted French bread slices, for serving

Directions:

1. Preheat the smoker to 275°F with the mesquite wood.
2. In a large bowl, stir together the mozzarella, Colby, Parmesan, sour cream, tomatoes, salt, pepper, basil, oregano, red pepper flakes, garlic, and onion powder. Transfer the mixture to a small metal or aluminum-foil pan. Place the pan in the smoker for 1 hour until hot and bubbly.
3. Serve hot with crackers or toasted French bread slices.

Rack Of Lamb

Servings: 7 Or 8
Cooking Time: 20 Minutes

Ingredients:

- FOR THE PASTE
- ½ cup olive oil
- ½ cup dry mustard
- ¼ cup hot chili powder
- 2 tablespoons freshly squeezed lemon juice
- 2 tablespoons dry minced onion
- 1 tablespoon smoked paprika
- 1 tablespoon dried thyme
- 1 tablespoon Worcestershire sauce
- 1 teaspoon salt
- 1 American rack of lamb (7 or 8 chops), membrane along the back of the rack removed
- FOR THE MINT SAUCE
- ¼ cup fresh mint leaves, chopped
- ¼ cup hot water
- 2 tablespoons apple cider vinegar
- 2 tablespoons firmly packed brown sugar
- ½ teaspoon salt
- ½ teaspoon freshly ground black pepper

Directions:

1. TO MAKE THE PASTE
2. In a small bowl, whisk together the olive oil, mustard, chili powder, lemon juice, onion, paprika, thyme, Worcestershire sauce, and salt. Set aside.
3. Preheat the smoker to 200°F with the apple, cherry, lilac, or oak wood.
4. Rub the paste all over the lamb and place it on the smoker rack. Smoke for 1¼ hours until it reaches an internal temperature of 145°F.
5. Remove the lamb from the heat and let it rest for a few minutes before serving with the mint sauce.
6. TO MAKE THE MINT SAUCE
7. While the lamb smokes, in a small bowl, stir together the mint, water, vinegar, brown sugar, salt, and pepper. Set aside until serving.

PORK RECIPES

Cola Spareribs

Servings: 6 To 8
Cooking Time: 30 Minutes

Ingredients:
- 2 racks pork spareribs (6 to 8 pounds)
- ¼ to ½ cup Basic Barbecue Rub (page 19)
- FOR THE SAUCE:
- 1 (12-ounce) can Coca-Cola
- 2 cups prepared ketchup
- 2 tablespoons apple cider vinegar
- ¼ cup light brown sugar
- 2 tablespoons Basic Barbecue Rub (page 19)
- 2 cloves garlic, finely minced

Directions:
1. Prepare the spareribs by removing the thin membrane on the back side (see page 56). Pat the ribs dry with a paper towel and then liberally apply barbecue rub all over, including the ends and side pieces. Place the ribs in a large zip-top plastic bag and refrigerate for at least an hour, or overnight.
2. Prepare the smoker's water pan according to the manufacturer's instructions and preheat the smoker to 225°F. While it heats, fill a medium bowl with water and add 3 or 4 handfuls of wood chips to soak.
3. Using tongs, place the ribs on the smoker racks with the meat side facing up. Add a small handful of the soaked wood chips to the chip loading area, and keep adding more chips at least every 30 minutes.
4. While the ribs are cooking, combine the sauce ingredients in a medium saucepan. Heat on the stovetop over medium heat until sugar has dissolved and then reduce heat and simmer for about 15 minutes, stirring occasionally. The sauce will thicken slightly as it cooks.
5. Smoke the ribs for 5 to 6 hours, basting them with the sauce several times during the last hour of cooking. The ribs are done when the bones start to show and the meat is tender but not falling off the bone. Let rest for 15 minutes under a foil tent, cut the ribs apart to serve, and serve with additional sauce on the side.

Smoked Candied Bacon

Servings: 4
Cooking Time: 10 Minutes

Ingredients:
- 12 slices thick-cut bacon
- ¾ cup packed light brown sugar
- 3 tablespoons maple syrup
- 2 teaspoons freshly ground black pepper

Directions:
1. Preheat the smoker to 275°F.
2. Arrange the bacon slices on a wire rack. Set on the middle rack of the smoker and smoke the bacon for 15 minutes. Flip the slices over and cook for 5 more minutes.
3. Meanwhile, in a small bowl, mix together the brown sugar, maple syrup, and pepper.
4. Take the bacon out of the smoker and brush both sides with the maple syrup mixture. Return the bacon to the smoker and smoke for another 15 minutes, or until the edges are crisp and the center is caramelized. For a deeper flavor, keep basting with the maple syrup mixture every 5 minutes.

Smoked Sichuan-honey Spareribs

Servings: 4
Cooking Time: 4 Hours

Ingredients:
- 2 tablespoons Chinese five-spice powder
- 6 pounds pork spareribs, membranes removed
- Flaked sea salt
- Freshly ground black pepper
- ½ cup rice wine
- Grated zest of 2 oranges, plus juice of 2 oranges
- 4 garlic cloves, finely chopped
- 3 tablespoons wildflower honey
- 3 tablespoons dark soy sauce
- 3 tablespoons hoisin sauce

- 3 tablespoons dark brown sugar

Directions:

1. Preheat the electric smoker to 250°F. Ensure the drip tray is clean and in place. Seal the door.

2. Place the wood chips in the smoking tray or firebox, get a good smoke rolling, and seal the door.

3. Rub the Chinese five-spice powder evenly over both sides of the ribs. Season them with salt and pepper. Arrange the ribs on smoking trays, flesh-side up, leaving space between them. Smoke for about 2 hours; the meat will begin to shrink from the bones.

4. In a medium bowl, whisk together the rice wine, orange zest, orange juice, garlic, honey, soy sauce, hoisin sauce, and brown sugar. Transfer to the middle of a large sheet of aluminum foil.

5. Place the ribs, flesh-side down, on the sauce mixture. Tightly wrap the foil to seal the ribs and return them to the smoker for about 2 hours more. The ribs are done when the meat has shrunk from the bones and the flesh is tender.

6. Remove the ribs from the smoker and let them rest for 20 minutes. Unwrap the foil, remove the ribs, cut them into individual ribs, and serve them with the sauce from the foil.

3-2-1 Smoked Ribs

Servings: 6
Cooking Time: 20 Minutes

Ingredients:

- 3 racks St. Louis-style pork ribs
- 1 to 2 cups Pork Rub
- 1 cup apple juice
- 3 cups Bacon-Flavored BBQ sauce (optional)

Directions:

1. Preheat the smoker to 225°F.

2. Remove and discard the membrane from the bone side of the ribs. Cover both sides of the ribs with the pork rub.

3. Smoke the ribs for 3 hours.

4. Take the ribs out and place them on a board. (Those ribs will be hot, so handle them with BBQ mitts.) Using a spray bottle, give them a squirt or two of the apple juice on both sides.

5. Tightly wrap each rack of ribs with the butcher paper.

6. Place the wrapped ribs in the smoker and smoke for 2 hours.

7. Then take them out and unwrap them. If desired, spread the sauce all over some (or all) of the ribs.

8. Return them to the smoker and smoke for 1 hour. If some of the ribs are sauced, place them below the unsauced ribs.

9. Carefully take the ribs out of the smoker and let them rest for 15 minutes before serving.

Applewood-smoked Baby Back Ribs

Servings: 4 To 6
Cooking Time: 4 Hours

Ingredients:

- FOR THE SPICE RUB
- 3 tablespoons cumin seeds, whole
- 3 tablespoons coriander seeds, whole
- 3 tablespoons fennel seeds, whole
- 1 tablespoon allspice berries, whole
- 3 tablespoons paprika
- 3 tablespoons chili powder
- 1 tablespoon garlic powder
- 1 tablespoon onion powder
- FOR THE BABY BACK RIBS
- 8 pounds baby back pork ribs, trimmed and membranes removed
- Flaked sea salt
- Freshly ground black pepper
- 2 cups packed dark brown sugar
- 2 cups dark molasses
- 2 cups wildflower honey
- 2 cups apple cider
- ½ cup bourbon (or brandy)

Directions:

1. TO MAKE THE SPICE RUB

2. Preheat a heavy-bottom pan over medium heat on the stovetop.

3. Combine the cumin, coriander, fennel, and allspice. Toast the spices for about 5 minutes, until they're

fragrant and smoky, gently tossing them to toast evenly. Let cool slightly. Grind the spices in a mortar with a pestle or in a clean spice or coffee grinder until smooth. Transfer to a small bowl.

4.   Stir in the paprika, chili powder, garlic powder, and onion powder. Store in an airtight container.

5.   TO MAKE THE BABY BACK RIBS

6.   Preheat the electric smoker to 250°F. Ensure the drip tray is clean and in place. Seal the door.

7.   Place the wood chips in the smoking tray or firebox, get a good smoke rolling, and seal the door.

8.   Rub the spice mixture evenly over both sides of the ribs. Season them with salt and pepper. Arrange the ribs on smoking trays, flesh-side up, leaving space between them. Smoke the ribs for about 2 hours; the meat will begin to shrink from the bones.

9.   On a large sheet of aluminum foil, prepare a bed of brown sugar drizzled with the molasses and honey.

10.   Place the ribs, flesh-side down, onto the sugar bed. Add the apple cider and bourbon. Tightly wrap the ribs in the foil and return them to the smoker. Smoke for about 2 hours more. Remove the ribs from the smoker and let rest for 20 minutes.

11.   Unwrap the foil, remove the ribs, and serve with the sauce that developed in the foil.

Stuffed Smoked Pork Tenderloin

Servings: 6
Cooking Time: 2-3 Hours

Ingredients:

*   2 pounds of 2 pork tenderloins, trimmed
*   ½ cup of prosciutto, thin slices
*   ¼ cup fresh bread crumbs
*   3 tablespoons fresh parsley, minced
*   1 teaspoon fresh rosemary, minced
*   2 cloves of garlic, minced
*   4 tablespoons extra virgin olive oil
*   Salt and black pepper to taste

Directions:

1.   Preheat the smoker to 225 degrees F for 40 minutes, by adding the cherry wood chip into the smoker box.

2.   Take a cutting board and place the two tenderloins on it.

3.   Place the prosciutto slices over one of the tenderloins, so it hangs from all the sides.

4.   In a separate bowl, combine the bread crumbs, rosemary, parsley, and garlic.

5.   Place it over the prosciutto.

6.   Lay tenderloin on top, and then ties it with kitchen string.

7.   Transfer the tenderloin on a rimmed foil-lined baking sheet.

8.   Place the tenderloin inside the smoker.

9.   Attach the digital thermometer for reading the temperate.

10.   Smoke until it reaches the internal temperature of 205 degrees F.

11.   Let the tenderloin rest 20 minutes before removing the string.

12.   Then slice and serve.

Smoked Memphis Ribs

Servings: 4
Cooking Time: 3 To 4 Hours

Ingredients:

*   6 tablespoons fine pink Himalayan salt
*   6 tablespoons dark brown sugar
*   2 tablespoons paprika
*   1 tablespoon garlic powder
*   1 tablespoon onion powder
*   1 tablespoon freshly ground black pepper
*   1 teaspoon dried thyme
*   1 teaspoon dried marjoram
*   1 teaspoon dried oregano
*   1 teaspoon ground cumin
*   1 teaspoon dried mustard
*   1 teaspoon ground fennel
*   ½ teaspoon ground cayenne pepper
*   2 (3-pound) racks St. Louis-cut pork spareribs, trimmed
*   1 cup apple cider
*   1 cup apple cider vinegar
*   ¼ cup molasses

Directions:

1.   In a medium bowl, whisk together the salt, sugar, paprika, garlic powder, onion powder, black pepper,

thyme, marjoram, oregano, cumin, mustard, fennel, and cayenne to combine. Rub half of the spice mix into the ribs on both sides. Tightly wrap the pork ribs with plastic wrap and refrigerate them for 24 hours.

2.   In a large bowl, stir together the remaining half of the spice mix, the apple cider, vinegar, and molasses. Set aside for basting.

3.   Preheat the electric smoker to 225°F. Ensure the drip tray is clean and in place. Seal the door.

4.   Place the wood chips in the smoking tray or firebox, get a good smoke rolling, and seal the door.

5.   Arrange the ribs on smoking trays, flesh-side up, leaving space between them. Smoke them for about 1 hour; the meat will begin to shrink from the bones. Baste both sides of the ribs using the cider mixture. Continue to smoke for 2 to 3 hours more, basting every 30 minutes with enough basting liquid to coat the ribs. The ribs are done when the meat has shrunk from the bones and the flesh is tender.

6.   Remove the ribs from the smoker, baste once more, loosely tent them with aluminum foil, and let them rest for 10 minutes before serving.

Honey And Maple Glazed Ham In An Electric Smoker

Servings: 4
Cooking Time: 3 Hours 40 Minutes

Ingredients:

- 4 pounds of boneless ham, spiral sliced
- Glaze:
- ⅓ cup of maple syrup
- ½ cup of spicy honey
- ½ cup dark brown sugar
- ¼ cup ground red pepper
- ¼ cup apple juice
- ¼ teaspoon minced ginger
- ¼ teaspoon cinnamon
- ¼ teaspoon allspice powder
- ¼ teaspoon garlic powder

Directions:

1.   First, preheat the electric smoker grill to 225 degrees F.

2.   Take a small cooking pot and heat it over medium flame.

3.   Now add all the ingredients of glaze to the cooking pot and let it cook for about 5 minutes.

4.   Once the sugar dissolves, the glaze is ready.

5.   Now place the ham in a casserole dish, cut side down.

6.   Drizzle half of the glaze over the ham and brush it for even coating.

7.   Cover the ham with aluminum foil tightly.

8.   Place the casserole dish on a middle rack of electric smoker and cook it for 3½ hours.

9.   Afterward, remove the ham from the electric smoker.

10.   After removing the aluminum foil, drain off the juices.

11.   At this stage, apply the reserved glaze over the ham.

12.   Replace wood chips with new fresh ones.

13.   When smoke gets heavy, put the ham back in the smoker uncovered.

14.   Let it cook for 10 more minutes.

15.   Remove the ham from the electric smoker; let it sit for 20 minutes.

16.   Then, slice and serve.

Smoked Pork Shoulders

Servings: 6
Cooking Time: 12 Hours

Ingredients:

- 6 pounds pork shoulder, Boston butt
- ½ cup molasses
- 10 ounces pickling salt
- 6-8 cups of water
- 2 teaspoons ground cumin
- 1 teaspoon ground fennel
- 1 teaspoon coriander
- 2 tablespoons chili powder
- 2 tablespoons onion powder
- ½ tablespoon paprika

Directions:

1.   Combine molasses, pickling salt, and water in a large bowl to make brine.

2. Put the pork into the brine for about 8 hours before starting the cooking process.

3. Pat dry the meat.

4. Apply all the rub ingredients evenly all over the pork.

5. Now start the cooking process by adding the wood chips to the smoker.

6. Place the meat on the sheet pan and transfer to the top most rack of the smoker.

7. Next, insert the probe thermometer for heat measurements inside the meat.

8. Close the electric smoker door and then cook for12 hours at 225 degrees F.

9. Once the internal temperature reaches 190 degrees F, the meat is done.

10. Let the pork rest for 20 to 30 minutes before serving.

Smoked Pork Belly Ends

Servings: 6
Cooking Time: 30 Minutes

Ingredients:
- 1 cup Pork Rub
- 1 tablespoon cayenne pepper
- 8 tablespoons light brown sugar, divided
- 2 pounds pork belly, skin removed
- 4 tablespoons (1 stick) unsalted butter, cut into pats
- 1 cup Bacon-Flavored BBQ Sauce

Directions:
1. Preheat the smoker to 275°F.

2. In a small bowl, mix together the pork rub, cayenne, and 2 tablespoons brown sugar. Cut the pork belly into 1 ½-inch squares and generously sprinkle the seasoning all over them. Arrange them on a wire rack.

3. Smoke the pork belly squares for 2 hours.

4. Remove the pork belly squares and put them on a sheet pan. Sprinkle with the remaining 6 tablespoons brown sugar and dot with the butter.

5. Return to the smoker and smoke for 1 hour.

6. Take the pan out of the smoker, add the BBQ sauce to the pork belly, and stir it all together. Return the pan to the smoker and cook for 15 more minutes.

7. Let the pork belly rest for 5 to 10 minutes before serving.

Pork Italian Sausage Fatty

Servings: 4
Cooking Time: 30 Minutes

Ingredients:
- 12 bacon slices
- 1 pound Italian pork sausage, well chilled
- ¼ cup marinara sauce, divided
- 1 cup pepperoni slices
- 4 slices capicola, well chilled
- 4 slices genoa salami, well chilled
- 4 slices ham, well chilled
- 1 bell pepper (any color), sliced
- 1 small onion, sliced
- ½ cup marinated banana peppers, or spicy giardiniera peppers
- ¼ cup Italian dressing

Directions:
1. Preheat the smoker to 225°F with the oak wood.

2. On a sheet of plastic wrap, place 6 bacon slices side by side vertically and weave another 6 pieces through them horizontally in an over-under pattern.

3. On another sheet of plastic wrap, spread the sausage to create a circle 10 to 12 inches in diameter.

4. Spread 2 tablespoons of marinara over the sausage round like a pizza, leaving a 1-inch border all the way around.

5. Layer on the pepperoni, capicola, salami, ham, bell pepper, onion, and banana peppers like a pizza, again leaving that 1-inch border.

6. Top with the remaining 2 tablespoons of marinara and sprinkle the Italian dressing over the top.

7. Carefully lift the edges of the sausage round and bring them together. Pinch and press the sausage together to seal the seam and create a stuffed tube. Using the plastic wrap as a support, roll the raw sausage fatty onto the center of the bacon weave. Discard the layer of plastic wrap that was under the sausage.

8. Use the plastic wrap under the bacon to roll and seal the bacon edges around all sides of the sausage roll. Secure with toothpicks and use the plastic wrap to transport it to the smoker grate. Gently roll the fatty so its seam is on the bottom. Smoke for up to 2 hours or until the internal temperature hits 160°F.

Smoked Pork Crown Roast With Pan Gravy

Servings: 12
Cooking Time: 8 Hours

Ingredients:

- 8 pounds crown roast of pork
- Salt and pepper, to taste
- 10 garlic cloves, minced
- 4 tablespoons honey Dijon mustard
- 2 tablespoons apple cider vinegar
- 2 tablespoons dark brown sugar
- A handful of fresh sage
- 1 cup butter
- 6 cloves garlic, minced
- ¼ cup flour
- ½ cup white wine
- ⅓ cup of chicken broth
- 3 tablespoons fresh parsley, minced
- Salt and black pepper

Directions:

1. Grind the trimmings of the meat crown.
2. Preheat the electric smoker to 225 degrees F for about 30 minutes.
3. Place the rack in the lowest position.
4. Fill the water pan for the wood chips.
5. Season the pork with salt and pepper.
6. Rest it for one hour at room temperature.
7. When the electric smoker is heated, start with the cooking process.
8. In a bowl, combine minced garlic, Dijon honey mustard, apple cider vinegar, and sugar.
9. Brush the mixture well over the pork.
10. Adjust the digital thermometer inside any meat part.
11. Place the crown pork roast in the electric smoker.
12. Cook it until the temperate reading is 180-200 degrees F.
13. Remove the pork from smoker and preheat the gas grill.
14. Finish it over the grill flames for a more texture outer layer.
15. Meanwhile, prepare the gravy by heating butter in a large skillet over medium heat.
16. Add the dripping from the pan inside the smoker.
17. Add the broth and bring mixture to boil.
18. Afterward, reduce heat and let it simmer.
19. Add salt, pepper, garlic, flour, white wine, and parsley.
20. Place the crown roast on a serving plate and drizzle pan gravy on top.
21. You can serve the gravy individually as well.
22. Serve with a garnish of fresh sage.

Sweet & Tangy Baby Back Ribs

Servings: 6 To 8
Cooking Time: 20 Minutes

Ingredients:

- 14 to 16 pounds baby back pork ribs (about 4 racks)
- 1 cup Basic Barbecue Rub (page 19)
- 1 cup Tangy Smoked Barbecue Sauce (page 17), or sauce of your choice

Directions:

1. Prepare the ribs by removing the thin membrane from the back side (see page 56). Pat the ribs dry with a paper towel and liberally apply the Basic Barbecue Rub all over, including the ends and side pieces. Place the ribs in a large zip-top plastic bags and refrigerate for at least an hour, or preferably overnight.
2. Prepare the smoker's water pan according to the manufacturer's instructions and preheat the smoker to 225°F. While it heats, fill a medium bowl with water and add 3 or 4 handfuls of pecan wood chips to soak.
3. Use tongs to remove the ribs from their bag and place them directly on the smoker racks, meat side facing up. Add a small handful of the soaked pecan chips to the chip loading area, and keep adding more chips at least every 30 minutes. Smoke the ribs for 4 to 5 hours, until the bones start to show and the meat is tender but not falling off the bone.
4. For a crispy rib, finish the ribs on the grill. Preheat the grill while the ribs finish smoking, then grill over medium heat for just 3 to 4 minutes per side, basting with the barbecue sauce or your own choice of sauce.
5. Let rest for 15 minutes under a foil tent, cut ribs apart to serve, and serve with additional barbecue sauce.

Holiday Ham

Servings: 10 To 12

Cooking Time: 35 Minutes

Ingredients:

- 2 tablespoons prepared yellow mustard
- 2 teaspoons hot sauce
- 1 (5- to 7-pound) precooked bone-in half ham, scored with a sharp knife in straight and parallel lines, making a square pattern
- ½ cup Bill's Best Barbecue Rub, divided
- 1 (14.5-ounce) can sliced pineapple
- 1 small jar maraschino cherries
- Pineapple–Brown Sugar Sauce

Directions:

1. Preheat the smoker to 275°F with the cherry or hickory wood.
2. In a small bowl, stir together the mustard and hot sauce, and spread this on the ham.
3. Generously coat the ham with about 6 tablespoons of the rub.
4. Decorate the ham with pineapple slices and place maraschino cherries in the middle of each slice, secured with toothpicks.
5. Sprinkle the remaining 2 tablespoons of the rub on top of the fruit.
6. Put the ham in the smoker and cook it for about 2 hours.
7. Cover the ham loosely in aluminum foil and continue to smoke for 3 hours more, until the internal temperature reaches 160°F.
8. During the final half-hour of cook time, generously slather the ham with the sauce every 10 minutes, and again just before taking it off the heat.
9. Let the ham rest for 15 to 20 minutes before carving.
10. Serve alongside Smoked Onion Bombs, if desired.

Jamaican-style Jerked Pork

Servings: 6

Cooking Time: 9 Hours

Ingredients:

- 1 (4- to 6-pound) boneless pork shoulder, butterflied (see Tip)
- 6 tablespoons olive oil
- 1 tablespoon chopped Scotch bonnet pepper
- 1 tablespoon granulated garlic
- 2 tablespoons onion powder
- 2 tablespoons light brown sugar
- 1 tablespoon dried parsley
- 2 teaspoons salt
- 2 teaspoons cayenne pepper
- 2 teaspoons smoked paprika
- 1 teaspoon ground allspice
- 1 teaspoon dried thyme
- 1 teaspoon freshly ground black pepper
- ½ teaspoon ground cumin
- ½ teaspoon ground nutmeg

Directions:

1. Score the pork shoulder's fat layer and the meat with a sharp knife, then brush it all over with the olive oil.
2. With a sharp knife, poke holes about ½ inch deep all over the pork.
3. In a small bowl, mix together the Scotch bonnet, granulated garlic, onion powder, brown sugar, parsley, salt, cayenne, smoked paprika, allspice, thyme, black pepper, cumin, and nutmeg. Rub the seasoning into the pork. Then cover it in plastic wrap. Refrigerate for 8 hours. Then, let the pork sit at room temperature for 1 hour before smoking.
4. Preheat the smoker to 225°F.
5. Smoke the pork for 3 hours, or until the internal temperature reaches 145°F.
6. Wrap it in aluminum foil and smoke it for 1 hour longer.
7. Unwrap it and cook for 1 more hour.
8. Let it rest for 30 minutes before serving it to your hungry friends.

Smoked Pork Shoulder Sandwiches With Apple-onion Chutney

Servings: 8

Cooking Time: 10 Hours

Ingredients:

- FOR THE SPICE RUB
- 3 tablespoons paprika
- 3 tablespoons chili powder
- 3 tablespoons ground chipotle pepper
- 3 tablespoons ground ancho chile pepper
- 1 tablespoon garlic powder
- 1 tablespoon onion powder
- FOR THE PORK SHOULDER AND APPLE-ONION CHUTNEY
- 1 (8- to 10-pound) bone-in pork shoulder, trimmed
- Flaked sea salt
- Freshly ground black pepper
- 1 tablespoon unsalted butter
- 1 tablespoon canola oil
- 8 shallots, thinly sliced
- 4 Golden Delicious apples, cored, peeled, and cut into 8 wedges
- 4 thyme sprigs, leaves stripped and finely chopped
- 2 cups apple cider
- 2 cups hard cider
- Pretzel buns, for serving
- Whole-grain mustard, for serving

Directions:

1. TO MAKE THE SPICE RUB
2. In a small bowl, stir together the paprika, chili powder, chipotle pepper, ancho chile pepper, garlic powder, and onion powder until blended.
3. TO MAKE THE PORK SHOULDER AND APPLE-ONION CHUTNEY
4. Preheat the electric smoker to 250°F. Ensure the drip tray is clean and in place. Seal the door.
5. Preheat a large cast iron pan on a smoking rack.
6. Evenly rub the spice mixture over all sides of the pork shoulder. Season it with salt and pepper. Place the pork in a shallow pan on a smoking rack (the pan will collect the cooking liquid). Insert a probe thermometer (if available) into the thickest part of the meat, not touching the bone. Set the target temperature for 190°F. Smoke for about 4 hours; the meat will begin to shrink from the bones.
7. In the preheated cast iron pan, combine the butter, canola oil, shallots, apples, and thyme. Season with salt and pepper.
8. Remove the pan with the pork shoulder from the smoker, then remove the pork from the pan. Collect the cooking liquid from the pan and strain it through a fine-mesh sieve set over a bowl. Using an injection needle, inject the shoulder with the liquid. Space your injections evenly around the shoulder. Place the shoulder back in the smoker on a rack. Give the apples and shallots a quick toss. Smoke for 4 to 6 hours, tossing the chutney occasionally.
9. When the apples and shallots are tender, stir in the apple cider and hard cider to deglaze the pan, scraping up any browned bits from the bottom. Continue to cook the apples and shallots until your desired consistency is reached. Remove and set aside.
10. Once the internal temperature of the pork reaches 190°F, remove the pork and loosely tent it with aluminum foil. Let it rest for 1 hour. Using two forks, shred the pork.
11. Build your sandwich by layering the buns with pork, topped with apple-onion chutney and mustard.

Smoked Pork Loin

Servings: 4

Cooking Time: 20 Minutes

Ingredients:

- 5 pounds pork loin
- ¼ cup olive oil
- ½ cup Pork Rub
- 1 tablespoon light brown sugar

Directions:

1. Preheat the smoker to 275°F.
2. With a sharp knife, crisscross the layer of fat on the pork loin. Then brush the pork with the olive oil.
3. In a small bowl, mix the pork rub and brown sugar together. Rub it all over and into the pork loin.

4. Smoke the pork for 2 hours 30 minutes, or until the internal temperature reaches 145°F. Do not overcook it!

5. Remove the pork from the smoker and let rest for at least 15 minutes. Serve warm.

Smoked Pork Chops

Servings: 4
Cooking Time: 10 Minutes

Ingredients:

- ½ cup Pork Rub
- 1 tablespoon light brown sugar
- 8 boneless center-cut pork loin chops (at least 1 inch thick)
- 2 tablespoons olive oil
- 1 tablespoon apple cider vinegar
- 1 cup apple juice

Directions:

1. Preheat the smoker to 225°F.

2. In a small bowl, mix the pork rub with the brown sugar. Brush the pork chops with the olive oil and season them on both sides with the pork rub mixture.

3. Mix the apple juice with the tablespoon of apple cider vinegar in a spray bottle. Place the chops in the smoker and cook them for 1 hour and 15 minutes. Every 30 minutes or so, spritz them with the apple juice mixture. When their internal temperature reaches 145°F, the chops are ready to come out.

Cherry-spiced Maple Glazed Ham

Servings: 3
Cooking Time: 2-3 Hours

Ingredients:

- 1 cup cherry preserves
- ⅓ cup light brown sugar, packed
- ⅓ cup maple syrup
- ½ cup water
- 1-ounce honey whiskey
- 2 tablespoons Dijon mustard
- 1 teaspoon cinnamon
- Cayenne pepper, to taste
- 1 teaspoon ground cloves
- ½ teaspoon garlic powder
- 2 tablespoons butter
- Other Ingredients:
- 2 pounds of spiral cut ham
- Kosher salt and black pepper, to taste
- 2 tablespoons of canola oil
- 4-6 ounces of cherry juice

Directions:

1. Combine all the glaze ingredients in a pot, and let it cook for a few minutes until sugar dissolved.

2. Then set aside for further use.

3. You can puree it in a blender after cooling, for a fine consistency.

4. Add more water if the consistency is too thick.

5. Preheat the smoker for 20 minutes at 225 degrees F.

6. Combine cherry juice and 1 tablespoon oil in a separate bowl, which will be used further for basting.

7. Drizzle one tablespoon of the reserved oil over the ham and rub well.

8. Season the meat with salt and pepper.

9. Cook inside the electric smoker for 2-3 hours.

10. Keep basting the ham after every 30 minutes with prepared basting mixture.

11. When the internal temperature reaches 205 degrees F, the ham is ready.

12. Let it sit at room temperature for 30 minutes before serving.

13. Brush a final layer of basting mixture, and then serve with prepared sauce as a side serving.

14. Enjoy.

Beer Pork Steak

Servings: 4
Cooking Time: 2 Hours

Ingredients:

- 4 pork shoulder steaks
- 1 cup of BBQ sauce
- 1 can of beer of your choice
- Oil spray, for greasing
- 6 tablespoons paprika
- Salt, to taste
- Black pepper, to taste
- 4 tablespoons brown sugar

- 3 tablespoons garlic powder
- 2 tablespoons onion powder

Directions:

1. Preheat the electric smoker to 225 degrees F for 30 minutes by adding apple wood chips.
2. To start cooking, first, combine all the rub ingredients in a bowl to prepare a rub.
3. Rub the steaks with the prepared rub well and then marinate for 30 minutes in the refrigerator.
4. Combine the beer and BBQ sauce in a small bowl.
5. Brush the steak with BBQ sauce mix and place inside the smoker for cooking for about 45 minutes.
6. After 10 minutes of cooking, brush with more BBQ sauce mixture to the pork steak to keep it moist.
7. Cook for additional 45 minutes at 325 degrees F.
8. Once the internal temperature reaches 185 degrees F, the steak is ready to be served.
9. Take the steak out of the electric smoker and then serve with more BBQ sauce if liked.

Crispy Pork Belly With Caramelized Cipollini Onions

Servings: 8
Cooking Time: 4 Hours

Ingredients:

- 2 tablespoons extra-virgin olive oil
- 2 tablespoons unsalted butter
- 24 cipollini onions
- 4 pounds pork belly, trimmed
- 3 tablespoons fennel seeds, whole
- 4 thyme sprigs, leaves stripped and finely chopped
- Flaked sea salt
- Freshly ground black pepper
- 3 fresh bay leaves
- 1 cup white wine

Directions:

1. Preheat the electric smoker to 225°F. Ensure the drip tray is clean and in place. Seal the door.
2. Place the wood chips in the smoking tray or firebox, get a good smoke rolling, and seal the door.
3. Place a large cast iron skillet on a smoking rack to preheat, then pour in the olive oil and add the butter to melt.
4. Prepare an ice bath by putting 4 cups of ice in a large mixing bowl and filling it three-quarters full with cold water.
5. Bring a large pot of water to a boil over high heat. Place the onions in the pot and blanch them for 15 seconds. Using a slotted spoon, transfer the onions to the ice bath to cool. Drain, trim, and peel the onions. Set them aside.
6. Using a paring knife, score the skin on the pork belly, making parallel cuts through the skin but not into the flesh. Turn the pork 45 degrees and cut parallel scores in the opposite direction.
7. Vigorously rub the fennel seeds and thyme into the pork skin and between the cuts. Season all sides of the pork belly with salt and pepper. Place the pork on the smoking rack, skin-side up. Insert a probe thermometer (if available) into the thickest part of the meat, not touching the bone. Set the target temperature for 165°F.
8. Add the onions and bay leaves to the preheated skillet, tossing them to lightly coat them with the oil and butter. Season with salt and pepper. Smoke the onions for 20 to 25 minutes until tender.
9. Gently stir in the white wine to deglaze the skillet, scraping up any browned bits from the bottom. Continue to smoke the sauce for another 15 minutes. Remove it from the smoker and set aside.
10. Continue to smoke the pork belly until the internal temperature reaches 165°F and the meat is tender and pulls apart easily.
11. Transfer the pork to a work surface. Loosely tent it with aluminum foil and let it rest for 20 minutes.
12. Gently slice the pork belly into portions and serve with the sauce and the onions.

Cuban Mojo-marinated Pork

Servings: 8 To 10
Cooking Time: 20 Minutes

Ingredients:

- FOR THE MOJO SAUCE
- 1 cup freshly squeezed orange juice

- ½ cup freshly squeezed lime juice
- ¼ cup olive oil
- ¼ cup finely minced garlic
- 1 tablespoon salt
- 1 tablespoon Mexican adobo seasoning
- FOR THE CUBAN RUB
- ¼ cup Cuban seasoning (I use McCormick)
- 1 tablespoon onion powder
- 1 tablespoon garlic powder
- Zest of 1 orange, divided
- FOR THE PORK
- 1 (6- to 8-pound) bone-in Boston butt
- ¼ cup honey
- 1 avocado, sliced, for serving
- 1 red onion, thinly sliced, for serving

Directions:

1. TO MAKE THE MOJO SAUCE
2. In a small bowl, stir together the orange juice, lime juice, olive oil, garlic, salt, and adobo seasoning. Set aside.
3. TO MAKE THE CUBAN RUB
4. In a small bowl, mix the Cuban seasoning, onion powder, garlic powder, and half of the orange zest. Set aside.
5. TO MAKE THE PORK
6. Rub the butt with the Cuban rub.
7. With a meat injection syringe, inject the mojo sauce throughout the meat, except on the bottom. Place the meat on a pan and wrap tightly with plastic wrap. Refrigerate overnight.
8. Preheat the smoker to 225°F with the applewood.
9. Remove the meat from the refrigerator and let it come to room temperature. Remove and discard the plastic wrap. Place the meat in the smoker and smoke for 12 to 14 hours until the internal temperature reaches 200°F. Remove from the heat.
10. Drizzle the butt with the honey and the remaining orange zest. Wrap the butt tightly in aluminum foil and place in a cooler to keep warm and rest for about 40 minutes.
11. Cut into chunks and serve with the avocado and red onion slices.

Pork Tenderloin Recipe

Servings: 5
Cooking Time: 2-3 Hours

Ingredients:

- 2 cups ketchup
- ½ cup dark brown sugar
- 4 tablespoons apple cider vinegar
- 2 tablespoons Worcestershire sauce
- 2 teaspoons BBQ sauce
- Salt, to taste
- Ground black pepper, to taste
- ½ teaspoon garlic powder
- ½ teaspoon of chopped onion
- 2 tablespoons apple juice
- Kosher salt, to taste
- 2 teaspoons garlic pepper seasoning
- Meat and Rolls:
- 2 pork tenderloins (4 pounds), remove the silver skin
- Butter substitute spray
- 16 sweet Hawaiian rolls

Directions:

1. Preheat the electric smoker to 225 degrees F.
2. Take a saucepan and heat all the sauce ingredients in it for about 6 minutes.
3. Once it's done, let it cool aside for further use.
4. Now in a separate bowl, mix together the dry rub ingredients.
5. Take tenderloins and fold the thin edges under the tenderloins and tie it with a string.
6. Season the tenderloins with the rub.
7. Grease the tenderloins with the butter spray.
8. Add wood chips to the side tray of the electric smoker. Place the pork tenderloins on the middle rack.
9. Cook until the thermometer read 205 degrees F of internal temperature.
10. Remove the pork from the grill and allow resting for 5 minutes.
11. Slice the tenderloin, and place between toasted buns or rolls.
12. Drizzle with prepared sauce and serve.

Smoked Pork Pinwheels

Servings: 15

Cooking Time: 20 Minutes

Ingredients:

- 8 ounces cream cheese, at room temperature
- 2 tablespoons chopped fresh chives
- 1 tablespoon garlic powder
- 2 pounds pork tenderloin, butterflied to lay flat, pounded to ¾ inch thick, and cut into (about 15) long, 1-inch-wide strips
- 2 teaspoons salt
- 2 teaspoons freshly ground black pepper

Directions:

1. Preheat the smoker to 275°F with the hickory wood.
2. In a small bowl, stir together the cream cheese, chives, and garlic powder.
3. Spread each pork strip with a thin amount of the cream-cheese mixture. Roll the strips into pinwheels and secure with toothpicks or kitchen twine.
4. Sprinkle the pinwheels with the salt and pepper and transfer them to a grill pan with a closed bottom. Smoke for about 45 minutes until the internal temperature hits 160°F.

Delicious Smoked Pork

Servings: 4-6

Cooking Time: 4 Hours

Ingredients:

- 4 pounds pork shoulder
- Kosher salt, to taste
- 2 tablespoons smoked paprika
- 3 tablespoons lemon Pepper
- 2 tablespoons cayenne pepper
- 1 tablespoon garlic powder
- 1 tablespoon black pepper
- ½ cup of yellow mustard
- 4 tablespoons of Worcestershire sauce
- ⅓ cup of apple cider vinegar
- 1 cup apple juice
- ½ cup water

Directions:

1. First, wash the pork shoulder under hot water, then pat dry.
2. In a bowl, combine salt, paprika, lemon pepper, cayenne pepper, garlic powder, and black pepper.
3. Put the pork shoulder on a large cookie sheet.
4. Spread the Worcestershire sauce all over the pork and then rub mustard over the shoulder gently.
5. Rub the bowl, spice mixture over the pork and then wrap the shoulder with a plastic wrap.
6. Marinate it for 12 hours in a refrigerator.
7. After 12 hours have passed, remove the pork shoulder from the fridge and let come to room temperature.
8. Bring the smoker to 220 degrees F.
9. Combine apple cider vinegar, water and apple juice in a spray bottle
10. Soak smoking chips in water in a bucket by the smoker.
11. Place the handful of smoking chips into the smoking basket and place the marinated pork shoulder inside the smoker.
12. Spray it with bottle liquid every 45-60 minutes.
13. Add additional wood chips when needed.
14. Cook for about 4 hours.
15. Let it sit for one hour before serving.
16. Enjoy.

Hickory-smoked Pork Loin

Servings: 3 Or 4

Cooking Time: 15 Minutes

Ingredients:

- ½ quart apple juice
- ½ quart apple cider vinegar
- ½ cup sugar
- ¼ cup salt
- 2 tablespoons freshly ground black pepper
- 2 teaspoons hickory liquid smoke
- 1 (4-pound) pork loin roast
- ½ cup Greek seasoning (Cavender's Greek seasoning is good)

Directions:

1. In a container large enough to hold the brine and pork, make the brine by combining the apple juice,

vinegar, sugar, salt, pepper, and liquid smoke. Stir to dissolve the salt and sugar.

2.   Add the loin and enough water to submerge it. Cover and refrigerate overnight.

3.   Remove the loin and discard the brine. Do not rinse the meat.

4.   Preheat the smoker to 250°F with the hickory wood.

5.   Generously coat the meat with the Greek seasoning and place it in the smoker. Smoke for about 3 hours until the internal temperature reaches 160°F.

Smoked Italian Sausage

Servings: 6 To 8
Cooking Time: 5 Minutes

Ingredients:

- 2 pounds (8 to 12 links) Italian sausage, in casings
- 8 to 12 hot dog buns
- Condiments of choice

Directions:

1.   Preheat the smoker to 250°F with the hickory wood.

2.   Place the fresh sausages in their casings on a grill rack. Smoke for 3 to 4 hours until the internal temperature reaches 165°F.

3.   Wrap the buns tightly in aluminum foil and stick them in the smoker for the final 10 to 15 minutes of cook time.

4.   Serve the sausages with the heated buns and desired condiments.

Smoked Spicy Baby Back Ribs

Servings: 8
Cooking Time: 8 Hours

Ingredients:

- 8 pounds baby back ribs
- 1 cup Pork Rub, divided
- 1 teaspoon coarse salt
- 1 teaspoon ground cumin
- 1 teaspoon chipotle powder
- 2 teaspoons cayenne pepper
- 1 tablespoon red pepper flakes
- 1 cup apple cider
- ½ cup apple cider vinegar

Directions:

1.   Remove the membrane from the bone side of the ribs with a small, sharp knife.

2.   In a bowl, mix together ¾ cup pork rub, the salt, cumin, chipotle, cayenne, and red pepper flakes. Rub the pork rub mixture all over the ribs. Wrap them tightly in plastic wrap and refrigerate for 8 hours.

3.   Preheat the smoker to 250°F.

4.   In a bowl, mix together the apple cider, vinegar, and the remaining ¼ cup pork rub.

5.   Place the ribs in the smoker bone-side down. Smoke for 2 hours, basting them with the vinegar mixture every 30 minutes, until the internal temperature reaches 145°F.

6.   Let the ribs rest for at least 10 minutes before serving.

Smoked Pork With Veggies

Servings: 4
Cooking Time: 20 Minutes

Ingredients:

- 1 pound Brussels sprouts, halved
- 6 slices bacon
- 1 teaspoon coarse salt
- 1 teaspoon freshly ground black pepper
- 1 tablespoon minced fresh or granulated garlic
- 1 (3-pound) pork tenderloin, cut into 8 slices
- ¼ cup olive oil
- 2 tablespoons Pork Rub
- ½ cup Bacon-Flavored BBQ Sauce
- 2 tablespoons apple cider vinegar
- ½ cup maple syrup

Directions:

1.   Preheat the smoker to 275°F.

2.   Place the halved Brussels sprouts on a sheet pan.

3.   In a skillet on the stovetop over medium heat fry the bacon until half cooked. Take it out of the pan and cut it into pieces. Add the bacon with the pan drippings to the Brussels sprouts. Sprinkle with the salt, pepper, and garlic and toss to mix.

4.   Pat the pork slices dry with some paper towels. Brush them with the olive oil and rub them with the pork rub.

5.   Place the pork slices in the smoker with the pan of Brussels sprouts underneath. Smoke for 45 minutes.

6.   Brush the pork with the BBQ sauce. Add the vinegar and maple syrup to the pan of Brussels sprouts and mix them together.

7.   Smoke for another 45 minutes, or until the internal temperature of the pork reaches 145°F.

8.   Let the pork rest for 10 minutes. Then cut the pork into 1 ½-inch pieces and mix it up with the Brussels sprouts. Serve immediately.

Applewood-smoked Pork Jowl

Servings: 4
Cooking Time: 3 Hours

Ingredients:

- 2 pork jowls, excess fat removed
- 2 cups rice wine
- 1 cup hoisin sauce
- ½ cup soy sauce
- 3 tablespoons sesame oil
- 2 tablespoons dark brown sugar
- 2 tablespoons wildflower honey
- 2 teaspoons Chinese five-spice powder
- Flaked sea salt
- Freshly ground black pepper

Directions:

1.   Using a paring knife, score the fat on the pork jowls, making even parallel cuts down to the flesh, but not through it. Turn the pork 45 degrees and make parallel cuts in the opposite direction. Transfer the pork to a large food-grade plastic bag.

2.   In a large bowl, whisk together the rice wine, hoisin sauce, soy sauce, sesame oil, sugar, honey, and Chinese five-spice powder. Transfer to the bag with the pork. Remove as much air as possible from the bag and seal it. Refrigerate for 24 hours, turning the pork occasionally.

3.   Remove the jowls from the bag, reserving the marinade in the refrigerator.

4.   Preheat the electric smoker to 250°F. Ensure the drip tray is clean and in place. Seal the door.

5.   Place the wood chips in the smoking tray or firebox, get a good smoke rolling, and seal the door.

6.   Season the pork on all sides with salt and pepper and place it on a smoking rack. Insert a probe thermometer (if available) into the thickest part of the meat, not touching the bone. Set the target temperature for 165°F. Smoke for about 1 hour. Baste each jowl with the reserved marinade. Smoke for about 1 hour more. The jowls are done with they reach an internal temperature of 165°F.

7.   Remove and loosely tent the meat with aluminum foil. Let it rest for 20 minutes before serving.

Hickory-smoked Maple Bacon

Servings: 20
Cooking Time: 2 To 3 Hours

Ingredients:

- ½ cup pure maple syrup
- ¼ cup coarse sea salt
- 3 garlic cloves, minced
- 3 fresh bay leaves, finely chopped
- 2 thyme sprigs, leaves stripped and finely chopped
- 2 rosemary sprigs, leaves stripped and minced
- 2 tablespoons peppercorns, whole
- 2 tablespoons fennel seeds, whole
- 2 tablespoons caraway seeds, whole
- 5 pounds skin-on pork belly

Directions:

1.   In a food processor, blend the maple syrup, salt, garlic, bay leaves, thyme, rosemary, peppercorns, fennel, and caraway. Process until smooth and combined. Rub the cure all over the pork.

2.   Place the pork belly in a large food-grade plastic bag. Remove as much air as possible from the bag and seal it. Refrigerate it flat on a tray for 7 days, turning 2 or 3 times.

3.   Rinse the pork with cold water and pat it dry with a paper towel.

4.   Preheat the electric smoker to 200°F. Ensure the drip tray is clean and in place. Seal the door.

5.   Place the wood chips in the smoking tray or firebox, get a good smoke rolling, and seal the door.

6.   Place the pork belly, skin-side up, on a smoking tray; cut it in half, if necessary, and use multiple shelves. Insert a probe thermometer (if available) into the

thickest part of the meat, not touching the bone. Set the target temperature for 165°F. Smoke for 2 to 3 hours, or until the internal temperature reaches 165°F.

7.   Transfer the bacon to a cutting board. Loosely tent it with aluminum foil and let it rest for 20 minutes before slicing.

Apple Cider Brats

Servings: 6 To 8
Cooking Time: 20 Minutes

Ingredients:

- 2 (12-ounce) cans or bottles hard apple cider
- 1 large red onion, quartered
- 1 large apple, quartered
- 6 to 8 fresh bratwurst sausages
- 6 to 8 large, hearty hot dog buns (optional)
- grainy mustard, for serving
- FOR THE CARAMELIZED ONIONS AND PEPPERS:
- 1 tablespoon olive oil
- 2 white or yellow onions, sliced
- 2 or 3 large bell peppers (any color), seeded and sliced

Directions:

1.   Prepare the smoker's water pan according to the manufacturer's instructions and preheat the smoker to 250°F. While it heats, fill a medium bowl with water and add 3 or 4 handfuls of apple wood chips to soak.

2.   In an 8 × 12-inch disposable foil pan, combine the cider, onion, apple, and sausages. Place in the smoker and add a small handful of the soaked apple wood chips to the chip loading area. Adding more chips at least every 30 minutes, cook the brats until they've reached an internal temperature of 160°F, about 1½ to 2 hours.

3.   While the sausages cook, heat the olive oil in a large skillet on the stovetop over medium-high heat for 30 seconds to a minute. Add the sliced onions and peppers and let them caramelize, stirring frequently over medium-high heat to keep them from burning. They are done when soft and lightly browned, about 10 to 15 minutes.

4.   Take the brat pan out of the smoker and use tongs to remove the brats from the cider. Serve immediately, with or without buns, topped with the caramelized onions and peppers and the mustard.

Smoked Chops With Cast Iron Leeks And Beans

Servings: 4
Cooking Time: 2 Hours

Ingredients:

- 2 tablespoons extra-virgin olive oil, plus more for brushing
- 4 bone-in pork chops
- Flaked sea salt
- Freshly ground black pepper
- 8 fingerling potatoes, halved lengthwise
- 4 leeks, quartered lengthwise and thinly sliced
- 1 garlic bulb, halved
- 4 cups cannellini beans, drained and rinsed
- 1 cup white wine
- 1 cup chicken stock
- 3 parsley sprigs, leaves stripped and minced
- Grated zest of 1 lemon, plus juice of 1 lemon

Directions:

1.   Preheat the electric smoker to 275°F. Ensure the drip tray is clean and in place. Seal the door.

2.   Place the wood chips in the smoking tray or firebox, get a good smoke rolling, and seal the door.

3.   Place a large cast iron skillet on a smoking rack to preheat and pour in 2 tablespoons of olive oil.

4.   Brush the pork chops with olive oil, season with salt and pepper, and place them on a smoking rack. Insert a probe thermometer (if available) into the thickest part of the meat, not touching the bone. Set the target temperature for 145°F. Smoke the pork chops for about 1 hour; the meat will begin to shrink from the bones.

5.   In the skillet, combine the potatoes, leeks, and garlic. Toss to coat in the olive oil. Season with salt and pepper.

6.   Add the beans, white wine, chicken stock, parsley, lemon zest, and lemon juice. Season with salt and pepper. Smoke for about 1 hour.

7.   Stir the bean mixture and nestle the chops into the beans. Smoke for 1 hour more, or until the internal temperature of the pork reaches 145°F.

8.   Remove the skillet from the smoker. Loosely tent the pork chops with aluminum foil and let them rest for 10 minutes.

9.   Serve each chop on a bed of the white beans.

Smoked Sausage Hash

Servings: 4

Cooking Time: 30 Minutes

Ingredients:

- Nonstick cooking spray
- 2 garlic cloves, finely minced
- 1 teaspoon dried basil
- 1 teaspoon dried oregano
- 1 teaspoon onion powder
- 1 teaspoon salt
- 1 teaspoon freshly ground black pepper
- 4 to 6 cooked Smoked Italian Sausage, sliced
- 1 large bell pepper (any color), diced
- 1 large onion, diced
- 3 potatoes, cut into 1-inch cubes
- 3 tablespoons olive oil
- French bread, for serving

Directions:

1.   Preheat the smoker to 225°F with the applewood.

2.   Cover the smoker's grill rack with aluminum foil and coat it with nonstick cooking spray.

3.   In a small bowl, mix together the garlic, basil, oregano, onion powder, salt, and pepper.

4.   In a large bowl, toss together the sausage slices, bell pepper, onion, potatoes, olive oil, and spice mix to coat. Spread the mixture on the foil-covered rack. Place the rack in the smoker and smoke for about 45 minutes until the potatoes are soft and easily cut with a fork.

5.   Serve hot with torn bread.

Pulled Pork Hoagies

Servings: 8

Cooking Time: 8 Hours

Ingredients:

- FOR THE MARINADE
- 4 cups apple cider
- 12 garlic cloves, halved
- 3 shallots, very thinly sliced
- 1 jalapeño pepper, sliced
- 3 star anise, whole
- 3 thyme sprigs
- 3 rosemary sprigs
- 1 tablespoon fennel seeds, whole
- 1 tablespoon coriander seeds, whole
- 1 tablespoon allspice berries, whole
- 5 pounds pork shoulder, trimmed
- FOR THE SLAW
- 1 Savoy cabbage, trimmed, cored, and finely sliced
- 1 fennel bulb, trimmed, cored, and finely sliced
- 1 carrot, grated
- ½ cup mayonnaise
- ½ cup apple cider vinegar
- 2 tablespoons wildflower honey
- 2 tablespoons whole-grain mustard
- 1 tablespoon finely grated fresh ginger
- 3 mint sprigs, leaves stripped and finely sliced
- Grated zest of 1 lemon, plus juice of 1 lemon
- Celery seed, for seasoning
- Flaked sea salt
- Freshly ground black pepper
- FOR THE HOAGIES
- Flaked sea salt
- Freshly ground black pepper
- 8 hoagie rolls, halved, lightly buttered and grilled
- Whole-grain mustard, for serving

Directions:

1.   TO MAKE THE MARINADE

2.   In a large bowl, whisk the apple cider, garlic, shallots, jalapeño, star anise, thyme, rosemary, fennel seeds, coriander seeds, and allspice to combine. Transfer to a large food-grade plastic bag and add the pork. Remove as much air as possible from the bag and seal it. Refrigerate for 24 hours, turning the pork occasionally.

3.   TO MAKE THE SLAW

4.   In a large mixing bowl, combine the cabbage, fennel, and carrot.

5.   In a small bowl, whisk the mayonnaise, vinegar, honey, mustard, ginger, mint, lemon zest, and lemon juice to blend. Add the dressing to the cabbage mixture and stir to coat all the ingredients. Taste and season with

celery seed, salt, and pepper. Cover and refrigerate overnight.

6.   TO MAKE THE HOAGIES

7.   Preheat the electric smoker to 250°F. Ensure the drip tray is clean and in place. Seal the door.

8.   Place the wood chips in the smoking tray or firebox, get a good smoke rolling, and seal the door.

9.   Drain the pork and pat it dry with a paper towel. Discard the marinade. Season the pork on all sides with salt and pepper. Place the pork in a shallow pan to collect the cooking juice and place the pan on a smoking rack. Insert a probe thermometer (if available) into the thickest part of the meat, not touching the bone. Set the target temperature for 190°F. Smoke for about 3 hours; the meat will begin to shrink from the bones.

10. Remove the pan with the pork from the smoker, then remove the pork from the pan. Strain the cooking liquid through a fine-mesh sieve set over a bowl. Using an injection needle, inject the pork shoulder using all the liquid. Space your injections evenly around the shoulder. Place the shoulder back in the smoker on a rack. Smoke for 2 to 3 hours more, or until the internal temperature reaches 190°F.

11. Transfer the pork to a cutting board. Loosely tent it with aluminum foil and let it rest for 20 minutes. Using two forks, shred the pork.

12. Serve the pulled pork on a buttered, grilled hoagie roll, topped with the slaw and whole-grain mustard.

Smoked Bone-in Pork Loin Chops

Servings: 4

Cooking Time: 1 Hour 30 Minutes

Ingredients:

•   1 tablespoon extra-virgin olive oil, plus more for brushing

•   1 tablespoon unsalted butter

•   4 bone-in pork chops

•   2 tablespoons flaked sea salt

•   Freshly ground black pepper

•   ¼ cup smoked paprika

•   8 rosemary sprigs

•   2 Bosc or Bartlett pears, halved and cored

•   2 limes, halved

Directions:

1.   Preheat the electric smoker to 275°F. Ensure the drip tray is clean and in place. Seal the door.

2.   Place the wood chips in the smoking tray or firebox, get a good smoke rolling, and seal the door.

3.   Preheat a large cast iron skillet on a smoking rack, then pour in the olive oil and add the butter to melt.

4.   Brush the pork chops all over with olive oil. Season with salt, pepper, and paprika. Press 2 rosemary sprigs into the oiled surface of each chop.

5.   Place the chops, rosemary-side down, on the smoking rack. Insert a probe thermometer (if available) into the thickest part of the meat, not touching the bone. Set the target temperature for 145°F. Smoke for 1 to 1½ hours until the internal temperature reaches 145°F.

6.   Place the pears in the skillet, flesh-side down. Cook for about 20 minutes, until tender. Remove and set aside.

7.   Transfer the pork to a cutting board. Loosely tent it with aluminum foil and let it rest for 10 minutes.

8.   Serve the chops topped with any of the liquid that accumulated while resting, a thinly sliced pear, and half a lime for squeezing.

Homemade Bacon

Servings: 60

Cooking Time: 20 Minutes

Ingredients:

•   2 tablespoons pink curing salt

•   2 tablespoons sugar

•   1 tablespoon freshly ground black pepper

•   1 (6- to 8-pound) pork belly, skin removed, cut into 3 or 4 pieces

Directions:

1.   In a small bowl, stir together the curing salt, sugar, and pepper.

2.   Rub the pork pieces with the spice mixture, and place each piece in a resealable plastic bag or on a dish. Cover tightly. Refrigerate for 8 to 10 days to cure.

3.   When ready to smoke, preheat the smoker to 200°F with the apple or hickory wood.

4. Rinse the pork-belly pieces and pat them dry. Place them on the smoker's grill rack and cook for about 4 hours until the internal temperature reaches 150°F.

5. Cool the meat for 30 to 40 minutes. Refrigerate it for several hours before slicing it to your desired thickness.

Pernil-style Smoked Pork

Servings: 8

Cooking Time: 6 Hours

Ingredients:

- 3 cups water
- ¼ cup coarse salt
- ¼ cup light brown sugar, plus 2 teaspoons
- 2 cups ice cubes
- 2 tablespoons apple cider vinegar
- 6 tablespoons sherry, dry or sweet, divided
- 1 (8-pound) bone-in pork shoulder
- 4 tablespoons olive oil
- ½ cup Pork Rub
- 2 tablespoons minced garlic
- 2 teaspoons dried oregano
- 1 teaspoon dried sage
- 1 teaspoon dried thyme
- 1 teaspoon freshly ground black pepper

Directions:

1. In a medium pot, heat the water to almost boiling. Add the salt and stir until it's dissolved. Add ¼ cup brown sugar and stir until it's dissolved. Remove the brine from the heat and cool it off with the ice. Add the vinegar and 4 tablespoons sherry.

2. When the brine solution is cool, score the fat side of the pork with a sharp knife, place it in a large zip-top bag, and add the brine. Close the bag, squeezing out all the air. Refrigerate for about 4 hours.

3. Pat the pork dry with paper towels. Leave it out on the counter for 1 hour.

4. Preheat the smoker to 250°F.

5. In a small bowl, mix together 2 tablespoons olive oil, the pork rub, garlic, oregano, sage, thyme, pepper, and the remaining 2 tablespoons sherry and 2 teaspoons brown sugar. Brush the pork with the remaining 2 tablespoons olive oil, then rub the pork rub mixture into the pork, all over.

6. Smoke the pork for 3 hours.

7. Take it out, wrap it in aluminum foil, and return it to the smoker for another 2 hours.

8. Remove the aluminum foil and let it smoke for 1 hour longer, or until the internal temperature reaches 205°F.

9. Let it rest for at least 30 minutes before serving.

Delicious Pork Loin Recipe

Servings: 6

Cooking Time: 3 Hours

Ingredients:

- 4 pounds of pork loin, whole boneless
- 1-½ tablespoon of five-spice powder
- Sea salt, to taste
- Black pepper, to taste
- 1 teaspoon of garlic powder
- ½ teaspoon of nutmeg
- 2 tablespoons of safflower oil
- Apple juice, unsweetened (as needed)
- Water, as needed

Directions:

1. First, rinse the pork loin and pat dry with a paper towel. Trim the excess fat from the loin. Transfer the pork loin to a sheet pan.

2. Take a small bowl and combine five-spice powder, salt, pepper, garlic powder, and nutmeg.

3. Then add oil to it and make a paste.

4. Rub this prepared paste all over the loin and let it sit at room temperature for 60 minutes.

5. Afterward, preheat the electric smoker to 225 degrees F.

6. Place water and apple juice in a bowl at the base of the electric smoker.

7. Now add wood chips to the side tray of the electric smoker. Then place the pork loin, fat side up, on the middle rack. Next, insert the probe thermometer, for heat measurements.

8. Close the electric smoker door and then cook for 3 hours.

9. Check the pork loin every 45 minutes for an internal temperature of 180°F.

10. Add more wood chips if the smoke is not enough.

11. Add water and apple juice if needed.

12. Now remove the pork from the electric smoker and place it on a cutting board.

13. Allow the meat to rest for about 15 minutes before cutting.

14. Slice it thinly and serve it with your favorite's salad or side serving.

Bacon, Pastrami, And Smoked Pork Cheeseburgers

Servings: 4
Cooking Time: 15 Minutes

Ingredients:
- 2 pounds ground pork
- ¼ cup jarred garlic puree
- Salt
- Freshly ground black pepper
- Granulated garlic
- 4 slices smoked bacon
- 1 pound pastrami, sliced
- 12 arugula leaves
- 4 large hamburger buns, split and toasted
- 4 slices beefsteak tomato
- 4 slices cheese, such as provolone, cheddar, American, or Swiss
- Favorite burger sauce, for serving

Directions:
1. Preheat the smoker to 275°F.

2. In a bowl, mix together the ground pork and garlic puree.

3. Divide the burger mixture into 4 equal portions (about 8 ounces each) and shape them into balls. Then flatten them out a bit into patties. Use a soup spoon to make a dent in the center of each patty to help it cook more evenly and keep its shape.

4. Sprinkle both sides of the patties with a generous amount of salt, pepper, and granulated garlic to taste.

5. Smoke the burgers for 40 minutes.

6. Arrange the bacon and pastrami on two different cooking racks and set in the smoker. Continue to smoke the burgers, bacon, and pastrami for another 20 minutes, or until the internal temperature of the burgers reaches 160°F.

7. To assemble, place 3 arugula leaves on the bottom of each bun. Add a slice of tomato, a burger, a slice of cheese, some pastrami, and a slice of bacon to each burger. Squirt your favorite sauce over the burgers, add the top bun, and serve.

Pulled Pork Sandwiches

Servings: 6
Cooking Time: 15 Minutes

Ingredients:
- 1 cup Pork Rub
- ¼ cup packed light brown sugar
- 4 to 6 pounds boneless Boston butt
- 1 cup Dijon mustard (or your favorite)
- 1 cup apple juice
- 6 kaiser rolls, split and toasted
- Favorite sauce, for serving

Directions:
1. Preheat the smoker to 225°F.

2. In a small bowl, mix together the pork rub and brown sugar. Slather the meat with the mustard, then generously sprinkle the pork rub mixture over the meat, rubbing it all over.

3. Smoke the pork for 4 hours. Fill a spray bottle with apple juice.

4. Remove the pork, spray with the apple juice, and wrap tightly in butcher paper. Smoke it for another 2 hours, or until the internal temperature reaches 195°F.

5. Let the pork rest for 1 hour, then shred it.

6. Serve on toasted kaiser rolls with your favorite sauce.

Simple Smoked Pork Shoulder

Servings: 16
Cooking Time: 15 Minutes

Ingredients:
- ½ quart apple juice
- ½ quart apple cider vinegar

- ½ cup sugar
- ¼ cup salt
- ¼ cup soy sauce
- 1 (5- to 7-pound) picnic pork shoulder roast
- ¼ cup firmly packed light-brown sugar
- 1 tablespoon paprika
- 1 tablespoon ground turmeric
- 1 tablespoon ground cumin
- 1½ teaspoons freshly ground black pepper
- 1 teaspoon dried rosemary
- 1 teaspoon dried sage
- Hot Pepper Vinegar Barbecue Sauce, for serving
- 16 hamburger buns

Directions:

1. In a container large enough to hold the brine and pork, make the brine by combining the apple juice, vinegar, sugar, salt, and soy sauce. Stir to dissolve the sugar and salt.
2. Add the shoulder and enough water to cover the meat. Cover and refrigerate overnight.
3. Remove the shoulder and discard the brine.
4. Preheat the smoker to 200°F with the hickory wood.
5. In a small bowl, mix together the brown sugar, paprika, turmeric, cumin, pepper, rosemary, and sage. Coat the shoulder with this rub and place it in the smoker. Smoke for 8 to 9 hours until the internal temperature reaches 195°F to 205°F, for fall-off-the-bone goodness.
6. Remove the pork and let it rest for 20 minutes. Shred the meat with forks before serving with the buns and sauce.

Pig Candy

Servings: 30 To 40
Cooking Time: 20 Minutes

Ingredients:

- Nonstick cooking spray
- 2 pounds bacon slices (see Homemade Bacon, if you want to make your own)
- 1 cup firmly packed brown sugar
- 2 to 3 teaspoons cayenne pepper
- ½ cup maple syrup, divided

Directions:

1. Remove the grill rack from the smoker and cover it with aluminum foil. Use two racks if necessary. Spray the foil with nonstick cooking spray.
2. Lay the bacon out in a single layer, leaving a tiny space between each slice so they don't stick together.
3. In a small bowl, mix together the brown sugar and cayenne, using more or less cayenne to control the heat.
4. Using a brush, generously baste the bacon with ¼ cup of maple syrup.
5. Sprinkle half the rub on top of the bacon.
6. Place the rack(s) in the smoker and smoke the bacon for 1 hour.
7. Flip the bacon, baste this side with the remaining ¼ cup of maple syrup, and sprinkle with the remaining rub.
8. Smoke for 1 hour more until done. The bacon will be brown, firm, and bubbly. Cool and serve, or refrigerate for later use.

Pork Shoulder Steaks Recipe

Servings: 10
Cooking Time: 7 Hour 30 Minutes

Ingredients:

- ½ cup hoisin sauce
- ⅓ cup honey
- ½ cup soy sauce
- ¼ cup dry sherry
- 3 teaspoons Chinese five-spice powder
- 4 tablespoons five-spice powder
- 2 tablespoons dark brown sugar
- 2 tablespoons sea salt, or to taste
- Meat Includes:
- 7 pounds of 1 boneless pork Boston butt

Directions:

1. Whisk together all the sauce ingredients to make a sauce in medium bowl.
2. To prepare a rub, take a separate bowl and combine all the rub ingredients.
3. Rub the seasoning all over the pork butt meat.
4. Coat evenly and then place it in a resealed plastic bag.
5. Now, turn on the smoker and adjust it out 255 degrees F.

6. Then add wood chips and wait once the wood starts producing smoke.

7. Now, place the meat inside the smoker and then smoke it for 7 hours.

8. Meanwhile, pour all the sauce ingredients into the saucepan and bring the mixture to boil.

9. Reduce heat of the pan to low and simmer for 10 minutes.

10. Once thickened, turn the heat off.

11. Once the pork cooked, brush sauce over the meat evenly.

12. Continue to smoke it for 30 more minutes.

13. Serve when done.

Zesty Mustard Smoke Pork Tenderloin In A Smoker

Servings: 2

Cooking Time: 3 Hours

Ingredients:

- 2 pork tenderloins
- 4 tablespoons of BBQ sauce
- Pork Rub Ingredients:
- ¼ cup cane sugar
- ¼ teaspoon chili powder
- ½ tablespoon granulated onion
- ½ tablespoon granulated garlic
- ½ tablespoons dried chilies
- ¼ tablespoon dill weed
- ½ tablespoon lemon powder
- ½ tablespoon mustard powder

Directions:

1. Combine all the rub ingredients in a large bowl and set aside.

2. Start the smoker and add apple wood chips.

3. Adjust the setting to 225 degrees F.

4. Meanwhile, trim the pork fat and silver skin.

5. Rub the seasoning over the pork loin.

6. Place the pork in the smoker.

7. Cook for 3 hours until internal temperate reaches 200 degrees F.

8. Brush the BBQ sauce on the pork and then left it to sit for 20 minutes.

9. Then serve and enjoy.

Pork Tenderloin Brochettes

Servings: 4

Cooking Time: 1 To 2 Hours

Ingredients:

- ½ cup mirin
- ½ cup soy sauce
- ½ cup fish sauce
- ½ cup sake
- ½ cup packed dark brown sugar
- 2 pork tenderloins, membranes removed, diced
- 1 pineapple, trimmed, peeled, quartered lengthwise, cored, and cut into large dice
- 2 red bell peppers, stemmed, cored, and cut into large dice
- 1 red onion, quartered

Directions:

1. In a large bowl, whisk together the mirin, soy sauce, fish sauce, sake, and brown sugar. Transfer to a large food-grade plastic bag and add the diced pork. Remove as much air as possible from the bag and seal it. Refrigerate for 24 hours, turning 2 or 3 times.

2. Remove the pork from the marinade, reserving the marinade in the refrigerator.

3. Preheat the electric smoker to 225°F. Ensure the drip tray is clean and in place. Seal the door.

4. Place the wood chips in the smoking tray or firebox, get a good smoke rolling, and seal the door.

5. Build the brochettes by alternating pork cubes, pineapple, red pepper, and red onion on 8 (12-inch) bamboo or stainless steel skewers. Arrange the brochettes on smoking trays, leaving space between each one. Baste with the reserved marinade. Insert a probe thermometer (if available) into the thickest part of the meat. Set the target temperature for 165°F. Smoke for about 20 minutes. Baste all sides of the brochettes with the reserved marinade. Continue to smoke, basting every 20 minutes, until the internal temperature reaches 165°F, for 40 to 80 minutes more.

6. Remove the brochettes from the smoker. Loosely tent them with aluminum foil, and let them rest for 10 minutes before serving.

Peppercorn Pork Tenderloin

Servings: 6 To 8
Cooking Time: 10 Minutes

Ingredients:

- 2 small (1- to 3-pound) pork tenderloins, any remaining silverskin removed
- 2 tablespoons olive oil
- 1 tablespoon peppercorns, crushed in a mortar and pestle
- 2 teaspoons turbinado sugar
- 1 teaspoon red pepper flakes

Directions:

1. Preheat the smoker to 225°F with the applewood.
2. Coat the tenderloins with the olive oil.
3. In a small bowl, thoroughly combine the peppercorns, sugar, and red pepper flakes. Rub the spices across the entire surface of each piece of meat. Place both tenderloins in the smoker, allowing for good air and smoke flow. Smoke for 2 to 3 hours, or until the internal temperature reaches 145°F.
4. Let them rest for 10 minutes before slicing and serving.

Apple Wood Smoked Pork Loin In A Digital Smoker

Servings: 6
Cooking Time: 5 Hours

Ingredients:

- 5 pounds of pork loin, trimmed
- 2 tablespoons canola oil
- 3 tablespoons garlic powder
- 2 tablespoons dried rosemary, chopped
- ¼ cup salt, or to taste
- ½ cup dry pistachios, chopped and roasted
- 6 tablespoons ground black peppercorns

Directions:

1. Load the electric smoker grill with apple wood chips and preheat it for 50 minutes at 225 degrees F.
2. Rinse and pat dry the pork and then brush it with oil.
3. Now rub all the listed spice over the pork and then let the pork rest for 10 minutes.
4. Next, insert the probe thermometer for heat measurements inside the meat.
5. Close the electric smoker door and then cook for 3-5 hours until internal temperate reaches 200 degrees F.
6. The pork is done, take it out and let it sit for a few minutes before serving.

Mexican-style Smoked Carnitas

Servings: 12
Cooking Time: 11 Hours

Ingredients:

- 2 cups Pork Rub, divided
- 1 tablespoon coarse salt
- Juice of 2 limes
- Juice of 1 orange
- 4 bay leaves
- 6 tablespoons olive oil, divided
- 1 (8-pound) bone-in pork shoulder
- 1 tablespoon dark brown sugar
- 1 teaspoon chili powder or cayenne pepper
- 1 teaspoon chipotle powder
- 1 teaspoon ground cumin
- 1 teaspoon dried oregano

Directions:

1. In a small bowl, mix together 1 cup pork rub, the salt, lime juice, orange juice, bay leaves, and 2 tablespoons olive oil.
2. Place the pork shoulder in a 2-gallon zip-top bag. Pour the marinade over the pork, seal the bag, and refrigerate for 10 hours.
3. Take the pork out 1 hour before smoking it. Pat it dry with paper towels.
4. Preheat the smoker to 225°F.
5. Brush the pork with 2 tablespoons olive oil. In a small bowl, mix together the remaining 1 cup pork rub, the brown sugar, chili powder, chipotle powder, cumin, and oregano. Rub the mixture into the pork on all sides.
6. Smoke the pork for about 6 hours, or until the internal temperature reaches 165°F.

7. Take the pork out of the smoker and place in a large metal baking dish. Brush the top with the remaining 2 tablespoons olive oil and cover the pork.

8. Increase the smoker's temperature to 350°F and cook the pork for 4 hours, or until it reaches an internal temperature of 205°F.

9. Remove the pork and let it rest for 1 hour. Keep the pan drippings. Shred the pork.

10. Increase the temperature of the smoker to 400°F and preheat a cast-iron skillet. Add 2 tablespoons of the drippings to the skillet and let it get hot. Then add the pork to the skillet and sear until it's browned, about 5 minutes.

11. Serve warm.

Herb-crusted Pork Loin

Servings: 6 To 8
Cooking Time: 15 Minutes

Ingredients:
- 3 pounds pork tenderloin
- 10 cloves garlic
- salt and black pepper
- ½ cup Dijon mustard
- ½ cup chopped fresh rosemary
- FOR THE SWEET MUSTARD SAUCE:
- 2 tablespoons Dijon mustard
- 2 tablespoons light brown sugar
- ½ tablespoon apple cider vinegar
- ½ cup vegetable or chicken stock or broth
- 2 teaspoons cornstarch
- ⅓ cup water
- Salt

Directions:
1. Prepare the smoker's water pan according to the manufacturer's instructions and preheat the smoker to 250°F. While it heats, fill a medium bowl with water and add 3 or 4 handfuls of mesquite wood chips to soak.

2. Prepare the tenderloin by poking 10 holes in the meat with a sharp knife all over the tenderloin and stuffing each hole with a clove of garlic. Season with salt and pepper before rubbing Dijon mustard over the entire tenderloin, making sure to coat all surfaces. Then press the chopped rosemary over the whole tenderloin, gently pressing it into the mustard to make sure it stays on.

3. Place the tenderloin directly on the smoker rack and add a small handful of the soaked mesquite chips to the chip loading area. Adding more chips at least every 30 minutes, cook the tenderloin until the internal temperature has reached 155°F, about 2½ to 3 hours.

4. While the tenderloin is cooking, prepare the sauce. In a medium saucepan, combine the mustard, brown sugar, vinegar, and stock. Bring to a boil on the stovetop over medium-high heat, then reduce heat and let simmer for 5 minutes. Meanwhile, in a small bowl stir together the cornstarch and water; slowly pour and whisk into the mustard sauce, which should thicken the mustard sauce almost immediately. Remove the sauce from the heat and season to taste with salt.

5. Let the tenderloin rest under a foil tent for 15 to 20 minutes before slicing. Spoon the sauce over the top to serve.

Sweet And Spicy Pork Shoulder

Servings: 6
Cooking Time: 4 Hours

Ingredients:
- 4 pounds pork shoulder, roasts
- Shoulder Rub Ingredients:
- ¼ cup brown sugar
- ½ cup white sugar
- ½ cup paprika
- ⅓ cup garlic powder
- 2 tablespoons white salt
- 1 tablespoon chili powder
- 1 teaspoon cayenne pepper
- 2 teaspoons black pepper
- 1 teaspoon dried oregano
- 1 teaspoon cumin
- Injection Liquid Ingredients:
- ¾ cup apple juice
- ½ cup water
- ½ cup sugar
- 3 tablespoons salt
- 2 tablespoons Worcestershire sauce

Directions:

1. Combine all the rub ingredients in a large bowl.
2. In a separate bowl, combine all the liquid ingredients.
3. Inject the liquid into the meat using the injector.
4. Pat dry the top surface of the meat, and then rub the spice mix all over meat evenly.
5. Let the meat sit for 2 hours at room temperature.
6. Cook it in an electric smoker for 4 hours, at 225 degrees F.
7. Serve and enjoy.

Argentine-style Smoked Boston Butt

Servings: 4
Cooking Time: 30 Minutes

Ingredients:
- 4 to 6 pounds boneless Boston butt
- 1 cup defatted chicken stock
- 3 tablespoons light brown sugar, divided
- 1 teaspoon Worcestershire sauce
- ¼ cup Pork Rub
- 1 tablespoon chipotle powder
- 1 teaspoon cayenne pepper
- 1 cup apple juice

Directions:
1. Preheat the smoker to 250°F and fill the water pan.
2. If the pork has a fat cap (layer of fat), separate it from the meat with a sharp knife. Set aside.
3. In a measuring cup, mix together the chicken stock, 1 tablespoon brown sugar, and the Worcestershire sauce. Pull it into the meat injector and inject it into the pork all over.
4. In a small bowl, mix together the pork rub, chipotle powder, and cayenne. Rub it all over the meat.
5. Replace the fat cap on the side of the meat it came from and tie it in place with butcher's twine.
6. Smoke the pork butt for 3 hours. Fill a spray bottle with the apple juice.
7. Spray with the apple juice and tightly wrap the pork with aluminum foil. It's a good idea to place wrapped meat on a small baking dish so it doesn't get punctured.

8. Return the meat to the smoker and smoke for another 3 hours, or until the internal temperature reaches 205°F.
9. Unwrap the pork and let it rest for 15 minutes before cutting into it.

Smoked Pork Leg

Servings: 10
Cooking Time: 9 Hours

Ingredients:
- 1 cup Pork Rub
- ½ cup packed light brown sugar
- 2 tablespoons coarse salt
- 1 tablespoon dried thyme
- 1 tablespoon ground cumin
- 2 teaspoons cayenne pepper
- 1 (12- to 14-pound) bone-in leg of pork
- 1 cup apple juice
- 1 tablespoon fresh lime juice

Directions:
1. In a medium bowl, mix together the pork rub, brown sugar, salt, thyme, cumin, and cayenne. Rub generous amounts of the mixture onto the leg of pork. Wrap it in plastic wrap and refrigerate for 8 hours.
2. Take it out of the fridge and let it come to room temperature, about 1 hour.
3. Preheat the smoker to 275°F.
4. Smoke the pork leg for 4 hours, or until the internal temperature reaches 145°F.
5. Mix the apple and lime juice in a spray bottle. Take the pork leg out of the smoker, spray it with the juice, then set it on a sheet of aluminum foil. Pour the rest of the juice on the meat, then wrap it up in the foil.
6. Return the wrapped pork leg to the smoker and smoke for 6 to 8 hours, or until the internal temperature reaches 205°F.
7. Take the pork leg out of the smoker and keep it covered for about 1 hour. Then unwrap it and carve away.

Ham Steaks With Pineapple Salsa

Servings: 6 To 8
Cooking Time: 15 Minutes

Ingredients:

- 2 (1 to 1½-pound) ham steaks
- 1 cup diced fresh pineapple
- ½ cup diced red onion
- 1 jalapeño chile, seeded and diced
- 1 tablespoon chopped fresh cilantro
- ½ lime, juiced
- pinch of salt

Directions:

1. Prepare the smoker's water pan according to the manufacturer's instructions and preheat the smoker to 220°F. While it heats, fill a medium bowl with water and add a handful of wood chips to soak.
2. Using tongs, arrange the ham steaks directly on the smoker racks. Add the handful of soaked wood chips to the chip loading area; this is the only time that you'll add chips.
3. While the ham smokes, in a small bowl combine the pineapple, red onion, jalapeño, cilantro, lime juice, and salt; set aside. When the ham has been smoking for about 30 minutes, transfer the warm steaks to a serving platter. Top with the pineapple salsa to serve.

Herb-crusted Rack Of Pork

Servings: 8
Cooking Time: 2 To 3 Hours

Ingredients:

- 1 cup panko bread crumbs
- 4 garlic cloves, finely chopped
- 2 shallots, finely chopped
- ½ cup fresh flat-leaf parsley leaves, finely chopped
- 3 tablespoons fresh thyme leaves, stripped and finely chopped
- 3 tablespoons fresh rosemary leaves, minced
- 3 tablespoons whole-grain mustard
- 1 tablespoon paprika
- Flaked sea salt
- Freshly ground black pepper
- 3 tablespoons extra-virgin olive oil
- 1 (8-rib) bone-in pork loin, excess fat trimmed
- 2 lemons, quartered lengthwise

Directions:

1. In a large bowl, whisk together the bread crumbs, garlic, shallots, parsley, thyme, rosemary, mustard, and paprika. Season with salt and pepper. Add the olive oil and whisk everything together until a paste forms. Rub the paste all over the pork.
2. Wrap the pork loin tightly in plastic wrap and refrigerate it at least 12 hours, or overnight.
3. Remove the pork from the refrigerator 20 minutes before smoking.
4. Preheat the electric smoker to 225°F. Ensure the drip tray is clean and in place. Seal the door.
5. Place the wood chips in the smoking tray or firebox, get a good smoke rolling, and seal the door.
6. Place the pork on a smoking tray in the center of the smoker. Insert a probe thermometer (if available) into the thickest part of the meat, not touching the bone. Set the target temperature for 165°F. Smoke for 2 to 3 hours, until the internal temperature reaches 165°F.
7. Transfer the pork to a cutting board. Loosely tent it with aluminum foil and let it rest for 20 minutes. Serve slices of pork with a wedge of lemon to brighten the flavor.

Smoked Pork Chops With Apple And Onion Compote

Servings: 4
Cooking Time: 4 Hours

Ingredients:

- 4 boneless pork chops
- ½ cup of BBQ Rub
- 2 tablespoons canola oil
- 2 tablespoons water
- 2 Spanish onions
- 2 apples, Granny Smith
- 2 tablespoons butter
- ¼ teaspoon cinnamon
- ½ teaspoon dry mustard
- ⅓ teaspoon nutmeg

- Salt and pepper, to taste

Directions:

1. Preheat the electric smoker and place apple wood chips in the smoke box. Let it heat for about 50 minutes.
2. Meanwhile, season the pork chops with BBQ rub by placing it on a baking sheet.
3. Then, covered it with the aluminum foil.
4. Set the temperature of the preheated smoker to 225 degrees F.
5. Insert the digital thermometer in the thickest part of the pork chop.
6. Set the internal temperate to 200 degrees F.
7. Place baking sheet with the chop into the smoker.
8. Smoke the chops for about 4 hours.
9. Meanwhile, make the compote by adding oil to the skillet and heat it over the low flame.
10. Now add onion and cook until soft.
11. It took about 15 minutes at low heat.
12. Take out the onion and add apples with water, and cook until turn golden.
13. Melt the butter in the same pan and add cinnamon, dry mustard, and nutmeg.
14. Add onions back to the pan and mix well.
15. Season it with salt and pepper.
16. Once chops are cooked, serve it with prepared compote.

Smoked Pork Ragù Over Pasta

Servings: 8

Cooking Time: 4 Hours

Ingredients:

- FOR THE BRINE
- ¼ cup coarse sea salt
- 2 tablespoons fresh thyme leaves, finely chopped
- 3 lemons, thinly sliced
- 3 fresh bay leaves
- 1 quart water
- 2 pounds pork shoulder (Boston or collar butt), trimmed
- FOR THE RAGÙ
- Flaked sea salt
- Freshly ground black pepper
- ½ cup extra-virgin olive oil
- 1 cup diced carrots
- 1 cup diced celery hearts
- 1 cup diced yellow onions
- 8 garlic cloves, minced
- 2 cups red wine
- 4 cups diced Roma tomatoes
- 1 quart water
- 3 fresh bay leaves
- 1 tablespoon fresh thyme leaves, finely chopped
- 1 tablespoon fresh oregano leaves, finely chopped
- 1 pound dried pasta
- Finely grated Parmesan cheese, for serving

Directions:

1. TO MAKE THE BRINE
2. In a large bowl, whisk the salt, thyme, finely chopped lemon slices, bay leaves, and water to combine. Transfer to a large food-grade plastic bag and add the pork. Remove as much air as possible from the bag and seal it. Refrigerate for 24 hours, turning the pork occasionally.
3. TO MAKE THE RAGÙ
4. Preheat the electric smoker to 250°F. Ensure the drip tray is clean and in place. Seal the door.
5. Place the wood chips in the smoking tray or firebox, get a good smoke rolling, and seal the door.
6. Place a large cast iron Dutch oven on a smoking rack to preheat.
7. Remove the pork from the marinade and discard the marinade. Pat the pork dry with a paper towel and season the pork all over with salt and pepper. Place the pork on a smoking rack. Insert a probe thermometer (if available) into the thickest part of the meat, not touching the bone. Set the target temperature for 190°F.
8. In the preheated Dutch oven, combine the olive oil, carrots, celery, onions, and garlic. Season with salt and pepper and return to the smoker. Smoke for about 20 minutes, stirring occasionally.
9. Stir in the red wine to deglaze the pan, scraping up any browned bits from the bottom.
10. Stir in the tomatoes, water, bay leaves, thyme, and oregano. Smoke for about 1 hour.
11. Check the internal temperature of the pork, not touching the bone. Continue to smoke the pork until the internal temperature reaches 190°F, then transfer

the pork to a cutting board. Loosely tent the pork with aluminum foil and let it rest for 1 hour. Using two forks, shred the pork and add it to the Dutch oven. Return the Dutch oven to the smoker and smoke for 20 to 30 minutes until the sauce is reduced to your desired consistency. Remove and discard the bay leaves. Taste and season with salt and pepper, as needed.

12. Cook the pasta according to the package instructions. Then strain the pasta, reserving the cooking water to adjust the consistency of the ragù, as needed.

13. Serve the pasta topped with the ragù and Parmesan cheese.

Competition Baby Back Ribs

Servings: 4

Cooking Time: 15 Minutes

Ingredients:

- 2 full slabs baby back ribs, back membranes removed (use paper towels for a good grip)
- 1 cup prepared yellow mustard
- 1 cup Bill's Best Barbecue Rub
- 1 cup apple juice, divided
- 1 cup brown sugar, divided
- 1 cup Spicy Hickory-Smoked Barbecue Sauce, divided

Directions:

1. Preheat the smoker to 225°F with the hickory wood.

2. Coat the ribs with the mustard to help your favorite rub stick to all parts of the slabs.

3. Coat the ribs with the rub. Place them in the smoker and start with 3 hours of indirect smoking. This is when you get all the smoke flavor, so use wood (I like hickory) smoke via plenty of hardwood chips.

4. After 3 hours, the smoke should have done most of the "flavoring" that can be absorbed. Now's the time for the "Texas Crutch." It has nothing to do with Texas barbecue, really. Simply put, you wrap and seal each slab individually in heavy-duty aluminum foil. Before sealing the foil wrapping, add ½ cup of apple juice and ½ cup of brown sugar to each pouch. Ride out the next 2 hours on electric heat—no more woodchips are needed.

5. Finally, unwrap the ribs and coat each slab with ½ cup of the barbecue sauce. Continue to smoke for 1 hour more while the dry heat tightens the surface of the ribs. Look for a firm, reddish crust or bark and, notably, the meat will clearly pull away from the ends of the bones. Mother Nature's pop-up thermometer!

Carolina Pulled Pork Bites

Servings: 15

Cooking Time: 15 Minutes

Ingredients:

- 1 pound Simple Smoked Pork Shoulder, pulled
- 2 cups panko bread crumbs
- ⅔ cup Carolina Mustard Sauce, plus more for dipping
- 1 egg, beaten
- 1 (8-ounce) block smoked Gouda cheese, cut into 15 cubes
- 1 pound bacon slices

Directions:

1. Preheat the smoker to 250°F with the pecan wood.

2. In a large bowl, mix the pork, bread crumbs, sauce, and egg until combined. Roll the mixture to form about 15 meatballs.

3. Push a cheese cube into each meatball and reform into a ball.

4. Wrap a bacon slice around each ball, completely covering it, and place it on a grill pan or Frogmat. Smoke for about 2½ hours until the internal temperature reaches 160°F.

5. Remove from the heat and serve with additional Carolina Mustard Sauce for dipping.

Smoked Italian Sausage With Peppers And Onions

Servings: 6

Cooking Time: 1 Hour

Ingredients:

- 3 pounds hot or sweet Italian sausage links
- ½ cup whole-grain mustard
- 2 tablespoons chopped fresh cilantro
- 1 cup chimichurri, store-bought or homemade (here)

- 1 teaspoon freshly ground black pepper
- 2 large yellow or red onions
- 2 large red or green bell peppers

Directions:

1.   Pat the sausages dry with paper towels and set them uncovered in the refrigerator for 1 hour to let them dry some more.

2.   Preheat the smoker to 250°F.

3.   Place the sausages in the smoker. Make sure there is space between the links to let the smoke flow freely around them. Smoke for 3 hours, or until the internal temperature reaches 165°F.

4.   Meanwhile, in a bowl, mix together the mustard, cilantro, chimichurri, and pepper. Cover and refrigerate until serving.

5.   About 15 minutes before the sausages are done, cut the onions into ½-inch slices. Cut the top off the peppers, remove the seeds, and cut into rings and then half-rings.

6.   On the stovetop in a skillet over medium heat fry the onions and peppers until browned and slightly charred, about 5 minutes. (Or if you have a pellet smoker, increase the temperature to 425°F and cook them on the grill.) When they're done, place them on a serving board or a large platter.

7.   To serve, set the sausages next to the onions and peppers and brush everything with the reserved mustard/chimichurri sauce.

Glazed Easter Ham

Servings: 8 To 10

Cooking Time: 15 Minutes

Ingredients:

- 10-pound bone-in spiral-cut ham
- ½ cup canned pineapple juice
- ¼ cup light brown sugar
- 1 tablespoon Worcestershire sauce
- ½ teaspoon coarse kosher salt
- ¼ teaspoon ground cloves
- ¼ teaspoon ground nutmeg
- 1 teaspoon cornstarch
- ¼ cup water

Directions:

1.   Prepare the smoker's water pan according to the manufacturer's instructions and preheat the smoker to 275°F. While it heats, fill a medium bowl with water and add 3 or 4 handfuls of hickory wood chips to soak.

2.   Place the ham directly on a smoker rack and add a handful of the soaked hickory chips to the chip loading area. While the ham starts to smoke, prepare the glaze. In a small saucepan, combine the pineapple juice, brown sugar, Worcestershire, salt, cloves, and nutmeg. Heat on the stovetop over medium heat, stirring until the sugar is dissolved and the glaze begins to boil. Combine the cornstarch and water in a small bowl, mixing well, and slowly pour into the boiling liquid while whisking to break up any clumps. Let the mixture return to a boil for about a minute and then remove from the heat. Reserve half the glaze for serving.

3.   Baste the ham with the glaze and add more wood chips at least every 30 minutes. The ham is already fully cooked, but it will be warm through when it reaches an internal temperature of 140°F, after about 2 hours of smoking.

4.   Let the ham cool slightly before slicing. Serve warm along with the remaining glaze on the side, if desired.

RECIPE INDEX